I0234338

Still Learning to Fly

A Pilot's Life

Christopher Brown

Former Captain Press®

This Hardcover Edition published 2025

Copyright© Christopher Brown 2025

ISBN 978-0-9936242-6-1

Former Captain Press®
Montreal, Quebec, Canada

Cover design by:
Christopher Brown

Background Photo courtesy:
RUSSIAN INTERSTATE AVIATION COMMITTEE
AIR ACCIDENT INVESTIGATION COMMISSION

This book is dedicated to

Linda Creasey

my wife and darling companion

for generations

You

hold my hand

speak your beautiful voice

smile into my eyes

nothing is impossible

Table of Contents

Table of Contents

Three-Letter Acronyms:

a Quick Reference Guide

There are many technical terms in this book. Do not be discouraged. They will become more familiar as you proceed.

This **Three-Letter-Acronym Quick Reference Guide**

and the **Glossary**

FFESG (For Further Elucidation See Glossary)

at the end of the book

Comtain (almost) everything you want to know and more

ADIRU	Air Data Inertial Reference Unit	
ADF	Automatic Direction Finder	**FFESG**
AGL	Above Ground Level	
A/H	Artificial Horizon	**FFESG**
AHRS	Attitude and Heading Reference System	
ALTERNATE LAW		**FFESG**
ALT	Altitude hold mode	See also FMA
ALT*	Airbus altitude capture mode See Chapter 7 p. 130	
AoA	Angle of Attack	
A/P	AutoPilot	**FFESG**

ASRS	Aviation Safety Reporting System	**FFESG**
A/T	AutoThrust	**FFESG**
ATIS	Automated Terminal Information Service	

Blue Line Line on the airspeed indicator marking V_{YSE} – best single-engine rate of climb

Braided Steel Cables **FFESG**

CAP Gen Canada Air Pilot (**General**)

CAS Calibrated Air Speed

CAT II Approaches with a 100-foot Decision Height

CAVOK Ceiling and Visibility Unlimited

CDA Constant Descent Angle

CFIT Controlled Flight Into Terrain

CVR Cockpit Voice Recorder

DFDR Digital Flight Data Recorder

DIRECT LAW **FFESG**

DLC Direct Lift Control (see Chapter Eight)

DME	Distance Measuring Equipment	**FFESG**
DP	Decision Point	

ECAM Electronic Centralized Aircraft Monitoring (Airbus aircraft)

EICAS Engine Indicating and Crew Alerting System (Boeing aircraft)

Envelope Protection **FFESG**

Equilibrium		FFESG
ETA	Estimated Time of Arrival	
EXT PWR	External Power	
FAF	Final Approach Fix	
FCOM	Flight Crew Operating Manual	
FCU	Flight Control Unit	FFESG
FD	Flight Director	FFESG
FFESG	For Further Elucidation See Glossary	
FLA	Four Letter Acronym	
FLCH	Flight Level Change	See FMA
Flight Envelope		FFESG
FMA	Flight Mode Annunciator FFESG	See PFD
FMGC	Flight Management and Guidance Computer	
FPA	Flight Path Angle	See FMA
FPV	Flight Path Vector	FFESG
G	The force (actually, the acceleration) of Gravity	
GPS	Global Positioning System	FFESG
HDG	Heading	See FMA
HUD	Heads Up Display	FFESG
IAS	Indicated Air Speed	
ICBM	InterContinental Ballistic Missile	

IFR	Instrument Flight Rules	
ILS	Instrument Landing System	**FFESG**
IMC	Instrument Meteorological Conditions	
INS	Inertial Navigation System	**FFESG**
IRS	Inertial Reference System	**FFESG**
ITCZ	Inter-Tropical Convergence Zone (AKA the Doldrums)	
LIGO	Laser Interferometer Gravitational Wave Observatory (see Wikipedia)	
LOC	Loss Of Control Accidents	
LOC	Localizer	**FFESG**
LOC/DME	Type of approach using radio aids: Localizer and DME	
LNAV	Lateral Navigation approach (a type of GPS approach)	
LPV	Lateral Precision with Vertical approach (an other type of GPS approach)	
MAA	Missed Approach Altitude	
MAD	Mutual Assured Destruction	
MAP	Missed Approach Point	
MCAS	Maneuvering Characteristics Augmentation System	**FFESG**
MCT	Maximum Continuous Thrust	
MDA	Minimum Descent Altitude	

MEM (chip)	Micro Electro-Mechanical device	
METAR	Hourly Weather Report.	**FFESG**
Mickey	A 13 oz. bottle of (usually) whiskey	
MLG	Main Landing Gear	
Mode C	Transponder with altitude reporting capability	
MP	Manifold Pressure	
MSL	Above Mean Sea Level	
NEXRAD	Next-Generation **Rad**ar (Weather Radar)	
NORMAL LAW		**FFESG**
NTSB	National Transportation Safety Board	
PAPI	Precision Approach Path Indicator	**FFESG**
PF	Pilot Flying	
PFD	Primary Flight Display	**FFESG**
PM	Pilot Monitoring	
PMA	Pilot Monitored Approach	
PIO	Pilot-Induced Oscillation	
PIT	Pilot-Induced Turbulence	
POH	Pilots Operating Handbook	
PTC	Pitch Trim Compensator	**FFESG**
QNH	Altimeter Setting Q Code	**FFESG**
QRG	Quick Reference Guide	
QRH	Quick Reference Handbook	

RA	Radio Altitude. See also **AGL**.	
RPM	Revolutions Per Minute	
RWY	Runway	
SOP	Standard Operating Procedure	
SPD	Speed	See **FMA**
Speedbrake		**FFESG**
STAR	Standard Terminal Arrival	
TAS	True Air Speed	
THS	Trimmable Horizontal Stabilizer	
TLA	Three Letter Acronym	
TMI	Too Much Information	
TOGA	Takeoff and Go-Around Thrust	See **FMA**
TRK/FPA	Track/Flight Path Angle	See **FMA** **FFESG**
TDZE	Touch Down Zone Elevation	
V_{XXX}	Airspeed Reference V Speed **FFESG**	
V_{APP}	Approach Speed	
V_{FE30}	Max speed for Flaps Extended to **30**	
V_{LO}	Max Landing Gear Operating speed	
V_{YSE}	Best single-engine rate of climb speed	
VASIS	Visual Approach Slope Indicators	
VFR	Visual Flight Rules	

VMC	Visual Meteorological Conditions	
VNAV	Vertical Navigation **FFESG**	See **FMA**
V/S	Vertical Speed	See **FMA**
W1X1/4F	Pre-METAR code. It means *indefinite ceiling 100 feet obscured, visibility ¼ mile in fog. See METAR.*	
	FFESG	
WAAS GPS	Wide Area Augmentation System	
	FFESG	
ZFW	Zero Fuel Weight	

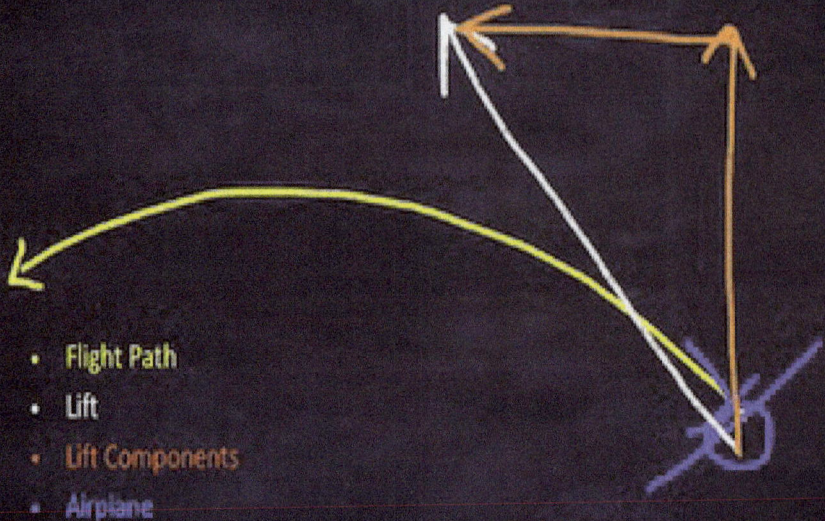

This is a diagram of an important concept. It is worth returning to often as understanding grows.

Not only does it describe how and airplane turns—it also shows how to fly crosswind takeoffs and landings safely.

Foreword

Chain of Experience

Nobody said it better than Andy Grove. He was the tough and brilliant manager who founded Intel in 1968 with Gordon Moore and Robert Noyce. He was writing about income distribution and sending jobs overseas to fatten the bottom line, but his words are just as much to the point in aviation:

> *Not only did we lose an untold number of jobs, **we broke the chain of experience** that is so important in technological evolution.*

Dear Reader: like many other occupations, flying is an apprenticeship trade. The technology of the trade evolves, therefore so must we – but *from* something *to* something. That is the point Andy Grove makes.

Understanding comes from seeing movement and change. Each new development is linked to the past. We must be able to have conversations between generations. That is what I hope to do with this book.

I was lucky. When I joined the airline in 1973 as a First Officer on the DC-9, apprenticeship was still very much a reality. True, some captains deselected themselves from teaching (*Not my job*) and it was probably just as well they did. But many – perhaps the majority of those I flew with – were just a few years out of a fighter pilot seat. They had a lot to offer and they passed it forward to me, each in his own way. Even though the DC-9 was not exactly the CF-86, the CF-101, or the CF-104, the chain of experience was real. The generations were linked. I saw where our skills came from, and my teachers saw where those skills were going.

Then Deregulation happened.

(President Jimmy Carter signed the Airline Deregulation Act into law on October 24, 1978. That was the first time in U.S. history that an industry had been deregulated. For further information, see Glossary)

Robert Crandall, then an executive at American Airlines, spoke against Deregulation at a Senate Hearing. What he said there has been filed far away, but what he said after Deregulation became law remains:

> *If anyone makes any money in this business ever*
> *again, it will be a f###ing miracle.*

Then he became President of American Airlines. Standing at his desk, he thought up *hub and spoke, airline miles rewards,* and *pricing for load management.* He set the standard. Other airlines, for the most part, just copied what he did. He had re-invented the airline business model.

Hub and spoke begat feeder airlines, which in turn begat turboprops and split seniority lists. DC-9's no longer prowled the Maritimes. Overseas routes proliferated, attracting senior pilots with larger airplanes and larger paychecks. If there was a junior pilot on those airplanes, he was a dozer. The pilots getting the real flying were at the feeders. The chain of experience was broken.

Two decades after Deregulation, re-invention in the airline business had become entirely financial. Airplanes and pilots alike were costs to be managed. Unions, still proud, didn't notice they had been castrated.

Officially, nothing was different. Airlines were merging. A few were even making money. But symptoms were appearing.

A feeder airline crashed a turboprop in Buffalo, killing all on board. A month or so later the New York Times Magazine published a profile of the pilots. It was heart-rending. The First Officer lived at home with her parents and had two jobs. In the year before her death, her earnings at the airline were $15,800.

The article stirred the pot. Some people paid attention, for a time. Then the article quietly disappeared. I can no longer find a reference to it.

The world has changed. The world is changing. We are all on a moving platform, trying to keep our footing.

You, Dear Reader. Most likely you have passed all your exams and wear all your ratings proudly on your licenses. Some of you wear wings and epaulettes, perhaps already at the airline of your choice.

Meanwhile, I am at the other end of my career and beyond. Fifty years ago, in my first job in aviation, I taught ground school. In my most recent position, I taught ground school.

I have learned that I love teaching a small class, seeing your smiles and tasting your wit. Watching your questing intelligence emerge, unashamed and bold. Hearing your voices. Touching each other with ideas.

Truth is as fluid as our skills and voices mingling. Flying with others and singing with others and learning with others has been one of the great joys of my life. Now, with COVID and old age (mine) I miss you.

I have to accept that for many reasons I will probably never meet most of you in person. That is my loss.

I have also accepted that for now I am not going to teach the class I want to teach: a seminar with you, pilots who have gone through all the hoops, passed all the exams. You who are at the beginning of your pilot careers.

We live in the now. We greet each new day and do what we can. And at my age I can't afford to wait for opportunity. Instead, I will write this book.

And who knows?

Maybe we *will* meet, somehow. The history of one soul touching another through writing and reading is a long and beautiful one. Maybe – together – we will be able to re-link the chain of experience.

§

Chapter One

And your life is filled with much confusion/Until happiness is just an illusion/
And the world around is crumbling down, darlin'

~ **Reach Out**/*I'll be There* – Holland-Dozier-Holland – *The Four Tops, 1966* ~

My starting point is today. It is easier that way to imagine myself in the world. Today's world is so different from the world of my coming of age, and indeed from the world of most of my career, that I have to start here in the present and hope that as I work my way back, memory will speak and those earlier worlds will live again. I hope they do, because we will both learn from the changes.

Learning is the key. As the world changes around us, *what we thought we knew* may need some adjustment.

Thought Experiment:

It is March, 2016. You are the captain of FlyDubai Flight FZ981, a B737-8. It is the latest version of an old aircraft design. Lots of new bells and whistles have been added to the sturdy old airframe.

You are hand-flying the approach into Rostov-on-Don, Russia. The weather is operational but windy. Your approach is tracking well within limits, because you are using the HUD and flying the "bird" onto the runway symbol.

Out of the blue there is a loud voice alert:

GO AROUND WINDSHEAR AHEAD

You make the understandable decision to go around. But it is messy. You find yourself pushing forward on the yoke to 62% of full deflection. In addition, you hold nose-down trim for four seconds. You bust flap speed and the missed approach altitude. Your heart is racing. But you have survived.

You are a long way from home; the alternates are – as is often the case – inconvenient. You and the crew consider what to do. You decide to hold.

Holding gives you time to think. That go-around scared you, but what did you do wrong? With a proper review – in the bar or at least on the ground after a successful landing – you might have remembered a couple of errors: you forgot to set QNH, and you set V_{APP} to V_{REF} + 10, instead of the V_{REF} + 18 recommended for the windy conditions.

But you're not in the bar. You're still flying, and unless you change your mind, the hold will lead you into doing another approach. And you still can't think of anything you did wrong. One minute you were tracking well within limits on the ILS, and the next you were performing the procedure you learned in the simulator: the *Low Level Windshear Escape Maneuver*.

Now you, reader, are yourself again. You have put yourself in this pilot's shoes, trying for empathy. What is his state of mind? What is he feeling? What about his confidence?

More questions arise, now that you are back to being you, and they are mostly *Why?* Why did the missed approach become sloppy and scary? Why was the aircraft so difficult to control? For that matter, why was there a missed approach at all?

There is another question – one that we are wisely holding in abeyance for now: *What would I/you have done?*

•

The majority of books and courses on flying are pitched at passing exams. But you, reader, have passed them all. Congratulations! Now you can start learning.

We are all in the same boat. After fifty-five-plus years as a pilot, I am still learning the trade. The world changes, and we struggle to keep up. We see *through a glass, darkly*. And that's fine with me. At my age, learning is one of life's greatest pleasures. I am content to know in part. Because – *and then, face to face, I shall know even as I also am known* – I think I know when that is. And I am in no hurry.

I have read many aviation books and taken many courses and passed a ton of exams. But many of my questions on the subject have been instigated by – and answered in – just two books:

- *Stick and Rudder*

- *Handling the Big Jets*

I recommend both to your reference library.

Wolfgang Langewiesche wrote Stick and Rudder in 1944, the year I was born. With good luck – I can't remember how it happened – I read it before I took my first flying lesson. But today I immediately remember two questions posed and answered in the book, each of them tied to a memorable illustration:

- How does an airplane fly?

- What happens (other things being equal) when you pull the stick back (not all the way) and hold it in the new position?

D.P. Davies became Chief Test Pilot at the British Air Registration Board in 1949. In that position he flew certification flights for most jet transports, up to and including the B-747 and the Concorde.

My copy of his *Handling the Big Jets* is a Third Edition from 1972. In this book Davies answers most of the questions important to a future airline pilot.

- What happens when you fly higher? Faster?

- What does it mean for the pilot when her aircraft is:

    - Larger

    - Heavier

    - Has a greater C of G range?

That's just a tiny sample of the subjects in *Handling the Big Jets*. It was my textbook during my airline career, from 1973 to 2004.

•

Propeller-driven aircraft have a *Service Ceiling,* above which they can no longer climb at 50 fpm. The altitude is largely determined by available thrust.

Airliners have an *Aerodynamic Ceiling,* known to jet fighter pilots as **coffin corner**. As air density decreases at higher altitudes, stall speed (in Indicated Air Speed) is steady, but you have to move faster (in True Air Speed) to get the same dynamic pressure.

As air temperature decreases at higher altitudes, sound waves slow. Mach 1 (where the airplane is moving exactly as fast as a sound wave) occurs at a lower True Air Speed. In a Standard Atmosphere at Sea Level (15°C), sound travels at 667 knots. At 35,000 feet and minus 56°C, Mach 1 is 574 knots.

On the airspeed tape, M_{MO} (Max Operating Mach) descends toward V_S (Stalling Speed) as altitude increases. Eventually they come together. That's the *corner.* You can't go faster, and you can't go slower.

Sounds scary. But it begs the question: *What happens if you do go faster or slower or higher?*

The test pilots did not, to my knowledge, explore those questions. But that *departure from the envelope* has been flight tested, and we have the data.

Thought experiment:

You are sitting in the right seat of an A330 at FL350. You are PF – pilot flying. The flight is approaching the ITCZ, the Inter Tropical Convergence Zone, known to sailors as *The Doldrums.* Air in the Doldrums meets and rises, causing surface calm and thunderstorms aloft. It is night. You have just entered cloud and the turbulence has started. The radar is showing bright returns ahead.

A few minutes ago you had a conversation with the Captain. You wanted to climb over the storms. He vaguely rejected the idea before going back to the First-Class cabin for a nap. But you are still pre-occupied with the idea of climbing out of the cloud.

Suddenly there is the loud noise of semi-solid precipitation hitting the windscreen. St. Elmo's fire dances around the wipers. The turbulence has increased. The first audio warning is *the cricket* as the autopilot disengages. The ECAM lights up with red and yellow messages. There is a confusion of audio alerts. The pitot-static instruments are dancing. The Flight Directors, still engaged, call for a climb.

So you do. You pull, and keep pulling. The flight controls have dropped from *Normal Law* into *Alternate 2 Law*. You have lost envelope protection, but the *Autotrim* is still active. Over a minute, as you hold up elevator, it runs the THS (Trimmable Horizontal Stabilizer) to full Nose-Up.

Still in cloud, the aircraft zooms, converting Kinetic Energy to Potential Energy on a ballistic trajectory. You don't know it, but you are exploring new territory. Using the aircraft's momentum, you have punched through *coffin corner* and out of the *Flight Envelope*. You are no longer flying.

Once again, reader, are yourself. You are no longer that right-seat pilot in the A330. But you feel uneasy. What is the airplane going to do now, and why?

Don't worry. We can find out. The DFDR (Digital Flight Data Recorder) was found. The Flight Test Data was intact. We know exactly what happened.

And once again we can defer the question: What would I/you have done? There is no need to explore that now, because someone else did it and we can learn from it. What you or I would have done is not only irrelevant. The thought – the question – might stand between us and our potential for learning. That would be contrary to our purpose.

•

I knew him as Uncle Eric. He was one of those too-rare adults who effortlessly treat children as equals. I looked forward to his visits.

He never let me off easy. But he would smile and make sure to engage me before countering one of my childish assertions.

Eric Leaver was a true autodidact, like Leonardo da Vinci. He contracted rheumatic fever as a child. Unlike Mozart, he survived the disease. It was England between the World Wars, and he was housed in an estate. There was a library. He took advantage of his good luck. He nurtured his youthful thirst for knowledge. He also developed what I believe what was for him a natural gift – a bright skepticism of orthodoxy and received wisdom. He became an inventor.

Eric was not my real uncle. He was a friend of my father's. The two had worked together at Electronic Associates Limited, just after World War II. During that era, when I was in elementary school, my father bought a surplus Link Trainer and set it up in our garage.

The Link was aviation's first simulator. Developed starting in 1928, and patented in 1931, it was largely ignored until the U.S. Post Office airmail system suffered a string of tragic accidents. In 1934 the Army Air Corps, now in charge, bought Link Trainers to help teach pilots to "fly blind". Edwin Link thus became one of the early inventors who made instrument flying possible. Others were the father and son team of Elmer Ambrose Sperry (gyro instruments) and Lawrence Burst Sperry (autopilot), Paul Kollsman (barometric altimeter), and – almost forgotten today – Eric W. Leaver.

At the same time as the other instrument flying pioneers – the early thirties, during the Great Depression – Uncle Eric was working on an automatic landing system for aircraft. During that project he invented – and patented and flight tested – an Inertial Navigation System.

In high school I was a car nut. I worked weekends and some evenings pumping gas. I was an apprentice mechanic. I could name every make and model year. I could find their hidden gas caps.

I also devoured *Popular Mechanics* and *Popular Science*. All I can remember from that reading is one article I scoffed at. It was about pigeons pecking a grid to guide the re-entry of an ICBM. I thought: Pigeons? Pecking? At 8 G's? The ICBM's need Uncle Eric's INS.

By that time, Eric had explained to me how his inertial system worked, and I had slowly understood. So when he told me how the U.S. Military had rejected his invention because "it doesn't take wind into consideration," I knew enough to laugh.

•

Thought experiment:

You are in geosynchronous orbit around Earth, like a GPS satellite. It is daytime. Earth is a brilliant blue and white, reflecting light. She is not under your feet – *down there*, like in low orbit – but *over there*. You can point at her. She is definitely spheroid and breathtakingly beautiful.

Your heartbeat slows. You watch as patterns of cloud swirl. You can plainly see that the atmosphere is of the Earth but not attached to Earth. Earth is spinning on her axis, but the clouds move to their own music.

You are overcome with the fragility of it all. The atmosphere is thin. It is not contained. It is attracted to Earth's surface by gravity. Why does it not blow away, as Mars' atmosphere has done?

Earth's magnetic field, you remember. Movement of the Earth's iron core generates a magnetic field, which deflects the solar wind safely around Earth and her atmosphere.

But for how long?

OK, Dear Reader, take a breath. You are back home. But some things are starting to make more sense.

Seeing is everything. You remember from the meteorology books how the tropopause is lower at the poles and rises where the atmosphere is warmer. Just now you could see that, plain as day. Indeed, the whole atmosphere – the whole blue beauty of it – bulges out unmistakably at the equator, and squishes down – like a flattened hat – at the polar ice caps.

You remember the swirls. You could see that the air near the ground was being dragged along by the spinning sphere, but aloft – where an airplane is cleaning up after takeoff – the air was on its own, rushing to fill in where air was rising; fanning out near the ground where air was sinking. And, varying with the sine of the latitude, the independent air was being bent by a force which isn't a force, the air's straight-line path describing a curve over Earth rotating beneath it.

Why is this Coriolis Effect so difficult to explain? I have been studying it and teaching it for years, each time believing I know what I'm talking about. And I'm still struggling.

There are more problems like this one. And there will be even more when we fly not in the atmosphere, but in interplanetary space. They are *frame of reference* problems. Relativity. Einstein.

We as creatures exist in a frame of reference. So it's hard for us to get our minds around problems with multiple frames. It takes Einstein's *thought experiment* technique to deal with them. But when you think about it, we pilots already operate in a system with two frames of reference. That's why takeoff and landing can get complicated. That's why there are word-pairs like:

- Airspeed/Groundspeed

- Heading/Track

- Vertical Speed/Flight Path Angle

Of course, if we don't want to think too hard, we can just say, *wind*. It's the *wind*.

I have a few thoughts about why further thought on this subject could be productive. Wind can be gusty. Large airplanes have large inertia. Let me begin with a story about *Ground Speed Mini*.

I flew the A320 from 1995 until I retired in 2004. During that time Airbus issued a number of supplements to the Flight Crew Operating Manual (FCOM). We called them *Blue Inserts*, because they were printed on blue paper. The insert in question was called:

A320/A321 FCOM BULLETIN No. 47

SUBJECT: GROUND SPEED MINI FUNCTION

I read it eagerly, because it was another example of how new data available – in this case from the three Inertial Reference Systems (IRS – the latest incarnation of Uncle Eric's INS), and the Flight Management and Guidance Computers (FMGC), can be used to help the pilots do their work. Data from these two could let the FMGC's (there are two) calculate the aircraft's momentum in real time. To put it more technically (or more scientifically), the IRS calculates the Flight Path Vector (FPV) *in reference to Earth*, and the FMGC (which knows the aircraft's current weight) could use the formulae ($p = mv$, and $E_K = 1/2mv^2$, respectively) to continuously calculate the aircraft's momentum and kinetic energy.

Why is that of interest?

Compare two aircraft, each on approach on a windy, gusty day, where there is likely to be *windshear*, defined as change of wind speed and/or direction with altitude.

The C172 is more like a leaf blowing in the wind. A leaf reacts instantly to gusts; its tiny Kinetic Energy is almost nothing compared to the density of the air throwing it around. In the same conditions a C172's airspeed will bounce up and down in reaction to wind gusts. The C172 has *some* momentum, after all. But with its low wing loading, the light airplane will react quickly, accelerating to regain its former speed *in reference to the air*.

No so the airliner. With its much larger momentum (mass times speed), the A320 will have a smoother ride and will largely conserve its momentum and its Flight Path Vector, which is its velocity *in reference to Earth*. It takes both energy *and* time to change this velocity. You could say that the C172 is stable *in reference to the air*, and the A320 is stable *in reference to Earth*.

Why does this matter?

Well, it doesn't. Not if the pilot can stay ahead of the airplane. Airline Standard Operating Procedures (SOPs) use a formula to add a gust factor to the approach speed. This provides a 'cushion' in case the bottom drops out right before the flare.

What did Airbus actually do in *Blue Insert N. 47?*

Preparing for descent in the A320, pilots enter the planned landing runway in the FMGC *Perf Approach* page. With the software revision that activated *Ground Speed Mini*, the pilots could also enter the tower or ATIS wind in the *Mag Wind* field, and it would be read by the FMGC.

The FMGC already calculates wind at the airplane in real time, using the FPV, TAS, HDG and vector addition.

In the clear air behind a rapidly-moving cold front, the wind at approach altitudes can still be quite strong. For our example, we'll say the wind aloft is 270/40. Our V_{APP} is 130. The tower advises the wind at runway 24L is 240/15G25, so we enter the wind (not the gusts) into the *Mag Wind* field.

Had we flown the approach at V_{APP}, our groundspeed would have been 130 − cos40, or 100 knots. That's 30 knots below the speed we want at the flare. We wouldn't have the time and/or energy to accelerate back to a safe airspeed.

Ground Speed Mini says, let's make sure we have enough Kinetic Energy at the flare. It does so by calculating a minimum acceptable groundspeed at the flare – a G/S that will most likely yield an airspeed of V_{APP}. V_{APP} (130) minus tower wind (15) gives 115 knots. Now, if the pilot uses managed speed (managed = magenta, so the speed bug is magenta) the autothrust will hold 155 knots airspeed (115 + 40).

That seems like a lot. You have to fly a few of these to become a believer.

There were many non-believers, though it was easy to see why. If you hadn't read the blue insert, you wouldn't enter the ground wind in the *Mag Wind* field. (As I recall, there was no Standard Operating Procedure (SOP) at the time that said you had to do so.) But if you didn't, the FMGC would assume a surface wind of zero, and your managed speed bug would be at 170 knots! No wonder an unbelieving pilot would pull the speed knob on the glareshield, turning the speed bug blue (blue = selected speed), and turn it down to something he was comfortable with.

Dare to leave the bug magenta, though, and wonders ensue. The bug is at 155 knots as you cross the Final Approach Fix (FAF). You glance at the groundspeed – 115. Light turbulence begins. At 1000 AGL the bug is down to 150 knots. You glance at the groundspeed – still 115. I am thinking of runway 24L at CYUL. There are hangars between the runways, their roofs at about 100 AGL. That'll be the shear, you think. Sure enough, there are a couple of sharp jolts. You sneak a quick peek at the airspeed. 130 knots. The thrust hasn't changed. You flare just as usual. Another normal landing.

~ Pilot Commandment Number Two ~
Know thy Airplane

In the Conclusion to *Handling the Big Jets,* there are two sections – *To Airline Pilots,* and *To Training Captains* – where the author is speaking directly to each. Each time I read this section I feel he is speaking directly to me. I realize now that I have internalized it to the point where I quote from it unwittingly, and sometimes incorrectly. But what follows is transcribed directly from my edition, p. 318:

> Finally, be aware of the inevitable dilution of fundamental aircraft type knowledge as generations of Training Captains succeed each other . . . As this knowledge is passed on . . . some parts of it get lost and the emphasis in certain areas weakens.

D.P. Davies is evoking a pipeline "directly from the manufacturer's pilots". This is a comforting image, but we should remember he wrote these words in 1972 – and as I write *these* words it is fifty years later.

I have always felt that pilots have a relationship with their airplane. Like people, aircraft types – and even individual airplanes – have personality. Like people, they need respect and care. They must be taken seriously. Neglect – whether intentional or not – can lead to a rough patch in the relationship.

Fifty years ago, Davies envisioned a pilot-to-pilot pipeline. The world was simpler then. Today there are other players in the drama. Other pilots. Robots. Builders and owners of aircraft. Nation-states and regulatory bodies. These supporting actors often have intercessor roles on the Flight Deck. Their intentions are good. But the essential relationship between aircraft and Pilot Flying can be eroded by well-intentioned intercession.

Thought experiment:

You are an Asiana A320 Captain. You have just completed your type training on the B777. Today will be the last flight in your Line Check. You are excited. You will be flying Flight 214 to San Francisco!

The weather is forecast to be CAVOK at KSFO. But doubt is gnawing away quietly at your confidence. NOTAM's say the glideslopes on both 28L and 28R are out of service. These are the landing runways at KSFO about 90% of the time.

What is so scary about doing a visual approach in daylight CAVOK conditions?

Well, you haven't done many visual approaches. Usually, you leave the autopilot engaged to 1000 AGL or lower. Your Chief Pilot recommends that you use at much automation as possible. You and your colleagues avoid flying manually, because you are concerned you might do something wrong and the company would blame you. You know that a contract simulator instructor at your airline has said that flying by hand at Asiana is "a big scare for everybody."

Now you are nine hours into this ten-hour flight. You flew as Pilot Flying for the first four hours. Then you took a five-hour break. Now you are back on the Flight Deck as PF. Top of Descent is about a half-hour away. The Relief Captain has briefed you that he has programmed the FMGC for the LOC 28L approach. He has also briefed you that the flight will likely be held at high altitude and/or high speed by Air Traffic Control for longer than normal during the approach to KSFO.

The Instructor Pilot – the Training Captain – has just returned to the cockpit. You strap into your seats for landing.

It is time for you to brief the approach. You brief for the LOC 28L. You have been thinking about how to do this approach on autopilot. You will use LOC mode for lateral guidance. You will use Vertical Speed mode to maintain the vertical profile. You include this in your briefing.

The flight is going very much as the Relief Captain predicted and you expected. Here, at 7.4 miles from the runway, you are gear down, flap 5, 184 knots, and 3100 MSL. That is about 650 feet above a 3° glideslope.

You can see you are high. You stick to your plan and roll the V/S wheel to -1500 fpm. Fifteen seconds later, the PM – the Training Captain – calls *One Thousand*.

That's strange, because you are nowhere near 1000 AGL. But you know what he is getting at. Asiana's guidelines for a stabilized approach recommend a rate of descent of *not more than 1500 fpm below 2000 AGL, and not more than 1000 fpm below 1000 AGL.*

You roll the V/S wheel back to -1000 fpm. As per your SOP's, you set the Missed Approach altitude of 3000 feet in the altitude window. You are still fast (30 knots plus over V_{APP}) and high (the PAPI lights are four white).

You call for and receive Flap 20. You call for Flap 30, but there is some discussion and delay, as you were 4 knots above V_{FE30}. You change the vertical mode to Flight Level Change – perhaps thinking this will get you down faster. Instead, the thrust begins to increase for the climb to the selected 3000 feet. Frustrated, you pull the thrust levers to idle. The Flight Mode Annunciator (FMA) reads;

HOLD | LOC | FLCH SPD

FLT DIR

You are flying by hand. At 500 AGL, you are on speed and on PAPI, except you are descending at 1200 fpm and the thrust levers are at idle.

At 50 AGL, a passenger seated behind the right wing notices a geyser of water where the engine exhaust kicks up the surface of the bay.

OK, reader, you are yourself again. I suspect you are thinking that this doesn't end well, and that is true for the airplane. It made it almost to the runway, but not quite.

•

The DC-9 autopilot has a vertical speed wheel. That was the choice if you didn't want to fly by hand. The throttles were strictly manual. (We were still saying *throttles* in those days, and *buckets* for the reversers.) But man and machine managed to operate with a high degree of mutual understanding.

As pilots (yes, mostly men in those days) we had the advantage of learning our trade before the new generation of autopilots arrived. It was not news to us that the DC-9 autopilot was using pitch to maintain a vertical speed. Without thinking about it we could control the airplane with high precision, whether we were using the autopilot or not. And when we dropped a hand down and rolled the V/S wheel into the zero detent, we knew exactly what Engine Pressure Ratio (EPR) to set for level flight, be it at Mach 0.78 at altitude, at 250 knots below 10,000 feet, or at 150 knots and flaps 15.

Today's pilots go directly to the new-generation auto-flight systems. These usually have at least three vertical modes:

- Pitch controls V/S

- Pitch controls airspeed

- VNAV

There is no standard nomenclature, or even standard function among manufacturers. For example, Boeing calls its *pitch controls airspeed* mode *Flight Level Change*. At Airbus it is *Open Climb*, or *Open Descent*. As far as I know, there is no course where young pilots learn the basics of autopilot function. There are only type rating courses, where you learn the type you are being trained on.

Questions are left open, and pilots changing types can be led astray. What does the auto-thrust do in a *pitch controls airspeed* mode? Airbus is clearer, with Climb Thrust in *Open Climb*, or IDLE in *Open Descent*. Set an altitude lower than the aircraft altitude and pull the knob, and you get:

IDLE | OP DES

Set a higher altitude and pull, and you get:

THR CLB | OP CLB

On a Boeing, if you set an altitude higher than the aircraft altitude and press FLCH, you get:

THR | FLCH SPD

So far, so good. But if you set a lower altitude and press FLCH, you get IDLE | FLCH SPD, but when the thrust levers reach the aft stop, that changes to:

HOLD | FLCH SPD

What does HOLD mean? It means there is no power to the thrust lever servos. The thrust levers are not going to move. In effect, it says to the human pilot, "You have control of the thrust levers."

On a Boeing, the thrust levers move. That's great feedback. Except if you touch them the Auto-Thrust effectively turns off. On an Airbus the thrust levers don't move, and if the A/T commands idle, the Flight Mode Annunciator (FMA) will say IDLE. And in *Open Climb*, if you pull the thrust levers back out of the climb detent, the FMA will change from

THR CLB | OP CLB

to

LVR CLB | OP CLB

Simple, eh?

Visual approaches are quite common in airline flying. Other things being equal, Air Traffic Control can handle more landings per hour using visual approach clearances, just as they were doing the day Asiana 214 arrived at KSFO. Perhaps there is a published visual approach, like the Expressway Visual Runway 31 at KLGA, or the Fairgrounds Visual Runways 30L/R at KSJC. Or maybe there's no traffic and you just want to fly a visual for fun and practice. In any of these cases, you can't just click the autopilot off with your thumb button. You have to think about what you want the A/T to do.

On the A320, we had a Standard Operating Procedure (SOP) for that. The PF would call:

Autopilot Off, Flight Directors Off

The PF would click the thumb button, and *the cricket* would sound as the autopilot disengaged. Then the PM would reach up with both arms and turn off both Flight Directors.

What? What do Flight Directors have to do with it? On an Airbus, turning off **both** Flight Directors pus the A/T in speed mode:

SPD | ---

The first two crashes of the A320 were caused by the pilots' ignorance of the A/T mode. In both cases the A/T mode was IDLE. In the second crash only **one** of the Flight Directors was off.

I know it seems like a roundabout way to tell the A/T what you want. In this situation (visual approach with autopilot off) it happens to be the only way. And just in case, our SOP had another way to catch this possible error. At the end of the Before Landing Check, the last call and response was:

Auto-Thrust . . .

The only acceptable responses were *Speed* or *Off*. If you are starting to think reading the FMA is important, you're right.

There's more. If you look closely at the Flight Control Unit (FCU) on the glareshield of the A320 you can see a button marked:

HDG/VS •TRK/FPA

This button changes the function of two selector knobs: *Heading*, and *Vertical Speed*.

Let's look at *Heading* first. Say you want to fly North, heading 360°. You turn the heading knob until 360° appears in the window, and *pull*. On Airbus aircraft, *pull* equals *selected*. The aircraft turns to a heading of 360°. The mode annunciator beside the heading window says HDG.

All this is familiar stuff. But what happens if you push that **HDG/ VS • TRK/FPA** button?

Try it. Two things change. The annunciator beside the window that says 360° now says TRK. And if you look to the right at the *Vertical Speed* window, its annunciator has changed from V/S to FPA – Flight Path Angle.

What does the airplane do as a result of your button-push? (You also have to pull again to select the track.)

If there's no wind, nothing. But if there is a west wind, the airplane turns left far enough to hold a track of 360°.

When you think about it, that's pretty cool. Imagine you were flying the ILS RWY 24R at CYUL. You are on LOC and G/S. You push that button and pull the HDG (oops, now it says TRK) knob.

(Remember – this is another thought experiment. Don't try this at home.)

The aircraft, which had been on the LOC and tracking it, will continue to do so. Just to be sure, you check the HDG/TRK window and make sure it says 237°, which the localizer track. If it doesn't, you set it to 237°.

Sure enough, the LOC needle stays centred. It actually makes sense. If you're on the LOC and you track 237°, you'll stay on the LOC. That's what I call *track steering*.

How does the A320 somehow know its track over the ground? Good question. Remember my *Uncle Eric*?

When Wolfgang Langewiesche published *Stick and Rudder*, in 1944, Uncle Eric had already invented, tested, and patented his Inertial Navigation System. The trouble was nobody believed it. Nobody believed it could work.

A generation later, when D.P. Davies wrote *Handling the Big Jets*, and I was a rookie at Air Canada, INS was just beginning to replace Navigators on overseas flights. Inertial was new – a high-tech replacement for the sextant and the Nautical Almanac. Davies doesn't mention inertial in his book.

In 1973 I was a wet-behind-the-ears First Officer on the DC-9, drinking from a firehose of learning. Litton LN-72 INS units were being installed on the DC-8.

I met the next-generation systems in 1982, when I transitioned to the B767. These were Inertial Reference Systems (IRS), also known as "strapdown systems".

At the Paris Airshow in 1983, GPS was demonstrated for the first time. There were only six satellites up, so there was only a three-hour window each day when enough satellites were visible to make the system work. Even so, it was a memorable milestone.

When I retired from the airline in 2004, our A319's had basic GPS systems which updated the IRS position. WAAS GPS, which reduced the GPS spherical error to about one metre, arrived in 2006, two years after I retired.

Now in my Bonanza, with a GTN650 WAAS GPS and an Aspen Primary Flight Display, I have more avionics capability than I had on the A320.

•

GPS and IRS – they do the same thing, don't they?

Yes. With each one you can get an accurate position and a Flight Path Vector. With either one you can do track steering. And a lot more besides.

But they are not identical. They are what I would call mathematical mirror images.

You already know about GPS. You grew up with it. It's on your phone, for Heaven's sake! Just for fun, let's do another thought experiment:

> You are in a railway boxcar. It is empty except for you. The door is closed. You are pretty sure the train is not moving – no swaying, no noise, no clickety-clack. You know you can't get out, at least for now. For some reason you are not worried. You start to doze off.

> Suddenly there is that long noise like very slow machine-gun fire as the hitches, one-by-one along the length of the train, take up their slack. Now you *are* moving, you think. But where? How fast?

> You pull out your phone and hit the Maps app. Yes! The pulsing blue dot is moving west along the track.

> You think about how the app knows that. There are satellites in geosynchronous orbit. Lots of them. Enough so that five or six of them are visible from just about any point on Earth. Or at any point in the atmosphere. Or, potentially, from any point in low Earth orbit. The clocks in these satellites are *very* accurately synchronized.

> A tiny chip in your phone can receive the signals from these satellites and calculate a distance to each. Then it does what we used to call – in two dimensions – triangulation. The chip makes a sphere (mathematically) which can contain all positions defined by the intersections of the surfaces of the time/distance spheres radiating outward from the satellites. Whew! I know that blows a brain fuse!

> Anyway, the sphere that your phone made to contain those intersections is your *spherical error*. Except your phone probably didn't. But an avionics GPS receiver does. More on that later. For now, let's leave the boxcar and ask about that other system – INS/IRS.

Inertial? How does that work? Could inertial tell you where your boxcar is going and how fast?

Let's start with Uncle Eric's invention.

Imagine a weight on a slippery track, held between two springs. There is an identical system at right angles to the first. The slippery tracks are on a platform that is held level with gyros.

Take this apparatus for a ride in your sports car. When you brake, the fore-and-aft weight will slide forward. When you turn, the sideways weight will slide to the outside of the turn. At a steady speed in a straight line, the weights will remain centred.

Eric Leaver flew that system in the early 1930's. We would now call those weights between springs on a slippery track *accelerometers*. You have some in your phone, in the form of MEMs (Micro Electro-Mechanical devices). Neat stuff on a tiny chip.

It is important to remember that accelerometers measure acceleration and nothing else. If your airplane is *in Equilibrium*, steady in cruise, climb, descent, or even approach, the accelerometers will read zero. So how can they navigate?

It was Eric Leaver's genius to recognize that indeed they can. They just need the help of an initial position and some math.

Eric linked the weights to potentiometers (variable resistors). These could be wired so that the moving weights produced a voltage proportional to the position of the weights. You could say that the voltage, over time, was an *analog* of the movement of the weights.

You probably know *analog* as *not digital*, or *before computers*. That's true. Today, analog devices have largely been eclipsed by digital technology.

But analog –

> *Of, or relating to, or being a mechanism or device in which **information** is represented by continuously variable **physical quantities***

– analog by its nature has advantages. Those voltages, changing with the position of the weights, are what mathematicians call functions, and they are a continuous record of the acceleration in each dimension over time. And back in the Thirties, before digital computers, it was handy that simple electronic circuits could be used to find the sum of all these accelerations.

•

I took calculus in college and didn't do well. The classes were at 8 AM, and I tended to skip them. I didn't study much, either. Somehow I got through the first year with D's both semesters. For some reason they let me register for second year.

The classes were still at 8 AM. I still didn't study. To get through the final exam, I got a friend to coach me on how to integrate a surface. It was enough to get me my D.

Still, it wasn't a wasted effort. The occasional moments where I caught a glimpse – a picture of what was going on – were magical. What has stayed with me is a great respect for mathematicians and their trade.

Let me pass on one of these glimpses:

GPS calculates position in 3D about once per second. Imagine those positions as dots in space.

Now – connect the dots. Each line between two dots is a *vector*. If you are moving fast – say, in an airplane – the dots are further apart. The lines are longer. Together, these lines are your Flight Path Vector.

Your GPS has used *change of position over time* to calculate your Velocity, which is a vector in 3D. In math, it might look like this:

$$V = ds/dt$$

That small *d* means difference. The small *s* is position. The V will often have an arrow over it to show that it's a vector. The equation says: *Velocity is change of position per unit time.* That, in turn, is the basis of all navigation.

•

Another thought experiment:

It is winter – March, 2015. Halifax, your destination, is blowing a north gale. You are the captain of Air Canada 624, an A320. You are pilot flying.

The two of you are a good crew. Your knowledge of, and adherence to, the SOP's is exceptional. Your team play with Flight Dispatch is also very good. You know that the company flight ahead of you missed its first approach but has now landed. Since its landing the weather has worsened:

METAR CYHZ 290200Z 35019G27KT ¼ SM R14
2600FT/N +SN VV002 M06/M06 A2962 RMK SN8

You are confident the weather will improve, and with the concurrence of dispatch have shortened your alternate from Montreal Dorval to Moncton, adding an hour or so to the hold time available.

You enter the hold at FL290. You and the First Officer plan and brief the approach meticulously, in accordance with Air Canada SOP's.

It is night. The approach in use is a LOC or LOC/DME RWY 05. You will use LOC for lateral guidance and FPA (Flight Path Angle) for vertical guidance. It is cold, so you calculate the cold temperature corrections.

You get this information from charts and tables in Air Canada's A320 Quick Reference Handbook (QRH). You correct the FAF altitude from 2000 to 2200, the MDA from 740 to 813, and the FPA from -3.08° to -3.5°. As you hoped, the weather has improved slightly:

SPECI CYHZ 290313Z 35020G26KT ½ SM
R14/3500V4500FT/N
SN DRSN VV003 M06/M07 A2963 RMK SN8
SLP040

You complete the briefings for the approach and go-around and do the In Range Check.

You are cleared for the approach. You intercept the LOC and, within 7nm from the FAF, descend to the corrected crossing altitude of 2200. Once the autopilot captures the altitude, you press the **HDG/VS • TRK/FPA** button, and check that the FPA is 0.0°. At 0.3nm from the FAF, you dial the FPA to -3.5° and pull. In the altitude window, you set the missed approach altitude of 3000.

You scan your PFD (Primary Flight Display). The FMA (Flight Mode Annunciator) says:

|SPEED| FPA -3.5 | LOC
| | API

|MDA 813 | 1FD2 | | A/THR

All is as it should be. The autopilot is tracking the LOC. The north gale is giving you 7° of drift. Your track is 053°, the charted track for the approach. Your heading is 046°.

You hear the automated male voice announce *Four Hundred*. You think of how the training captain who checked you out on the airplane a decade ago called him *"the German"*. Your First Officer calls *Minimum, Lights Only*. You look up and see lights. You disconnect the autopilot. The German calls *One Hundred*, and then *Fifty*.

To your surprise, you make a so-so carrier landing. The arrestor cable – the power lines on the perimeter road – snag the right engine, the right main gear, and the nose gear, slowing the aircraft. It slides to a stop on the runway, coming to rest near the normal touchdown point.

•

A friend I have known since kindergarten studies mathematics in his retirement. A decade or so ago he showed me his own derivation of *e*, the number which is its own derivative. That was the first time I even vaguely thought I understood. Speaking of things mathematical, he often uses words like *essence* and *beauty*. I expand on that in my head and say, perhaps even *truth*.

Both my friend and I are admirers of the late Richard Feynman. We are also daunted by him. My friend describes Feynman's teaching technique as *brutal*. He pictures Feynman as he writes symbols on the chalkboard in one of his physics classes, saying:

> *OK, gang, this is Quantum Electrodynamics. Follow
> me in – if you can!*

Both my friend and I read his books and lectures – slowly, and a little bit at a time. A very little bit at a time.

Gyros, and gyro instruments, are an important part of our trade as pilots. I have taught (or tried to teach) their operation in many ground school classes over the years. I welded extensions onto a bicycle wheel axle and put hand grips on them. I would get one student to hold the grips and another to spin the wheel. Then the student holding the grips would try to move the wheel in various ways. If the wheel was still spinning fast enough, she could feel how it behaved – up and down, or in and out, it feels the same as if the wheel were not spinning at all. But try to twist – to change the orientation of the axis – and it resists. It tries to escape from her grip. With the top of the wheel spinning away from her, if she tries to *bank* left, the wheel instead *yaws* left. I tell her to imagine this force she applies to the axis as a force applied to the rim of the spinning wheel. When the axis moves, the wheel moves as if the force had been applied 90°, or $\pi/2$ radians later in the rotation.

It boggles the mind. Here is what Feynman had to say about it. He has just derived this phenomenon mathematically. He puts down his chalk and turns to the class:

> We may now claim to understand the precession of gyroscopes, and indeed we do, mathematically. However, this is a mathematical thing which, in a sense, appears as a "miracle". It will turn out, as we go to more and more advanced physics, that many simple things can be deduced mathematically more rapidly than they can be really understood in a fundamental or simple sense. This is a strange characteristic, and as we get into more and more advanced work there are circumstances in which mathematics will produce results which **no one** has really been able to understand in any direct fashion. An example is the Dirac equation, which appears in a very simple and beautiful form, but whose consequences are hard to understand.

He returns to the chalkboard and the phenomenon of the gyro, and draws a diagram of a gyro moving in an even more mind-boggling way.

It is not for the faint of heart.

Let's take an old flying maxim . . .

> High to Low (and Hot to Cold), Look out Below.

. . . and explore it further using Feynman's technique – math first, understanding later.

High to Low is fairly straightforward. Our Kollsman barometric altimeter measures atmospheric pressure. We can correct for changes in the sea-level pressure by setting that pressure in the *altimeter setting window*, or – on the ground – by using the same knob until the instrument indicates the field elevation.

The effect of cold temperatures is a bit more subtle.

We'll use the Feynman technique and do the math first. We want to account for the squishing of the atmosphere at the poles, and for:

Hot to Cold, Look out Below.

We'll use a (only slightly) simplified version of the equation for finding air density in the atmosphere:

Density = Pressure/Temperature

Looking at the above equation, the only difference between Density and Pressure is Temperature, and cold air (a smaller denominator) increases the density of the air.

As Feynman might say, there we have it. Cold air is more dense. And our altimeter measures only pressure. Q.E.D.

Right. But now we have to try to understand it, as Feynman said, *in a fundamental or simple sense.*

It helps here to remember that our atmosphere is held close to Earth by gravity only, so it does not behave exactly as we learned in High School with Boyle's Law and Charles' Law. There is no container, so there is no constant volume. We'll also, for the moment, ignore the effect of water vapour on air density in the atmosphere.

Cold air sinks. On a clear night in a valley, air rolls downhill as it radiates its heat into space. At dawn, it is colder at the valley floor. If you walk uphill with your thermometer, you will see the temperature rise significantly.

The definition of density is mass per unit volume. Cold air is heavier. It has more mass per unit volume.

To simplify for a moment, imagine that sea-level pressure is the same everywhere on Earth. Imagine a tube going straight up – effectively a container open only at the top. The air is pulled toward the bottom of the tube by gravity. The pressure at the bottom of the tube depends on the weight of the air above. (If the tube has a cross-section of one square inch, that air weighs 14.7 pounds.) In our example, that weight is the same no matter where on Earth you put the tube, because the pressure is the same everywhere.

But where the air is colder, it is denser – it is packed together more tightly.

Imagine a point in the tube where the weight of the air above the point is the same as the weight of the air below it. The pressure there is half an atmosphere.

Where is that point? In warm air in the tropics, it could be at 40,000 feet. In the cold air at the poles, it could be at 20,000 feet.

The bottom line is that since the altimeter senses only pressure, it over-reads if the air is colder than a standard atmosphere. And the higher you go, the bigger the error.

As Richard Feynman might say, there you have it. Cold air is denser. Our altimeter reads only pressure. *Quod Erat Demonstrandum.*

But wait – do we really have to know all this? What does it have to do with flying an airplane?

•

Consider Chapter One of *Stick and Rudder*. The chapter title is *How a Wing is Flown*. Langewiesche doesn't waste time. In four pages he sets out the basics of how an airplane flies, and gives us a valuable lesson.

He summarizes his points thus:

- The Angle of Attack is the angle at which the wing meets the air

- The wing keeps the airplane up by pushing air down

- The wing is an inclined plane

- Forget Bernoulli

He explains why he brings up Angle of Attack in the second paragraph of the book:

> To understand this thing, however, requires real mental effort. There is only one way to understand unknown things – by comparison with known things . . . the Angle of Attack has no similes in our life on the ground.

In the fourth paragraph he explains what Angle of Attack is **not**, and makes the hugely important distinction between **Angle of Attack** and **Attitude**.

Then there is his admonition: **Forget Bernoulli.**

> While it is no doubt true, it usually merely serves to obscure to the pilot certain simpler, much more important, much more helpful facts . . . for a pilot it is useless knowledge . . . can be actually harmful if it is allowed to obscure the simpler, more fundamental facts of flight.

If you don't read any further into *Stick and Rudder*, you will still come away with plenty to think about, and to remember until the end of your flying career. Let's go backwards through what we have learned in those first four pages.

First, the valuable lesson.

Langewiesche has definitively answered our question, *do we need to know all this?*

No. We can safely ignore some of it – even some of the things we learned in order to pass exams. But . . .

Yes. If it is something that will determine whether we fly the airplane or it flies us, we do have to learn it. And that essential thing may be difficult to learn, because – as Langewiesche says – it has no simile in our life on the ground.

Second, the stuff about the wing. It is an inclined plane. Or it acts like an inclined plane. Sure – it has an airfoil section and flaps and slats

– but for our basic understanding the inclined plane will work just fine.

The laboratory is your car. The participants are you, your friend or companion, and a board. Let's say the board is a two-foot length of 1"x 3" pine. You are in the passenger seat with the board. Your friend is driving.

Perhaps you should not actually do this experiment. Perhaps thinking about it is good enough. But if you do, please observe speed limits and proceed cautiously, avoiding personal injury.

Your friend is driving the car at moderate speed. You open the passenger window and put your hand part-way into the airflow.

Perfect. Definite pressure on your hand, but it is non-violent.

You hold the board horizontally with both hands and, holding it flat on the window-frame, ease about 1/3 of it out into the airflow.

The board is content to lie on the windowsill, but it does push back on your right hand.

Now you will "fly" the board. You are prepared for the force your right arm will use to keep the exposed part of the board from moving toward the rear of the window frame. You find you can easily fly the board up and down by changing the angle at which it meets the air. Just for fun you turn the board so the cross-section is vertical. No lift – just drag. The board wants to pin itself to the rear of the window frame.

OK, you say, and bring the board inside.

Now you try the same thing with your hand. You squeeze your fingers together and bring your thumb up alongside. You look at the contour that makes. It looks quite a bit like an airfoil, with the thumb as the leading edge.

You fly your hand. It is part of you, so it flies better than the board. You're not trying to steady an unwieldy board with both arms, you're just flying your hand. And as long as you don't get overconfident and turn your hand vertical and bash your forearm against the door post, you'll be fine.

The board was the inclined plane. Your hand was a better-handling board. You understand that Angle of Attack is important. As you think about it, you might even ask, *Why don't airplanes have Angle of Attack indicators?*

•

The A320 has three Angle of Attack vanes, but no Angle of Attack indicator. For more about the rationale behind this, we go to another *Blue Insert.*

A320/A321 FCOM BULLETIN No. 46

SUBJECT: CHARACTERISTIC AND PROTECTION SPEEDS

The A320 has *envelope protection.* As long as everything is working and the flight controls are in *Normal Law,* the pilot cannot force the aircraft to go too fast or too slow. Or to bank too steeply or any number of other no-no's.

Angle of Attack, in Airbus lingo, is α, or alpha. Working up from the red area at the bottom of the airspeed tape, we have Vαmax, Vα-prot, and VLS. These are *alpha max, alpha protection, and Lowest Selectable Speed.*

Below *alpha max* the airspeed band is red. A yellow inverted (actually, rotated 180°) "L" runs from the red up to *alpha prot.* From there, a thinner, longer, rotated amber "L" continues to VLS.

VLS is just what it says – it is the lowest speed selectable by the pilot. All of these speeds are defined by α - Angle of Attack.

We know that the airspeed associated with an Angle of Attack depends on G – or, if the airplane is not maneuvering and is in equilibrium, on the weight of the airplane. And we have seen in *Blue Insert 47, Ground Speed Mini,* that the A320 knows its weight in real time. Of course, that is a necessity for envelope protection.

How does an A320 know its weight?

In two ways. The first is straightforward. The pilot enters the Zero Fuel Weight in the FMGC. The FMGC adds the current fuel weight. That's it.

The second way is more of a head-scratcher. It is, in effect, the speed calculation backwards. The FAC (Flight Augmentation Computer) first makes sure that the airplane is not maneuvering, and then compares the Angle of Attack and the Calibrated Airspeed. That AoA and airspeed combination (at 1 G) can only occur at one weight.

Same equation, different unknown.

Then the FAC uses that calculated weight in the equation again to calculate VLS, aka "the hook".

The bottom line, after all this, is that *the hook* is linked directly to Angle of Attack, while the approach speed bug above it is calculated in the FMGC from the Zero Fuel Weight. The two speeds are sourced independently.

On a normal approach, *the hook* is about 4-6 knots below the speed bug, which is V_{APP}. They are about ¼ inch apart. If they are closer than that, the Zero Fuel Weight you entered may be wrong. To be on the safe side, you pull the speed knob. The bug turns blue (selected speed) and you dial it up a bit to get that ¼ inch.

•

Do we need to know all this? This is a question we have to keep asking, because quantity is not quality. And the abstruse may not be useful.

Langewiesche's message still resonates. *Forget Bernoulli. Ponder Angle of Attack and Attitude.*

Teaching ground school over the years I have developed a module I call *Is Propwash Hogwash?*

The answer, in brief, is:

Yes.

No.

Unlike my ground school class, you have passed your exams. You have given correct answers to questions about these phenomena:

1. Torque

2. Spiral Slipstream

3. Gyroscopic Effect

4. P-Factor

All of these phenomena exist, but that's not the point. The questions we have to ask are:

- *Why does a single-engine propeller airplane yaw to the left?*

- *And when?*

- *And why?*

(Here I am speaking of most prop airplanes of our experience, where the prop, viewed from the cockpit, turns clockwise. There are exceptions of course: the Supermarine Spitfire with its Merlin engine, and the right engine of some twins.)

A couple of tailwheel examples will help to get us in the mood.

The original Beech 18, a tailwheel twin with radial engines and big, heavy props, was notorious for taking a dirty dart to the left on takeoff. Technique? Let the tail come up slowly, and be ready with right rudder.

An acquaintance bought a homebuilt – a low-wing, short-coupled tailwheel experimental. It did not have toe brakes – just a lever which applied brakes to both wheels. As far as I know, this pilot had no tailwheel experience.

At his home airport, if there is wind at all, it is a crosswind. He attempted takeoff with a left crosswind, and left the runway to the left.

To be sure, the crosswind has nothing to do with the prop. At least not directly. But in my Bonanza – which pulls strongly to the left in a calm – if I had a choice between a left or a right crosswind, which would I choose? And why?

Now let us deal with the four phenomena mentioned above and familiar from the written exams we have taken.

First, **Torque**. It is Newton's Third Law applied to rotation. The engine turns the prop to the right – clockwise from our viewpoint. There is an equal and opposite reaction. The prop turns the engine – and the airplane – counter clockwise.

Notice, though, that this is **not yaw**. It is **roll**. The Bonanza employs the standard design technique to deal with this: the left wing is rigged at a slightly higher angle of incidence than the right.

So torque exists. It causes roll, not yaw. The aircraft design deals with that. ***Forget torque.***

Next is the **Spiral Slipstream**, often called **Propwash**. This too exists. The air moving back along the fuselage is spiralling in a motion induced by the turning prop. The explanation has it that this spiralling air hits the vertical fin and rudder, pushing them to the right and causing a yaw to the left.

But what about my Bonanza? It has a V tail. And when you think about it, what about the horizontal tail? Does propwash affect only the rudder? And what net effect does it have?

As with torque, the effect is roll, not yaw. And the roll is taken care of by the way the airplane is rigged. Pilot technique not required. Even though it exists, propwash is hogwash. ***Forget Propwash.***

Then there is the **Gyroscopic Effect**, Richard Feynman's "miracle", the preservation of angular momentum as seen in real life. And it's real, all right. If you push forward to lift the tail quickly during takeoff in your Beech 18, that force is wholly converted – from a force twisting the axis of the props down, to a force twisting their axes to the left.

It is always a good idea to keep the behavior of whirling masses in mind, and to give them the respect they deserve.

Finally, there is **"P-Factor"**. Abstruse, but of great use.

The name – *P-Factor* – means *Prop Factor*. That is true, but it is not very helpful in explaining what is going on.

What *P-Factor* is about is Angle of Attack. Because the engine is bolted to the airframe, a change in the AoA of the wing necessarily involves a change in the AoA of the prop blades.

We have to remember what Wolfgang Langewiesche says in the first pages of *Stick and Rudder*:

> **Angle of Attack has no similes in our life on the ground.**

He also says **Angle of Attack is not Attitude.**

Assume for a moment that the axis of the engine crankshaft, and thus the propeller, is exactly aligned with the oncoming air, with the *relative wind*. (By design, this will be so, or nearly so, in cruising flight.) The down-going blade will have the same Angle of Attack as the up-going blade on the other side.

But increase the airplane's AoA, and the down-going blade will have a higher AoA than the up-going blade. The down-going blade will produce more thrust. The distribution of thrust across the prop disc will become unbalanced. More thrust will be produced by the right side of the prop disc. This will result in a yaw to the left, and that yaw will be entirely predictable, because it depends on just two factors, each ultimately in the pilot's control:

- Angle of Attack

- Power

That's why the need for right rudder persists in climb, but diminishes slowly with altitude (for a normally-aspirated engine). And why you don't think about right rudder during approach. Unless of course you have to do a go-around – or worse, a baulked landing. If you are not really strong and fit, if you do a baulked landing from just before the flare in my Bonanza, by the time you get cleaned up your right leg will be shaking.

So. P-Factor. Yes, it exists. But the best part is that the pilot understands the phenomenon, expects the yaw, and knows exactly when it will happen and how strong it will be. She can *stay ahead of the airplane*. As we shall see, that is the golden arrow in her piloting quiver.

•

You remember my friend-since-kindergarten, who taught me about *e*. He got his doctorate in physiology before deciding that he wanted to work with people. So he went back to Medical School, and then specialized in Emergency Medicine.

He remembers a physiology professor who developed a theory about an aircraft accident: the Air Canada DC-8 at Ste. Thérèse, Québec on November 29, 1963. For the time, the theory was *way out there*. Most people dismissed it. Some just thought the guy was crazy.

He proposed that a sensation originating in the body – the medical term is *somatogenic* – caused the crash by deluding the pilot, giving him the powerful sensation that the aircraft was rearing up like the Ferrari horse.

We will return to the Ste. Thérèse crash, because it was the first of a long, sad series of crashes involving the horizontal stabilizer, or *the stab*, as pilots call it. It was also possibly the first crash caused by what has come to be called the *somatogravic illusion*.

Do we need to know all this?

As we have seen, not always. Langewiesche says, **Forget Bernoulli.** Following in his footsteps, I developed a ground school module to help us think about deciding what we need to know. I said, **Forget Propwash.**

But ignorance of a complex subject is not always benign. The question instead becomes, *Could this kill me?*

That is the real question in our trade. Our job, like it or not, is survival. If we survive, the trusting people in the back will most likely also survive. So let's press on and keep learning, even though the subject might be abstruse. Because not only is learning fun in its own right, but it might just save our butt someday.

§

Chapter Two

Fly by feel, die by feel

Dear Reader, this time the "you" is not going to be you. I would not put you in these airplanes and expect empathy. But the people in these airplanes were human beings. And I think you should know their stories.

The problem – the reason I am going to ask you to watch from the sidelines – can be found in these pilots' legacies: the recordings of their work. The CVR (Cockpit Voice Recorder) transcript from Atlas Air 3591 is some of the most discouraging reading I have ever encountered. (If you, Reader, are curious and feeling stout of heart, you can find it in NTSB/AAR-20-02, starting on page 79.)

I read it the day before yesterday. That night I awoke at 4 AM with the sweats, hearing the pilots' voices. Arguing. Supporting each other in ignorance. Yesterday I couldn't think about them, let alone write about them.

But today is a new day, and I will stick to the facts as I address the pilot:

You, First Officer, are a man of faith. You also fudged your resumé when you joined Atlas Air. You did not mention that at Air Wisconsin in 2012 you *did not complete your initial First Officer training on the CRJ*. To be fair, you did mention your unsuccessful attempt to upgrade to Captain at Mesa Airlines in 2017, and your ride failures at Trans States in 2014. But you lied about the apparent employment gap for the time when you were really at Air Wisconsin.

Today – February 23, 2019 – you are First Officer on this B767 Freighter. You are Pilot Flying. Atlas Air 3591 is a cargo flight flown on behalf of Amazon Air. After departing from Miami the flight has to all appearances been normal. Conditions have been VMC all the way. Now, though, there is low cloud ahead as you start the descent in to

Houston, where a weak cold front has just passed through.

You have misunderstood the STAR Arrival for which you have been cleared and been gently corrected by the controller. You see returns on the radar, and ask for a diversion to the left. The controller says that would put you in the departure path and asks if you could instead divert to the right. You say *affirmative*. He gives you a vector and asks you to hustle down to 3000 feet.

You have extended the speed brakes and then asked for Flap 1, which extends the slats but also arms the Approach Mode in the FMGC. The speed is back to 230 knots. The captain is heads-down programming the FMGC. You – exactly according to your SOP – have your left hand on the speed brake lever, which is on the left side of the pedestal.

At 6300 MSL on descent, you simultaneously encounter IMC and light turbulence. Your wrist – or your watch – contacts the Go-Around Thumb Switch on the left Thrust Lever. If you had looked at the FMA, you would have seen:

GA | GA | GA

But you didn't look at the FMA.

The Thrust Levers have moved smoothly to TOGA Thrust. The autopilot has raised the nose to 4° nose-up to stop the descent. You are both startled. You, First Officer, say:

Oh! Whoa!
Where's my speed?
We're stalling!

You push. The captain, raising his head from the FMGC, says:

What's happening?

He pulls. He pulls hard enough to overcome the Control Column Override Mechanism. The elevators split – Captain's up, First Officer's down. The thrust is still at TOGA. The autopilot is still engaged. The airplane continues to pitch down and accelerate.

When you emerge into VMC at 3000 feet, the airspeed is 375 knots and the pitch attitude is 47.5° nose-down. You say:

Oh Lord have Mercy myself . . .
Lord have Mercy!
Lord!

The total elapsed time from entering cloud at 6300 feet to impact was 32 seconds.

We have to try not to get too discouraged about two people acting in ignorance. For what is a human being if not a miracle?

Art imitates life. And Uncle Eric's invention has evolved until it is more nearly what we have in, and between, our ears. The three Inertial Reference Units in the A320 are more than analogous to our own middle ear organs. They are (with some provisos – see *Glossary: Semi-circular Canals*) the same design.

You remember your early instrument training – partial panel, and all that. We practiced to gain competence and confidence. There is another exercise that can be done – not to teach you a skill, but to demonstrate your limitations. It goes like this:

> You are under the hood. I ask you to put your hands in your lap and your feet on the floor and to close your eyes. As smoothly and slowly as I can, I do a co-ordinated roll to the left to a bank of thirty degrees. Then I roll rapidly back to wings-level and say, open your eyes – you have control.

> Before you even get your eyes open, you begin a roll to the left. You see you are in a thirty-degree left bank. Somewhat unbelievingly, you roll back level.

What's going on here?

You have demonstrated that your semi-circular canals – your rotational accelerometers – have a threshold below which they feel nothing. That is an important piece of knowledge, just like the aircraft's limitations. Only this phenomenon is a physical limitation of the pilot.

In each ear we have six accelerometers. For each axis we have both a rotational accelerometer (the semi-circular canal) and a linear accelerometer (the otolith). They work just like Uncle Eric's weights on a spring, only they have tiny hairs bent by the movement of fluid in a canal, or tiny hairs with tiny rocks on their free end being bent by acceleration. These sensors are inertial. Like all inertial systems they need an initial reference. For our ear organs, that reference is eyesight. For pilots the sighted reference is the horizon.

Hold on, you say – didn't Uncle Eric's invention have three – or maybe only two – accelerometers? Why six?

You are right. There has been an evolution.

You remember that Eric put his accelerometers on a platform stabilized by gyros. This technology – a platform held level by gyros with three orthogonal linear accelerometers – reached its zenith of sophistication in 1959 with the Litton LN-3 in the Lockheed F-104 Starfighter.

Then in 1982 with the Boeing B767, and in 1988 with the Airbus A320, IRS (Inertial Reference Systems) arrived.

As mentioned above, IRS is very close in function to our own middle ear, with the same number and type of accelerometers. Adding the three rotational accelerometers, and using the theory behind Elmer Ambrose Sperry's True-North-seeking Directional Gyro (used in ships beginning in WW1), the IRS became not just a navigation device but also an Attitude and Heading Reference System (AHRS). Like INS, IRS needs to know an initial position. But IRS also needs to know its initial attitude. So it aligns when the airplane is parked. Using the rotation of the Earth, it fine-tunes an assumption of level attitude.

Imagine a plane tangent to the Earth's surface, touching the sphere at one point. The plane is what we, observing at that point, would call level.

That imaginary, sensed, and calculated plane is the new platform. The linear accelerometers now calculate where the 3D acceleration vector points in relation to that new, imaginary platform, even though they are actually "strapped down".

Software (or dedicated electronic circuitry) then integrates the acceleration vector so it becomes a velocity vector, and integrates again to resolve a new position.

Meanwhile, the rotational accelerometers, in addition to providing the platform, have done similar integration to yield Attitude and True Heading. Combined with the traditional pitot-static values (static and dynamic pressure), IRS has given us the means to fly by both of our pilot reference systems – relative to the air, and relative to the surface of the earth.

Whether you are flying an A320 or my Bonanza with its Aspen 1000 Pro PFD, you will see all the information you need to fly in either frame of reference. You have attitude and heading – which in our Earthly pilot world at least – are the same in both frames. But you also have track and groundspeed.

Note that you have two slightly different Flight Path Vectors, because the air you are flying in is moving relative to Earth's surface. There is wind, in other words. Note also that mathematically your FPV's are vectors, often represented as arrows. Because we are flying, these are vectors in 3D.

The difference between the two FPVs is the wind. If you go back to math and subtract one of your FPV's from the other, you can display wind on the PFD.

This is a tremendous leap forward for piloting. Imagine doing an ILS or LPV approach, flying it by hand. With track steering you can fly the whole approach with zero visible deviation of the track bar. And if you're having a good day, you can set the power to get the vertical speed you need (calculated after observing your groundspeed). Then the glideslope won't budge either. You'll feel good after that one.

•

Once again – and for the same reasons, Dear Reader – I ask you to watch from the sidelines as I go back thirty-odd years to address the captain of Skylink Flight 070. The aircraft is a turboprop, a Swearingen Metro III. It has a voice recorder and a five-channel data recorder. The only useable data from the data recorder after the accident are airspeed, altitude, and vertical speed. The date is September 26, 1989.

That is long enough ago to be before METARS. Instead, we had the SA, which as I recall stood for Sequence Aerodrome, or maybe Sequence Actual. We just called them sequences. Here is my translation of the 8 AM sequence for the flight's destination, Terrace, BC (CYXT):

METAR CYXT 261500Z 00000KT 5SM BCFG FU SCT006 SCT035 SCT120 BKN250 7/6 A2997 VIS S 1SM

In the old-style SA, the 5SM BCFG FU (visibility 5 miles in patchy fog and smoke) would have looked like this: 5FK -X (visibility 5 miles in Fog and smoKe, sky partially obscured).

Just as we still have (in Canada) the code CAVOK (Ceiling and Visibility OK), or FABO unofficially in Quebec (for fait beau), we used to have *W0X0F*, which we called *flat on its ass*. It stood for *indefinite ceiling zero obscured, visibility zero in fog.*

We have lost the symbols, but the concepts of obscuration and indefinite ceiling remain important, as we shall see.

It is just after 8 AM, Captain. You check the sequence. It doesn't look too bad. So why did that LearJet ahead of you miss his first approach?

You can see the drifting smoke from the slash burns that were started last night southwest of the airport. But here in the hold you are essentially VMC with scattered stuff below. It is unclear if the low stuff is fog or smoke or both. But it is moving, drifting slowly northeast.

Now the Lear has landed on runway 15 on his second approach, and reported that the south end of the runway is obscured by a 300-foot-thick bank of fog. The time is 0820.

You decide to follow the Lear to runway 15. You will do the LOC/DME to runway 33 and circle, breaking off for a left downwind to runway 33. Did you notice that on the sequence report that the visibility to the south was 1 mile?

You pass the XT Beacon (Final Approach Fix for the runway 33 approach). The visibility at the airport is now ½ mile. At 0826:07, your First Officer announces *100 Above*. At 0826:34, one of you announces *ground contact*. You are on a left downwind for runway 15, steady at 500 AGL.

At 0827:43, you say, *got 27.*

(Like many airports of the era, CYXT has three runways forming a triangle. Runway 15/33 has since been extended to the northwest. The thresholds of runways 21 and 27 are the same piece of asphalt, and are about halfway along this left downwind for runway 15.)

Your First Officer has already made two comments about the weather. Now, he says, Gees!

You say, OK, and start to descend.

Ten seconds go by. Your First Officer says, 145 descending, OK?

What he should have said was SINK RATE, because you were descending at 1687 fpm, presumably in a left turn for a short base and final to runway 15.

You call for full flap. Your First Officer responds Full Flap on the way.

As the flap movement begins the aircraft is descending at 1282 fpm. As the flaps move, the vertical speed changes abruptly to a climb of 783 fpm, then settles back to a descent of 536 fpm. The flap movement, balloon, and correction together take 14 seconds. You are at 150 feet AGL.

		V/S	Time
Capt	In the Missed		:21
F/O	OK		
Capt	Gear Up		:17
F/O	Gear's comin' up		
Capt	Flaps Up		
F/O	Flaps comin' up to half		:10
		-3000 fpm	
F/O	Descending . . .	-2500 fpm	:04
F/O	DESCENDING!	-2500 fpm	
			:00

As is usually the case with accidents, a number of factors have lined up to drastically reduce the odds of survival. We will, I hope, explore them all before we're done. But for now – did you notice something this Skylink Flight has in common with Fly Dubai and Atlas Air?

They are all doing go-arounds. (Admittedly, the Atlas Air go-around was unintentional.)

In a go-around, there is acceleration.

·

You deserve a break. How about a much more pleasant thought experiment?

It was a good trip but you're wacked. Fifteen flight hours in three days and now you're deadheading home. Your First Officer was a nice kid from Toronto Base. You got along well. But now he's deadheading home, just like you.

Your second martini sits, half-empty, on your tray-table. You look out the window, trying to guess your altitude. Low teens, you think. The seat belt sign will come on soon. And there's CYUL – home – sliding by on your right. Must be a lot of traffic. What are they going to do, give us vectors to Trois Rivières? Oh, well.

You realize you have a pretty good buzz on. No worries. Your Significant Other is picking you up. Wait – turning north? We diverting to Mirabel?

Whatever. It doesn't seem to bother you. You look at your martini and giggle. Not a ripple in it so far and it's dead level in the glass. You glance outside. Twenty-degree bank at least. Then back to the martini. Nice and level. Nice work up front guys! Keep that gin centered!

You've had a good sleep, and now you're drinking coffee. But the martini image stays with you as an indicator of local G. Local G is pretty important in our trade, you think, as you tilt your cup this way and that and watch the black liquid move.

Your Significant Other has gone to work and it's your day off, so you can afford to be a little dreamy. You find yourself doing a thought experiment. Your coffee is no longer on the kitchen table. In your head it is on your tray-table, which is down although it is supposed to be stowed.

Takeoff – ripples, for sure. But with the acceleration, what happens?

Landing – heavy braking, and then a hard turn to the right onto a 90° taxiway.

You think you know. That coffee is going to be all over the tray-table. And you think you know which edge it's going to spill over, and when.

Yes, you are having a lazy day. You are still at the kitchen table. Your thoughts have turned to the Swearingen Metro III, that long, thin twin turboprop that crashed at CYXT.

With your third cup of coffee and nothing you have to attend to immediately, you find yourself puzzling through those last minutes and seconds of the fatal flight.

They sure didn't stick to the plan.

The plan was to do the approach to runway 33, to get into VMC and circle. In VMC. How the heck do you get from that plan into IMC at 150 AGL? How do I even know they were in IMC?

Well, ten seconds after they began the descent, when the First Officer said, 145 descending, OK?, their altitude was less than 500 AGL and their descent rate was 1687 fpm. If they had been in VMC, they both would have had heart attacks and that would have been that.

Instead, the captain calls for full flap, and the aircraft balloons – 1282 fpm down to 783 fpm up, and back to 536 fpm down, all in 14 seconds.

You put down your coffee, visualizing this airplane reacting to flap extension at this very low altitude. Surely, you think, this guy has called for full flap hundreds of times. He knows how the Metro III reacts. Surely he does not balloon into a climb every time?

Hello, Dear Reader. I can hear you. What a treat it is for me! I have followed you from martini to coffee to IMC at 150 AGL. I love where you're going. Mind if I come along?

Huh. I'm a sceptic, you know. I'm not going to believe you're there, or here, or whatever, just because you say so.

That's fine. I'll try not to be too present. I am here to encourage you, that's all. Like I said, I love where you're going. It is somewhere important.

Well, this guy wasn't really flying his airplane, was he?

Why do you say that?

Look at that zoom with flap extension! And where is he? In deep shit. He's gotten himself into IMC and he's way below any minimum altitude for the airport and the only thing that can save his ass now is to fly instruments with great precision and that means flying attitude, like wings level, get 10° nose up or whatever and hold it as you bring the power up and clean up and that's gonna take concentration and so far he's all over the map and then he – he gets caught by his own acceleration – it's that thing you were talking about last chapter, right? A distortion of local G?

Yes, exactly.

What do you call it again?

The Somatogravic Illusion.

But it's really just local G, right? I mean, it's like – laterally it would be a slip or a skid. The ball is not in the centre.

Or the gin.

Yeah. But it's just vectors, right? G is a vector. Acceleration is a vector. I was thinking that with my coffee just now. If you accelerate, your coffee is going to be comin' at you – over the rim, off the back of the tray table, and into your lap.

And think of a carrier launch.

Wow, yeah. With that catapult pushing you, you fly attitude or die.

Yup.

Stick and Rudder, Page One of Chapter One.

Attitude. Attitude is not Angle of Attack.

Yeah. Yeah – this is going somewhere. Because together they define . . .

May I try, Dear Reader?

Sure!

The Flight Path Vector.

Yeah. Where the airplane is going. That's the pilot's job. To be aware of the FPV and to control it. That's what flying is!

Yup. That's the essence of it. By the way, it is also a ball that is sometimes dropped. But hey, Dear Reader – I have really enjoyed this. I know you have a life and a job and you have to get on with both, and I have to keep on writing. But just before you go – a very short story:

> I was a newbie First Officer on the DC-9 in 1973. We got a lot of practice hand flying in IMC as we did all-stops hops through the Maritimes. The captain that day had flown the CF-104, the Mach 2 fighter with the Litton LN-3 INS.

> I must have been fumbling in my flight bag or looking at a chart.

He very kindly said to me, "Chris, when you're flying instruments, move your eyes, not your head. That way you won't get the leans."

He would know. The Starfighter, Lawn Dart, Widow-Maker (CF-104 drivers do not like that last name) was not a forgiving aircraft.

●

Dear Reader. I hope I hear from her again. What shall I call her?

Captain. Captain, because she is, and I am no longer.

She spoke of Attitude and the Flight Path Vector – how being aware of them and taking charge of them is the essence of the pilot's job. While all of us always have more to learn, I'd say Captain is in good shape for survival, because she has reached that understanding.

Now is a good time to delve deeper into what we mean when we speak of attitude flying.

●

Attitude Flying

I will start with an anecdote about what attitude flying looks like, and how you can tell immediately if someone is flying attitude.

An Air Traffic Controller has joined the club, and I am checking him out on our C172. It is a lively, turbulent day.

It feels as though the C172 is on rails. Sure – you can feel the turbulence. But half of the bumps don't change the aircraft's attitude. And when the attitude doesn't change, the pilot does nothing. The airplane feels rock-solid.

It is the same in turns, where the bank angle remains steady in spite of the turbulence. And in maneuvers and changes of pace, the pilot knows ahead of time what attitude in pitch and roll will be required. Control movements happen only when needed – to hold or change attitude.

On the way back to the airport, he turned to me and said, "You're not saying anything. I guess that's good."

It turns out he has a Class I instructor rating in aerobatics.

Captain, just now, said, "together they define . . ."

She was speaking of the first two parameters mentioned in Stick and Rudder, on Page One of Chapter One: Angle of Attack, and Attitude. Together, she said, they define the aircraft's **Flight Path Vector**.

The Flight Path Vector is also known as where the airplane is going.

As we consider these parameters, it might be well to step back, out of the cockpit (at least in our heads) and look at them in the context of the two frames of reference in the pilot's world.

Attitude is always in reference to the horizon. On a clear day over flat country, our eyesight and perception can easily resolve the horizon as a line. The pilot's perception has a tougher job on a hazy day in mountainous terrain. On a hazy night with stars above and lights below, the pilot's perception cannot resolve a horizon, so he must revert to instrument flying.

You remember how Inertial Reference Systems, with "strapdown" linear accelerometers, maintain a virtual platform, which maintains its alignment with a plane tangent to the Earth's surface – a level plane. Our aircraft's attitude is defined in reference to that plane, to that artificial horizon.

How do Angle of Attack and the Flight Path Vector figure in?

Let's step back further and into another cockpit we have already visited: the A330 in the ITCZ. You remember how you punched through coffin corner on a ballistic trajectory and out of the Flight Envelope.

What's going to happen now? you asked.

As I mentioned earlier, we don't have to wonder – the DFDR was found.

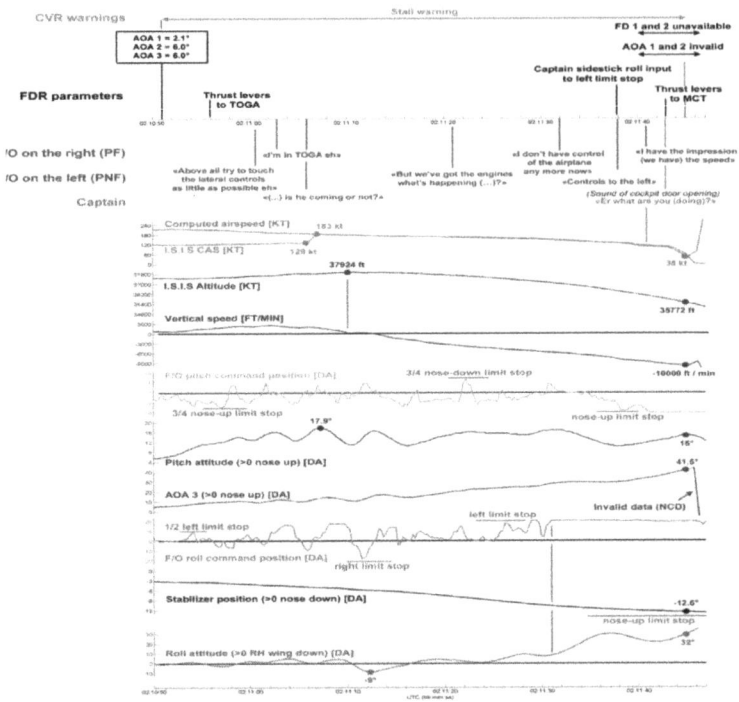

Figure 28: Parameters from 2 h 10 min 50 to 2 h 11 min 46

The traces above reveal what happened when Air France Flight 447 reached *coffin corner* at two hours, eleven minutes into the flight. This is a one-minute window:

- The vertical speed, which has been positive, sinks to zero at the maximum altitude of 37,924 feet.

- The aircraft, now ballistic, starts to sink.

- The actions of the First Officer on the sidestick are mostly Nose Up.

- The *Autotrim* runs the Trimmable Horizontal Stabilizer to full Nose Up.

- The pitch attitude varies, but is almost always greater than 15° Nose Up.

- As the sink rate increases so does the AoA, to 41.5° in less than a minute.

- Forty seconds after reaching coffin corner, the rate of descent is 10,000 feet per minute.

If you spend a minute trying to visualize these forty seconds, you will be able to see why the Angle of Attack changes as it does. The airplane is holding a more or less constant attitude, but its Flight Path Vector is that of a baseball or a bullet: a parabola – first up, then down.

As the descent continues, the aircraft maintains close to a level attitude in pitch, rolling back and forth in the falling leaf motion characteristic of many airplanes in deep stall. The AoA hovers around 80° – not quite 90° because the engines, still at MCT thrust, give the airplane some forward movement.

Essentially, the airplane is flat as a pancake and falling straight down.

As a point of reference, the stall AoA of most wings is 17°. That is the point where the wing starts to produce less lift and more drag. At 80°, it is like the board when you held it vertically and it wanted to go back and hit the door post.

By looking at this admittedly extreme (but actually flight-tested) example, we can clearly see the relationship of Attitude, AoA, and the Flight Path Vector.

OK, that's what happens at 90° AoA. So let's go to the other extreme – 0° AoA. What happens then?

Well, that has been flight tested too, and far too many times. The latest is China Eastern Flight MU5375. A video – apparently from a mining company security camera – captures the horrifying moment just before the crash. The aircraft is aiming – and going – straight down.

$$P + P = PP$$

That's Dan, one of my earliest mentors. There was a little smile he would get when he ventured into territory that might push the borders of his Catholicism. He would purse his lips slightly and scrinch up his nose. Sometimes he would snicker softly through his nose – a giggle with his mouth closed. If the subject was even vaguely racy he might lift his brows and look at you with big round eyes.

In the non-mathematical equation above, it was the schoolboy humour that triggered the snicker.

Pitch + Power = Predictable Performance

The same message can be found in Transport Canada's *Flight Training Manual*, in Exercise 6 – *Straight and Level Flight* (page 53 in my edition).

Attitude + Power = Performance

The translation into prose might go like this: ***If you want to stay ahead of the airplane, know the pitch attitude and power for the regime you want to establish.***

A practical example is me in my Bonanza. I am in *cruise* with 65% power. The TAS is 165 knots. I know that I will need a pitch attitude of 2° to 2 1/2°. Now if I want to do a *cruise descent* at 500 fpm, I will need 18 inches of Manifold Pressure and about 0° pitch.

I am not experimenting, not chasing airspeed or vertical speed. I *know* what will be required and I fly it by *flying attitude*.

There are some things to note about this example. I begin in the flight regime of *cruise*, where the power is fixed and I maintain altitude with tiny changes of *attitude*. I am (apart from the tiny changes) in *equilibrium*.

Now I want to descend at cruise speed or slightly higher. I fly the new attitude and watch as the airplane descends and accelerates to the new speed. I adjust the power to the new setting. During this change (I call it a *transition*) I am *not in equilibrium*. The Flight Path Vector is changing – in this case in both speed and direction. That means there is acceleration.

But I have complete confidence that 0° pitch and 18 inches of Manifold Pressure will soon result in a new equilibrium in the regime I want – say, 175 knots and 500 fpm descent. All I have to do is hold the 0° pitch and keep winding off some throttle to hold the 18 inches. (With constant throttle, the Manifold Pressure will increase as we descend).

We will keep returning to these concepts, exploring them in more depth:

- Attitude Flying

- Staying Ahead of the Airplane

- Equilibrium

- Transition

- Flight Path Vector

•

In any serious enquiry hard work, persistence, and genuine learning will reward with new insight. But that new insight is always a way-station on the journey. A hundred years ago physicists were working out quantum mechanics. In 2015 gravity waves were discovered. And today three scientists were awarded the Nobel Prize in physics. Their subject? Quantum entanglement. Einstein called it "spooky action at a distance." Today we know that this *entanglement* will open up a new era in computation and perhaps in communication.

Let's return – if not to Earth, to Earth's atmosphere. To flying airplanes.

What is the really good pilot really doing when she flies *attitude*? She is really flying the Flight Path Vector.

Hold on, you say. There may be an FPV, but it is invisible. The naked eye alone cannot find it.

You are right, in a way. If I showed you a photo – the view of the runway through the windshield of an airplane at 500 AGL on final approach – you could probably guess where the FPV is pointing, but you could not know for sure. Why? Well, imagine that the photo was taken not from an airplane, but from a helicopter on the same approach. And just to be ornery, the pilot had remained on the glideslope but slowed to hover.

It would be the same photograph.

However – if instead I showed you videos from the same flying machines, your eyesight and perception could indeed resolve a Flight Path Vector.

I think you heard me say, *hold on*, just now. I still say *hold on*. We can deduce the Flight Path Vector, even without an Angle of Attack indicator. We use Vertical Speed and altitude . . .

Captain?

Yeah.

Wow! Great to hear from you again. But I don't want to intrude in your life . . .

No prob. I'm on Reserve.

Oh. I spent years on Reserve. But that was a long time ago.

So you know the drill. It sucks. Your Significant Other is at work and you're not. So I thought I'd see what you were up to.

Great! Welcome! Anytime!

So, where were you going with this *I'm really flying the FPV* thing?

Well, it's like always when you are writing or teaching. You know what you're reaching for, but you don't know exactly how you're going to get there.

OK, fair enough. So try something on me.

A couple of things. Later on, I want to talk about low approaches – about obscuration and indefinite ceilings. When you can't resolve an FPV, and why. But more immediately, I want to remember Langewiesche's tricks for flying a visual approach when you *can* see. It's on page 275 in my edition:

> **The ground underneath is moving toward you. The ground far away is moving away from you. And the spot that isn't moving is where you're going.**

Yeah. And if the power lines are moving up you're going to hit them.

Or go under them.

Yeah, you wish. But you're right. We both use these techniques.

The problem is, these things are all linked. And now I want to talk about turns, where the pilot uses lift – the largest force under her control – to curve the FPV. But it is frustrating to talk about one thing at a time when what you want to get at is the whole thing at once. And when the thing can get needlessly and uselessly complicated, you want to pare it down to a view – no, what? Maybe a *conception* of the thing that actually helps the pilot – remember Langewiesche and Bernoulli? Or me and hogwash?

Hah! Great rant. I love it. I want more. Can I help?

Of course! Socratic Dialogue!

Let's start with turns. I'm thinking about how you said lift is the largest force under my control. I like the thought. Where are you going with that?

Yes. Where am I going? To a conception, that is, I hope, not needlessly complicated. That lets you fly the Flight Path Vector. Directly, with no intervening concepts.

Using Attitude.

Yes. And power. P + P = PP.

Huh. OK. But what intervening concepts?

Well, flight controls. Trim. Anything theoretical except vectors.

I can't use the flight controls?

Yes, sorry. Of course you can. I'm talking about the feedback loop. You are a closed-loop pilot. You are always aware of what your control inputs do.

Yeah. I watch attitude.

Right.

I've flown with a few open-loopers. Yuck. They're all over the place. They're always surprised by what the airplane is doing. Yeah, by the way, that little saying at the beginning of the chapter – *fly by feel, die by feel* – isn't that a bit harsh?

It's factual. I know it sounds harsh, but it's just the way it is, in too many cases. The next chapter is going to start with:

Fly by trim, die by trim.

I bet you actually mean the stab.

Yes.

Sigh. That's me, sighing.

And rightly so.

So – turns.

Yes. Good idea. Let's start with Langewiesche's long Chapter 12 – *The Turn*, most of which I want to skip. But on Page 200 in my edition there is an illustration titled '*An airplane turns because it is banked*'. The title says it all. But the illustration – an overhead view of an airplane lifting itself through a 180° turn in four stages, is prescient. In his way Langewiesche is re-inventing the Calculus, which he may not have known. Did you take Calculus?

Yes. I started out as an engineer.

So you know the derivation of the integral by using limits and quantizing the area below the curve with rectangles.

Yeah. Two sets of rectangles. Just above and just below the curve. As the number of rectangles in an area approach infinity, the two sets of rectangles approach the same limit from opposite directions. That's the area under the function. The integral.

Yes. Have you got *Stick and Rudder* there? Is that illustration on your Page 200?

Hold on . . . yes! I see what you mean. He is quantizing a continuous process.

I have a question I used to ask instrument students: *How do you hold a heading?*

Wait – you're not going to get me on this – the airplane turns because it is banked – you keep the wings level!

Yup. Good for you!

And people might say, aileron, rudder, slip, skid, blah blah blah . . .

And Langewiesche does, in that chapter . . .

But you don't need to.

No. Here's my illustration: it is a symbolic airplane seen from behind. The lift vector is an arrow perpendicular to the wingspan. The vertical and horizontal components of the lift vector are illustrated, making a triangle. The Flight Path Vector is curved.

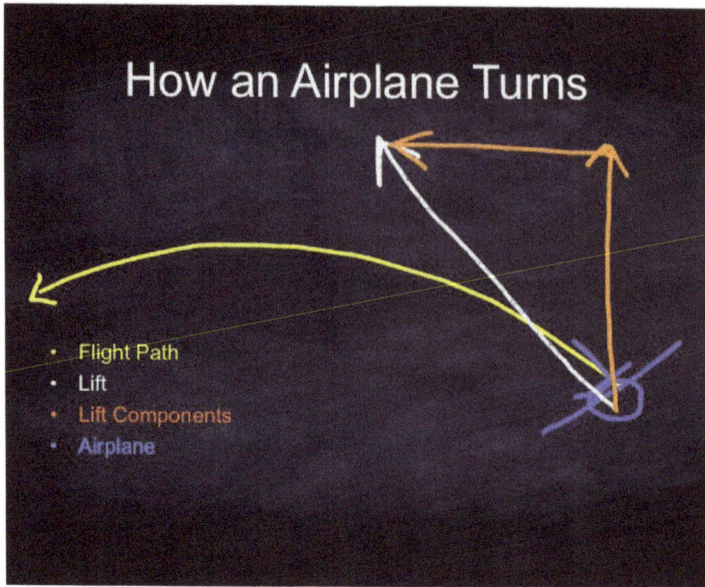

How an Airplane Turns

- Flight Path
- Lift
- Lift Components
- Airplane

Yeah. That's all the pilot needs, really. And I'm beginning to see what you mean about vectors. They're vectors, not scalars. And when they represent velocity, they stay the same unless some force causes an acceleration. And that acceleration can change the scalar speed – the length of the vector – or it can change its direction. As here, in a turn. The FPV is curved.

Exactly. Well put. And standby for further on that, sometime. We're going to use vectors for crosswind landings.

•

Fama di loro il mondo esser non lassa;
Misericordia e giustizia li stegna

To all memory of them, the world is deaf.
Mercy and justice disdain them.

~ Dante: Inferno – III, 49-50 ~

Today I was going to write about that turboprop that crashed in Buffalo. It was the first accident I studied in depth, and the first of a series that came to be called *loss of control* accidents. But it happened thirteen years ago and I wrote about it six years ago. So I had to go back and study.

Perhaps wrongly, I started with the NASA video entitled *Icing for Regional and Corporate Pilots*. I wound up feeling depressed.

Why?

The video is almost thirty-seven minutes long, full of information stemming from a lot of research. All of it real, important, and good to know.

Rationally, my blues may come from feeling as I did six years ago – that this video is an advanced graduate seminar, and it is not helpful for someone who has never enrolled in *Icing 101*.

Emotionally, it has made me reflect darkly on training that doesn't help, and on SOPs that don't help, and about how that training and those SOPs fit into the accidents we are studying.

The NASA video is a big piece of the puzzle in the Buffalo accident. Watching it today, after all that time, I kept asking, *who is this for?* For Regional and Corporate pilots, they say.

But I didn't see that. I saw only covering all the bases, and some butts besides. And I began to mourn the girl. She was twenty-four years old. The video didn't help her.

Today is a new day. I will do the best I can to tell you what happened. But Dear Readers – and Captain, if you're there – I am going to put you on the sidelines again. I am going to talk to the dear dead girl.

You sound like a good person and a good pilot. The only hitch in your career was that FAA Notice of Disapproval in May 2006 in your first try for your instructor rating. All other reports are positive to glowing. You are *ahead of the airplane*. You are *captain material*.

(Having held four different instructor ratings (two USA and two Canada), I can understand the hiccup. Teaching is an individual skill, and sometimes examiners want you to adopt their personal approach.)

You worked as an aircraft mechanic's assistant and as an aircraft dispatcher before getting your instructor rating. You took a pay cut to join Colgan. I understand. So did I. In 1973 I was earning $800/month as an instructor. My probation pay at the airline (the first two years as I recall) was $600/month.

You worked at a coffee shop while you were based at ORF with Colgan. But now that you have bid the EWR base, you have only the Colgan job. You and your husband have moved in with your parents in Seattle. The commute to Newark – usually on an overnight cargo flight via MEM – is less stressful than getting to and from Norfolk. Also, given your salary, living in Seattle is practical.

You sound like a healthy, cheerful person. You ski. People you meet like you. But that commute – it may be less stressful than the one from ORF, but it sure didn't do your immune system any good.

A day's skiing. A night's sleep. A day. An all-nighter deadhead on two different flights. A day waiting in EWR for an evening flight.

Then a sequence I know very well from too many EWR departures:

Sked is 1910. Pushback 1945. An hour later (2041) you remark, "I'm ready to be in the hotel room." You feel like shit. Takeoff clearance 2118. One hour later, you are no longer with us.

Dear Dead Girl,

I want you to be remembered, if not by name. I want you to be respected – not deleted, like that magazine article about you. I want pilots to see you with love as you – drip by torturous drip – get boxed in. As your escape options dwindle. As, in the final seconds, you awaken into an awareness that was most likely mistaken.

This time I **want** pilots to ask themselves what they might have done at that point. So, Dear Reader, follow me through as I recount the final minutes of Colgan 3407. Imagine you are *Pilot Monitoring*, like the dead girl. When do you start to feel uncomfortable? What options do you have at each point? When, do you think, is it too late?

It is a pattern I have seen before. A weak pilot is not enjoying what he is doing. He is uneasy, perhaps suspecting he is getting behind the operation. He fills the awkward gaps like someone desperate to avoid the truth. It is not so much that he is violating the *sterile cockpit* rules. It is that his conversation is sterile, violating his relationship with the Pilot Monitoring. When uneasiness escalates into raw fear, he loads up his PM with tasks, effectively taking her out of the loop. The stick shaker will start in four seconds.

Let's back up sixteen minutes. It is *start of descent*. The PF starts a story about a Houston controller who was known as *Mr. Happy*. The PF regales the PM with clever names for airplanes: *Bent-wing Pencil Jet, Barbie Jet*. That's funny, she says. He is encouraged. He keeps going. She responds to every line. It is like canned laughter. Then she says:

The guys that have fun and enjoy their jobs are so much more pleasant to work with

And he says:

Oh yeah

He starts another story. The PM responds to a radio call for another aircraft and is corrected. She gets it straightened out with the controller. The PF immediately goes on with the story, which he thinks is funny, but it is actually about poor radiotelephone technique and his own encouragement of it.

The poor technique extends to the in-cockpit communication. Back in climb the PF set the *REF SPEEDS* switch to *INCR* as part of the 24-hour Ice Protection Check. He said nothing. Sometime later the PM asks about the check, thinking about making a logbook entry. He says he did the check. There is still no mention of the position of the switch.

The pattern continues. The stories, jokes, and irrelevancies are basically non-stop. The SOP's are accomplished, but in an unprofessional manner, as if to do otherwise would be anti-social. The PF has been explaining how, on his last flight into Buffalo, he set the ILS track to 223° instead of 233°. He says to himself:

try not to be dyslexic

The PM laughs, but recently her responses have been sneezes and sniffles. She says:

alrighty your numbers. for flaps fifteen runway two three are eighteen and
fourteen.
sound of sniffle
Alrighty eighteen and fourteen.

They are setting their airspeed bugs for V_{APP} and V_{GA}. These are the regular, no-icing numbers for their situation. The *REF SPEEDS* switch is set to *INCR*. The stall warning – the *stick shaker* – will go off long before they slow to those speeds.

It is night and IMC and there is some icing, off and on. The approach controller is vectoring them for an intercept 3 miles from KLUMP, the outer marker. They are level at 2300 feet. They have to intercept the LOC before the GS, which crosses their altitude at least one mile before KLUMP. Their speed is 184 knots. A lot is going to happen very fast.

		Time
ATC	Colgan 3407 – 3 from KLUMP, left turn heading 260 for the intercept. Maintain 2300 until established on the LOC, cleared ILS 23.	1:38.5
CAPT	Approach armed	1:20.3
	power reduced to near idle	:52
Capt	Gear down. LOC's alive. Condition Levers to Max RPM	:48
	Low speed cue on A/S tape. Pitch attitude moving from 3 to 9 NU	:43
F/O	Gear's down. (A/S 145 kt.)	:31
Capt	Flap 15. Landing checklist. (A/S 135 kt.)	:28.5
F/O	Uhhh . . .	:25.4

	Stick shaker. A/P disconnect.	:24.2
	(A/S 131 knots, AoA 13°,	
	Pitch Attitude 18° Nose Up	
	Control columns move aft.	:23.8
	Power up to 75% torque	:23.2
	Pitch Attitude +30°, A/S 101knots	19.0
Capt	Jesus Christ!	:17.2
F/O	I put the flaps up	:16.6
Capt	(Grunt) ther bear	:09.8
F/O	Should the gear up?	:06.2
Capt	Gear up oh #	:05.2
	Increase in ambient noise	:04.9
Capt	We're down. (Thump)	:00.1
F/O	We're …… (scream)	
	End of recording	:00

•

It is good to follow the SOP's. But it is not enough. There has to be genuine communication among crew members. And even in today's two-crew cockpits, there are more than two in the crew.

Let's start with the humans.

You have probably heard of the party game. You sit in a big circle. The person who is *it* whispers a word to the person next to her. He in turn whispers the word to the person on his other side. And so on around the circle. Finally, with great laughter all around, the person who is *it* tells the group the original word, and the word that came back to her.

Let's look at some *best practices*. (That's what Industry calls them. I prefer to think of them as *strategies for survival*.) Some of these are not SOP's anywhere, as far as I know.

• If you move a switch or lever, you announce it:

- Landing Lights on

- Gear Lever Down

- Thrust Idle

• If you change attitude (or flight regime) you announce it:

- Go Around

- 15° Nose Up

- TOGA Thrust

Now for the third pilot. It is **essential** that both human pilots know – through the whole flight – what he/she/it is doing.

(It is helpful to pretend that the Autopilot/Autothrust is human. Somehow, we pay more attention that way. So she is *Fifi*, or he is *Otto*.)

• The PF is responsible for announcing any change on the FMA (or the PM, if that's who provoked the change).

Think of it this way: Fifi is mute, so you have to announce for her:

IDLE, OPEN DESCENT, 10,000 feet

Of course, there are exceptions. Remember *the German* on the A320? On every landing he will say to you:

Fifty
Forty
RETARD

More later on why he says that.

But the point here is that intra-crew communication is **essential**. It is also not easy. It takes concentration. It takes work. That, also, is the pilot's job.

Works in a relationship, too.

•

She got rolled, didn't she?

What?

Rolled. I think she got rolled. Trying to be too nice.

Captain?

Yeah. Sorry if I startled you . . .

S'OK. I just . . .

Uh – I know. She gets to me too.

The Dear Dead Girl.

Yeah.   *sigh*   That's me, sighing.   I liked your rant on communication, though.

Thanks . . .

Been thinking about myself with my Significant Other. Could do better . . .

Same for all of us.

Yeah. And I liked that you point out the crunch point on an approach. But you point it out mainly in the timeline. I think you might make it more specific. It is an important point.

Workload management . . .

Yeah. I mean – in this case the guy – the captain – was so far behind. And that situation was so tight. 184 knots. That's three miles per minute. He's three miles from KLUMP. Look at the vertical on the approach plate. They're at 2300 feet. The glideslope at KLUMP is 2187. Where does the G/S cross 2300? I figure it's a mile or so before KLUMP. What's that leave? About 40 seconds?

You're right. And he doesn't react right away, either. He pulls the power back some time after the approach clearance. And that's also when he says, *Approach Armed.*

There's something else. He's in altitude hold. The power is at idle, or nearly. That's a textbook approach to stall.

But something happens before the stall.

Yeah. The shaker. But they're not stalled.

Not yet.

A respectful silence reigns as they consider the Dead Girl, heads down, trying to get the checks done.

No. Not yet.   Why does she say – grunt – *uhhh*?

Yeah. I saw that in your timeline. She noticed something. Wait . . . was that the belated awareness you were talking about?

Maybe.

OK. But what? The *low speed* cue on the airspeed tape?

It's one second before the shaker. Maybe the attitude?

Yeah, what was it, again?

At the shaker it was 18° nose-up.

Jesus. And the AoA?

13°.

So not stalled.

No.

But he's 18° nose-up at idle thrust. And the condition levers are at high RPM. Those big six-bladed props are just huge fucking speed brakes.

Yes.

The ghost of the Dear Dead Girl hovers between them, her be-fogged awareness seeping into theirs.

And then the fucker pulls. I'm looking at your timeline. He puts the power up, but half a second before that, he's already pulling.

Yes. Pulling 1.4 G's.

So now it stalls. Pulled into an accelerated stall. And maybe she feels the break?

Yes. I think so.

And what's the attitude then?

30° nose-up.

Motherfucker!

Captain pauses, perhaps shocked by her language. But maybe not. She thinks about this Dash-8 Q400, 30° nose-up after the stall break, having turned into a falling leaf at 1600 AGL.

We think the same thing, don't we?

About her awareness . . .

Yeah. She's seen him put the power up. She's felt the G and then the stall break.

Then he says, *Jesus Christ!*

Yeah. She thinks he's doing a stall recovery.

Yes. And she puts the flaps up. Trying to help him.

And seals their fucking fate!

And it's too fucking late.

Oh why, Sweetie? Oh, poor thing, why?

She's performing her part of what's practiced in training . . .

Oh fuck yes. Recovery from *approach to stall*. Just like the Sim. Fucking Sim fucking training.

Yes.   *sigh*   That's me sighing, this time. She's really sick. Really foggy. Really scared, bless her. And with good reason.

So she reverts to training. Like Pavlov's poor, witless, lab dog, she . . .

. . . salivates. At the sound of the bell. So you know about that . . .

Yeah. Fuck it! What are they doing, with their training? They're the ones who are fucking witless . . .

But . . . well-meaning?

These aren't sighs. They are involuntary respiration, catchings of breath.

. . . I'm sorry, Captain. You're crying . . .

I am not writing. There is no Socratic Dialogue. There is nothing to say.

But there is communion. Together, we mourn the Dear Dead Girl.

•

On page 235 of my edition of *Stick and Rudder*, Wolfgang Lange-wiesche describes three methods of levelling off, of transitioning from *Climb* to *Cruise*. The third method is to climb several hundred feet above your target, set cruise power, and dive back down, "thus quickly picking up your cruising speed."

You may have heard the phrase *getting the airplane on the step*. That was hangar talk back in my era for Langewiesche's third method. It works. But who is going to do that in today's IFR environment? It would ring bells everywhere and set you up for a violation. But Langewiesche does say something interesting in that paragraph:

> This method is sometimes used on fast clean heavy airplanes because such ships, if levelled off in the usual manner, will take several minutes to accelerate to cruising speed, keeping the pilot busy unnecessarily.

Several minutes . . .   . . . pilot busy . . .   . . . unnecessarily . . .

These words lead us to something important.

Climb to *Cruise* is one of those segments I call *transitions*. The key fact about transitions is that the airplane is ***not in equilibrium***. In other words, there is acceleration. Things are changing. The pilot has to give that change her full attention.   *. . . pilot busy . . .*

Several minutes . . .   Yes. That transition in a C-172 – properly done – can take 15-20 seconds. But in the Bonanza, at 8000 or 9000 feet where the airplane is most efficient, that change will take at least a minute – or more, if I get interrupted by a radio call.   *. . . pilot busy . . . several minutes . . .*

Unnecessarily?

No. The transition must be made, and the pilot must pay attention.

Langewiesche's first method – nose down to get the speed, then set power "*so the flight will be level*" is close. I am embarrassed and reluctant to recount it, but there is a story here.

I am doing a cross-country with an instrument student in a C-172. It is one of those lively days with scattered to broken cumulus cloud. The bases are just above us. There are long stretches of updraft under the CU, and downdraft in the clear spaces.

The poor guy is really busy, and I am trying to figure out why. I noticed that when he levelled off he immediately pulled the power back to 2300 rpm. Then he did a *Carb Heat* check. For a few minutes, all was well. Then we hit the downdrafts. The altitude sagged. He pulled. The airspeed sagged, back to 85 mph. The RPM was 2150. Finally, he added power. But only to get back to altitude and 100 mph IAS. Then he pulled the power back to 2300 rpm.

The cycle repeated, over and over. He wasn't in *Cruise* flight, because he wasn't in equilibrium. What is going on? I wondered. What is he thinking?

At the time, I actually didn't know. He was checking *Carb Heat* a lot. As a guy who had a lot of C-150 time, that was understandable. But he also seemed to be using 2300 rpm as a *maximum* cruise power.

As often happens with new knowledge, the light bulb didn't go on right away. So I'm afraid I was no help to that pilot.

It was the next day when it dawned on me. The guy had a negative feedback loop going. The airplane was actually unstable in speed.

I went back to the Pilot's Operating Handbook for numbers. At our altitude, 2300 rpm was less that 60% power. The C-172 is designed to fly at 65% power, and the speed should be 120 mph, not 100.

So first, he never achieved design cruise speed. But what about that speed instability?

In my head, I replayed yesterday's flight, with updrafts, downdrafts, RPM, and IAS. Finally, the big light bulb came on. It's the prop! The fixed pitch prop!

Imagine you are driving on an autoroute. There are hills. Up and down every few kilometres. Instead of cruise control, you have a device to hold the throttle steady. It is a standard shift, and you are in high gear. You can't change gears. It is like a fixed pitch prop.

What happens?

You gain speed going downhill, and hit a maximum in the valley. Then, as you start uphill, the car slows. You (or the cruise control) are not pushing on the gas pedal, adding power. The throttle is fixed.

But as the car slows, so does the engine – it is connected to the wheels in a fixed ratio. As the engine slows, it produces less power. Power (at the fixed throttle angle) is dependent on RPM.

There's the instability, I thought. The negative feedback loop. When more power is required, the engine is producing less.

•

28 November 2022

I have already mentioned *indefinite ceiling* and *obscuration* as hazards in relation to a couple of accidents, and said that we would return to the subject and explore it in depth.

We will. But this morning brought news of the crash of a Mooney M20 F near Washington, D.C.

Inadvertently I am sure, the pilot managed to hit a high-tension tower dead centre at about 100 AGL. The aircraft lodged there. The time was 1730. The two people aboard were lowered to the ground, alive but injured and very cold, at about midnight.

You can see right away from the photos that the weather at the crash site was foggy. Indefinite ceiling. Sky obscured.

The approach to Montgomery County Airpark (KGAI) is the RNAV (GPS) RWY 14. WAAS-equipped aircraft can do an LPV (Localizer Precision with Vertical) approach to limits of 300/1 – Decision Altitude 789 MSL. The airport elevation is 539, so their altitude at impact was about 640 MSL.

I have found the towers they hit on Google Earth. There are two candidate sites, each with two towers staggered slightly apart. One is about 10° left of course. The other is slightly right of course. Since the aircraft appears to have been in a shallow right bank at impact, my money is on the latter site.

How can this – and the many accidents just like it – happen?

There are lights visible on the ground intermittently. The pilot looks out, and his gaze stays out for long seconds as he tries to make sense of what he sees. But there is nothing out there that makes sense, no information that will help him fly the airplane. In fact, it is worse than that. Obscuration gives him the illusion that he *will* see something if he just gets a little lower. But things are happening fast. In ten seconds he moves ahead 2000 feet and descends 120 feet.

30 November 2022

I was wrong. New photos of the crash site show definitively it was the left-hand (looking at the runway) or eastern set of towers. The towers are 3.5° left of the approach track, and 1.3 miles from the runway. There is no voice recorder, but the pilot, speaking to the 911 dispatcher, said:

> "We were looking for the airport. I descended to the minimum altitude and then apparently, I got down a little lower than I should have."

Both people were looking out. There was no way, looking out, to resolve a Flight Path Vector. So no one was flying the airplane.

What was *minimum altitude*? That depends on the GPS. If it was a WAAS GPS, the LPV approach has a *Decision Altitude* of 789 MSL. If not, the *Minimum Descent Altitude* is 980 MSL.

> "I got down a little lower than I should have."

True. 640 MSL is lower than either of those minima.

Why? In obscuration there is a very powerful illusion that can cause a pilot to *duck under*.

•

What does it mean to say that an airplane *flies like a jet*?

I found out, but I came at it backwards. In the early seventies a pilot friend bought an Aerostar 600. It is a mid-wing, monocoque-construction twin which holds the record for fastest piston aircraft. I got a few right-seat approaches and landings in it. Then, a year or so later, I had my first flight in the DC-9.

In those days the simulators didn't move. No whooshing hydraulic jacks. No artificial sensations of local G. So we had to get some training in a real airplane. We started with large circuits on runway 24L at Montreal Dorval. On my first takeoff and level-off (I think we did the circuits at 3000 feet) I thought, *this airplane flies just like the Aerostar! But with **a lot** more power!*

We had close to full fuel, but no cargo and only 3 of us on board. So to level off at 3000 feet and keep the speed below 200 knots, that power had to come **waay** back.

But the handling – the way it flew and responded – was very like the Aerostar. After the first circuit I was in love.

So what is different about a jet?

This is where *Handling the Big Jets* comes in, pointing out all the details, like *large speed range* and *large C of G range*. But the essence is *slippery*. A jet with gear up and a clean wing wants to go. And unlike prop aircraft, it does not want to slow.

Propellers with their engines at idle are effective speed brakes. In situations where they are in fine pitch (low gear) and torque is reversed (the props are turning the engines) they are **very** effective speed brakes.

Jet and turbofan engines do not generate much drag at idle thrust. Pull the power to idle at FL360 and maintain cruise Mach/IAS, and you are probably descending at 1500-2000 fpm. Slowing to 250 knots at 10,000 feet will take up to two minutes.

That's part of the problem. Then there's getting the approach speed back to where you don't need a drag chute, like the CF-104. That takes high-lift devices. Double or triple-slotted Fowler flaps. Leading edge slats.

And finally, landing. Once you're on the ground, you want to get the airplane's whole weight on the wheels as soon as possible.

So in addition to the high lift devices, you have speedbrakes/spoilers.

These are hinged panels near the trailing edge of the wing, ahead of the flaps and/or ailerons. When they are deployed, they open up a gap. Looking from a passenger seat behind the wing, you can see right through to the runway surface. The joke about the B-727 at touchdown was *activate full wing disassembly.*

There is another story here, an embarrassing one:

A friend had a Mooney – a nice turbocharged model. It had aftermarket speed brakes – panels with half-inch holes that, when deployed, would extend straight up out of a slot on the wing to about 2 inches above the surface. My friend always landed with speed brakes extended, which seemed odd after our jet experience.

Then, after retirement, I did a fair amount of instructing in an early Mooney with the manual "Johnson Bar" gear operation. I remember thinking that I couldn't own the airplane, because of an old snowboard injury to my right shoulder. I couldn't have made that complicated movement with my right arm.

Then a new friend took me for a day's flying in a later-model Mooney, and let me do the first landing. It was my first in a Mooney, odd as that may seem. It was my first where I was flying.

This is where it gets embarrassing. We had done an RNAV approach to the reciprocal runway, planning a circle-to-land. The VFR traffic dictated that we integrate into the pattern for a close downwind. I was busy, and without thinking used my Bonanza numbers. Turning base to final, I was in good position, but a good 10 knots fast. No sweat, I thought, unconsciously channeling the Bonanza.

Boy was I wrong. In that position in a Mooney, you are already screwed. Afterwards, I thought of a not-so-long-ago accident at Palo Alto where a Mooney, landing on runway 13 in wet weather, ran off the end into the marsh.

Fortunately, we had a long runway, and I could hold it off for 2000 feet in the flare.

Perhaps this is a good time to talk about the *drag curve*. Every airplane has one.

In *Handling the Big Jets* D. P. Davies has an excellent section with charts explaining how a jet's drag curve differs from a prop plane's. The bottom line is that the jet curve is a big shallow soup bowl, and the prop curve is a smaller-diameter, high-sided soup bowl.

This is one of those subjects that can easily draw itself away from the practical. The derivation – combine induced drag and parasite drag

– is interesting, and indeed essential knowledge. But the discussion too often veers into the unnecessarily arcane: *it's not really a drag curve but a thrust required curve, blah blah blah*. But though you might think it would, that part doesn't really help the pilot. What the pilot needs in his head is an image of that drag curve – the curve of the airplane he is now flying.

Why does the pilot need that image in his head?

So he doesn't screw up, like I did in the Mooney. Why did I screw up? Because I thought I was on the back side of the curve, and I wasn't. I was in the valley. In the bottom of the bowl.

Remember *speed stability*, and that poor guy in the C-172?

In his case it was the fixed-pitch prop that caused the instability. Even though he was on the right side of that asymmetric bowl (for the C-172, it looks more like a check mark with a rounded bottom), the fixed-pitch prop effect was enough to move the system from speed stable to neutral or unstable.

But every airplane, from fixed-pitch prop to jet, has a range on its drag curve that is speed-unstable. Pilots call it *the back side of the power curve*. It extends from the stall (left side of the soup bowl) to the *minimum drag* point (bottom of the soup bowl). In this range a lower speed (other things being equal) requires *more* power.

A pilot who has become good at it can pull the power to idle at FL360 and leave it there until he "catches the speed" at about 3 miles on final. He has timed selection of flaps and gear down and now, stable at about 700 fpm descent with the speed bleeding off toward V_{APP} he pushes the power up to the value he knows will hold that speed. If he is right about that power setting, he may not have to touch the thrust levers again until the flare, where – if he is flying an A320 – the German will prompt him, saying:

RETARD

If the pilot doesn't move the thrust levers all the way to idle right away, the German will keep calling **RETARD**.

So – saying that an airplane *flies like a jet* means *slippery*, which in turn means a long, shallow drag curve. As a soup bowl, it would be problematic. You wouldn't want to carry this bowl around if it was full of hot soup. With those almost-straight-line rims angling up from the wide bottom, you'd spill some for sure.

So, OK. *It is a thrust-required curve.* True enough. But the point remains: *the pilot needs to know where she is on the curve.* She needs to know whether she is speed-stable, and whether or not she is in equilibrium. In modern airline-and-regulator-speak, that would be *if she has achieved a stabilized approach.*

§

Chapter Three

Fly by trim and die by trim

Could we look at Atlas Air for a minute?

Captain?

Yeah. Slow day on Reserve.

I was going to start Chapter Three. But Atlas Air? Sure. Fire away.

I think maybe this **is** Chapter Three. You know, your header – *die by trim*? I think they did.

Wow. Good insight. I think so too. Now I don't feel so alone.

Well, can't we prove it? They found the DFDR, didn't they?

Yes.

So where was the stab?

We don't know. We know lots of stuff, but not that.

Unreadable?

There is nothing but foam left in my latte. I take a deep breath.

Chris? Are you there?

Sorry. Yes.

I know I should have read the whole report before talking to you

. . .

No – it's OK . . .

So I think I'm starting to get with your program. You know, this or that has been flight tested, as you put it.

Right.

So I was asking myself, just now – *if the elevators were split, flaps extended, TOGA thrust, how the hell does it get to 47.5° nose down?*

Exactly.

The F/O is on the thumb switches . . .

Yes.

Jesus.

He called him *Lord.*

Yeah. My coffee is cold.

Mine, too.

OK, so this is Chapter Three. He ran the stab full nose-down. But we can't prove it. Why? Tell.

The stab is not mentioned in the report. Anywhere. There is a full CVR transcript, but no DFDR traces.

Sensitive subject?

Yes. Atlas Air was the month before the second MAX crash. In between the flight tests, you might say.

Hah! So they bury it.

'Fraid so. Just *pilot error.* Aircraft not involved.

Wasn't there an article of that name sometime around then?

Yes, as a matter of fact. Bought and paid for.

Ooohh . . . but it **was** pilot error, wasn't it?

Yes.

So – no harm no foul?

I make a fruitless attempt to drain some foam from my cup. It's not going to happen without a spoon.

Chris?

There **is** harm. Burying facts keeps pilots from learning. They think, *I'm a good pilot. Couldn't happen to me.*

I'm still instructing. I know many pilots fly with trim. Without thinking about it. So I'm with you. This **is** Chapter Three. OMG! *Between the flight tests!*

•

Why is trim a problem?

Here we return to what Wolfgang Langewiesche wrote in 1944. The illustrations are on page 155 in my edition of *Stick and Rudder*; the chapter is called *The Flippers and the Throttle*.

First question: why does he call the elevators *flippers*? Is it just some quaint usage of the time?

No. He renames them on purpose, because he is uncomfortable with the implication of *elevators* – that pulling back makes the aircraft climb and pushing makes the aircraft dive. Because while that may be true in the short term, it masks a deeper truth essential for survival – *the elevators are the airplane's Angle of Attack control.* In the longer term, there is an exact correlation between elevator position and Angle of attack.

But wait, you say. Don't you control pitch attitude with elevator? And didn't you say that pitch attitude is not Angle of Attack?

Yes. All that is true. But let's parse out exactly what happens when you, the pilot, control pitch attitude with elevator.

If you have a copy of *Stick and Rudder*, you can follow me through with the illustrations on page 155.

The setting is a proscenium stage. In the top illustration the curtains are closed. The airplane enters stage left and exits stage right. In the bottom illustration the curtains are open, revealing what happened during the time the airplane was crossing the stage.

In the wings on stage left, the aircraft is gliding at 100 mph, slightly nose-down. A balloon shows the position of the stick.

Just before entering, stage left, the pilot pulls back on the stick and *holds it in the new position.* When the airplane emerges into the wings on stage right, the stick is still in the new position but the aircraft is in a more-or-less level attitude and the airspeed is 75 mph. Also – the stick is further back but the airplane is descending more steeply! This recalls the old adage:

Pull back, she goes up. Pull back further, she goes down.

Opening the curtain reveals what happened on stage. The aircraft zooms, exchanging some of its kinetic energy for potential energy. For a short time, the aircraft's flight path is level or even slightly climbing. Then – energy exchange complete – the aircraft settles into a *steeper* descent at a lower airspeed *and a higher Angle of Attack.*

For me, this is the most important – the essential – concept in the book, and it is beautifully explained and illustrated.

What does this have to do with trim being a problem? Let's instead ask, would you use trim in the above example? And if so, when? And why? And to answer, we'll zoom out to get an overview of Langewiesche's wonderful image.

What happens on the proscenium stage is what I call a *transition.* Were it a horse, the airplane would be slowing from a canter to a trot. It is not in equilibrium. Things are changing, including the Angle of Attack.

What happens if you trim during a transition?

Think about it: if you trim while things are changing, then at the end of the transition the aircraft will not be in trim. The pilot will have to trim again. Which leads to my riddle:

Q: How can you tell if a pilot is flying using trim?

A: His airplane is never in trim.

When his airplane exits stage right he expects it to be in trim because he has already trimmed. But it is not, because he trimmed *during* transition – for, say, 90 mph. So now the nose drops. He trims again, for the wrong reason. And on and on, in never-ending frustration. The pilot is flying by feel, which helps him not a whit. He is almost certainly not conscious of his attitude, at least not with any precision.

Trim itself is not the problem. Even his usage – trimming during transition – is not the problem.

I can think of three airplanes where I regularly *trim ahead*, moving the stab or the trim tab to the desired end-state after transition. In the DC-9, calling for slats and flap 5 at 280 knots, I would hold nose-up trim for one beep of the stab – ½ degree of movement. In the Bonanza and the Aerostar, I move the trim tab about 6 degrees nose-up when taking landing flap, anticipating the trim change required. Why? I don't want to be holding back pressure at the beginning of the flare, when I am about to need very accurate pitch control. It is much easier to modulate around zero stick force than around a 20-pound pull force.

So trim is not the problem. Even usage of trim is not the problem. The problem is *not thinking about trim* – not thinking about *why* you're using it, and *when*. And if you're not thinking about trim that way, you are probably also not aware of transition and equilibrium and perhaps also of pitch attitude. You are continually surprised by what the airplane wants to do. The bottom line is that the pilot must be aware of the position of the trim tab or the stab.

In a C-172 a pilot lacking that awareness is a sloppy, frustrated, and frustrating pilot.

In a jet with a moving stabilizer, he is seconds away from death.

•

*In dealing with the consequences of having a variable incidence tailplane one basic fact must be kept in mind – **it is very powerful**.*

· · ·

*The enormous power in a variable incidence tailplane can be a good servant when required **but an impossible master when not required**.*

•

You pissed me off, Chris!

Captain?

Yeah. And then I was more pissed off when I saw you were probably right.

Where?

Fly Dubai. In that go-around he held nose-down trim for four seconds. That's too much. That's flying with trim. And as you just said, in a jet that's seconds away from death.

Too true. Too many times.

And I know I should have gone and read the report, but you left me hanging. Did they do another approach?

Yes. After they held for two hours.

Two hours! Burning fuel. Reducing their options. Bad call!

You're right. They were setting themselves up.

So had the conditions changed? Got any better?

No. Pretty much the same.

So I have two questions. No, wait . . . probably more. But first – that *Windshear Ahead* warning. Never heard of it. What *is* that? Did they really have to go around? And that makes me think of *Groundspeed Mini*. I'm glad you talked about it because I'm using it all the time now. And on the same runway!

24 Left.

Yeah. and it works great, just like you said. I have amazed a few F/O's. Got some cred.

Good for you!

So was Rostov-on-Don like that? Did they *have* to go around?

No. It would have worked out OK. The approach wind was about 260/45. The surface wind was 240/21G29. They should have added 18 knots. They added 10 knots. So maybe a rough landing? But with 18 knots it would have worked out perfectly.

Whoa. And that *Low Level Windshear Escape Maneuver*. I *have* heard of *that*. And practiced it in the sim. But that's for when you're caught unaware and – God help you – you fly into a downburst like that L-1011 at Dallas. Shit! Now I'm getting echoes of our drill for *approach to stall*. And Colgan! Damn them! How butt-covering and short-sighted. Or the other way around.

I hear you.

And with the *Low Level Windshear Escape Maneuver* they have TOGA thrust. They're setting themselves up for the Somatogravic Illusion.

Absolutely. Much better to do a normal go-around. Come up smoothly on the power. Hold 15° nose-up. Et cetera.

Right. And it's not as if they were at Minimums, or something.

No. 1000 AGL.

But they smoked that one through.

Yes . . .

. . . and they do another approach. But they're lighter by two hours of gas. And the wind is more or less the same. So they go around again?

The second approach pops into my head, slowing my response time.

Same reason?

No. He gets a little fast. The F/O calls *Check the Speed*.

He's on a hair trigger. Primed for *Go-Around*.

Yes.

Does he do the *Low Level Windshear Escape Maneuver* again?

Yes.

Now it is Captain who just stops talking. I can feel her putting it together. Light airplane. TOGA thrust. There's going to be acceleration and pitch-up. And the very strong illusion of *more* pitch-up. And he has already used trim inappropriately on the first go-around.

. . . so where was the stab?

I found myself winging it. Too much so. I told her I would get back to her on that. I would go back to the *Final Report*, which is a model of completeness. I was sure I could find what I was looking for.

I did tell her that, as far as I knew, the captain was still trimming nose-down at impact.

•

28 December 2022

Ethiopia's *Final Report* on EA 302 – the second MAX crash – is out. One important new fact (new to me, at least) is proof that the airplane was catastrophically vulnerable to a single point of failure: the left Angle of Attack vane. There was, apparently, a bird strike on take-off which rendered the vane useless. Actually, worse than useless. We know from the DFDR that it sent an erroneous high AoA signal, triggering the MCAS.

Today the news came that the NTSB has issued a "comment" on that final report. They propose that another bullet point be added to the "causal factors":

> • the flight crew's inadequate use of manual electric trim and management of thrust to maintain

airplane control.

This is sad. Theory of flight, aerodynamics, and a century of experience are being ignored, and the knowledge gained therefrom dangerously distorted, all to further commercial and political interests.

Perhaps those who wrote the "comment" actually believe what they wrote. If so, that too is sad, because it exhibits a fundamental misunderstanding. As we have seen – trim, elevator, moveable tailplane by whatever name – these are the Angle of attack control, **not the speed control**. The two are not the same thing. And the implication – first aired in 2019 in the infamous *Pilot Error* article – is that **the pilots should have reduced thrust to regain control**. But don't worry. That, too, has been flight tested.

The year was 1989. A DC-10 had an uncontained failure of the center engine at cruise. Because the plumbing for the three hydraulic systems was routed together through the tail section, all three were damaged in the same place by debris from the failing engine. The result was the loss of all hydraulic fluid and thus the total loss of flight controls.

Nevertheless, the pilots maintained partial control by managing thrust on the wing engines to control attitude. Increasing thrust raised the nose; reducing thrust caused the airplane to pitch down. The airplane could be banked – and thus steered – with asymmetric thrust.

At touchdown on the airport, the speed was 220 knots and the vertical speed was 1850 fpm. Even so, 184 of the 296 passengers survived the crash landing.

The Ethiopian aircraft had two underwing engines. Thrust management would have had the same effect.

•

29 December 2022

Pilot Error

Heaven knows there is enough of it to go around. The industry-sized battle to prevent pilot error has spawned university departments, training programs, avionics, products, research, and academic degrees. No to mention a forest of three-letter acronyms. Yet accidents continue.

And these accidents don't just *happen*. There is always a story.

I think it came home to me that first year on the line. There are two of us up here and almost a hundred back there. Our job is to survive. If we save our own sorry asses, then most likely they too will be alive.

So – SOP's, regulations, and the best possible teamwork. But is that enough?

Part of my vision that first year was: no – it's not. We are human and there are going to be accidents. Accidents are inconvenient for airlines, aircraft manufacturers, and even regulatory bodies. But there is a fall guy: the pilot. There is a transaction: you sit in that seat and earn the big bucks and find joy in your trade, but if you screw up, you are responsible. It's your fault. And the transaction is doubly convenient if you're dead. It is hubris and nemesis and tragedy. Everyone else is washed clean and can move on. Poor old whatshisface. He sure fucked that one up.

At the other end of the scale is the *damn close thing*, like Waterloo.

It is my first year on the line in the DC-9. We routinely do all-stops hops through the Maritimes, in some of the worst weather anywhere. The captain that day was old Teddy. I had never flown with him before. But already I was getting a vibe, an alert: *Pay very close attention.*

Teddy is flying leg three into CYQY – Sydney, Nova Scotia. It is an ILS to runway 07 (today it has become runway 06) and the weather is on limits: 200-foot ceiling and ½ mile visibility. It is the first time I have done so with the airline, but I start talking. Coaching. Just like when I was a flight instructor. Knowing that if my words and my delivery don't have the desired effect I will have to take over. And trying really hard because I *really* don't want to have to take control, which for the First Officer (and despite all the *Cockpit Resource Management* training and protocol) will be messy and uncertain, even if the protocol is followed to the letter.

(Aside: years later, as Captain on the A320, I was doing a LOFT (Line Oriented Flight Training) simulator ride. My First Officer was a captain I didn't know. I suspected he was a plant. We had an engine fire after takeoff and did all the drills, but the engine was still burning. I elected to return to Calgary, even though the weather was near limits for the ILS on runway 16. It was the second half of the ride, after the break, so the right-seat guy was flying. As he intercepted the LOC, I noticed his flying was getting sloppy, like he wasn't paying attention. I started talking. I had to get quite forceful, barking headings in 2-degree increments, but he complied. In VMC at 200 feet, I took control and landed. *Why didn't you just take over right away?* They asked in the debrief. *It's a two-pilot airplane,* I said. *I didn't want to go solo unless it was absolutely necessary.* They looked doubtful, but I passed.)

In Sydney, I also managed to talk Teddy through. Perhaps that's why I did what I did in the LOFT. But Teddy wasn't so lucky. Later that same year he was flying an approach into Quebec City. The weather was at ILS limits, but the ILS was NOTAMed off. So he did the ADF approach.

As I recall, the beacon was offset from the runway centreline, so the final approach course was four or five degrees different from the ILS course, and he would have had to turn right to line up with the runway. With the weather what it was, he probably saw the runway too late to turn. He wound up in the mud to the left side of the runway.

No one was hurt. But Teddy didn't supervise the evacuation. He put down the airstairs and walked away, apparently without a word.

Teddy was a nice guy. Perhaps he still is. I hope so. Because his last act in aviation, weird though it may seem, was what had previously eluded him – a command decision.

•

30 December 2022

Because I am reading the EA 302 Final Report, I have to circle back to 1972 and *Handling the Big Jets*. In the same paragraphs quoted above, Davies makes another very important point:

– **it is *very powerful*.** *Because the elevator, when in* *trim, is always slipstreaming the tail it remains available over its full range and can be smaller than the elevator on a fixed-tail aircraft. This is simply because the stabilizer can be set to handle the bulk of the demand and the elevator remains to look after the rest of the demand. On a variable incidence tailplane, therefore, the elevator is smaller, and consequently less effective in isolation than it is on a fixed tailplane aeroplane.*

In the world of jets, C-172 experience is a suck-in, and particularly so for a pilot who flies by trim. For all practical purposes, the full range of pitch control is always available in a C-172, regardless of the trim position. If the pilot is basing what he "knows" on the C-172, he is in for a big surprise when things go for shit in a jet.

Davies says the elevators on a big jet are *less effective in isolation*, and that has proved to be true over the years from Davies' time to today, from flight tests to incidents and accidents. The stabilizer is there with its great power because a big jet has a wide speed range and a wide C of G range, not to mention larger configuration changes (flaps, slats, spoilers, gear).

A baulked landing with 40° flap in a C-172 is probably the most challenging maneuver in the type. The performance is marginal, and the airplane is **way** out of trim. The maneuver rates specific mention in the *Pilots Operating Handbook*, complete with the recommended procedure. I used to teach that taking 40° flap in a C-172 was akin to slowing below *Blue Line* in a twin. You are, in effect, committing to land. Or you should be.

In a big jet, the stab position is always part of the *Configuration Warning System*, because if a takeoff is attempted outside the green band, the aircraft may not be controllable.

In ET 302, both pilots were holding up elevator against the nose-down trim being applied by MCAS. They **did** get the stabilizer trim switches off, stymieing the software. They **did** verify that in that configuration the stab wasn't moving. They **did** try to move the stab manually, with the big trim wheels. They were unable to move the trim wheels. They had no way of knowing that by placing the stab trim switches to off, they were not just denying MCAS access to the stab. They were also denying their own access.

Today I have to remember the third point Davies makes in those same paragraphs. He clearly describes a *transition* (although he doesn't name it) and how to wait for the end of the maneuver before setting the stab . . .

Chris?

Oh – Captain?

Yeah, it's me. Got home late. But I have a coffee now, and I can't believe what you just said – they have no way of knowing? They don't know what these switches do? There *are* two switches, right?

Yes. On the back of the pedestal. Stand by. I'll send you a photo . . .

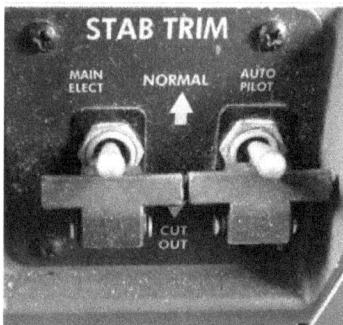

The labels presumably mean Primary and Backup.

B737-NG STAB TRIM CUTOUT Switches   B737-MAX STAB TRIM CUTOUT Switches

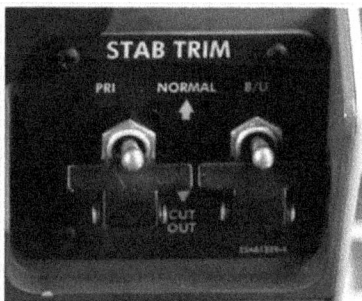

So see if I've got this – on the NG, they could turn off the right-hand switch and deny access to software – the autopilot, for example.

Right.

But now they've got new engines and there's a stick-force-per-G issue at high AoA.

Yes. You might have to push to keep it from over-rotating near the stall . . .

. . . and that's not certifiable . . .

Right.

. . . so they add software to run the stab nose-down?

Yes.

That's nasty. Couldn't they use a stick pusher on the elevator? Like the Colgan Q400?

Afraid I can't answer for them. But remind me in a month or two. I'd like to explore the whole idea of Mach trimmers and stick pushers with you.

So there's software that uses the stab. And it's there so the airplane will pass certification . . . wait – so they don't want the pilots to be able to turn it off?

Something like that.

So what did they do to the switches?

Rewired them. Put them in series.

Seriously? In series?

Yes.

So opening either switch . . .

Shuts everything down. A/P, MCAS, Speed Trim. And the thumb switches.

So they try to move the wheels by hand – and they can't. Why?

They are both holding up elevator. Pulling like crazy. Almost certainly that force jams the stab drive.

OK . . .

STILL LEARNING TO FLY

There is a history of this phenomenon. In flight tests. Real flight tests, I mean. With test pilots. Starting back with the DC-8. I think maybe Davies has a passage on it. I'll check. Anyway, if you have enough altitude, you can unload and then trim. Gently.

You mean like a recovery in aerobatics – push to 1G or less, then roll . . .

Exactly.

With neutral elevator, the stab would be moveable. But they didn't have the altitude.

No. And the stab was already so far Nose-Down that it was a losing battle with elevators alone.

I'm looking at what you wrote . . .they were pretty methodical. Got the switches off. Verified there was no more stab movement with the switches off. But they were losing the battle. They have to get the stab back more Nose-Up.

And it's stuck.

Yeah . . . so now the thumb switches are the only option. And reducing power would worsen the mistrim . . .

Yes.

OMG. So they . . .

Yes.

. . . so now they're fighting MCAS . . .

Yes. And they have no way of knowing how to win that battle. There was only one way . . . no, two possible ways, maybe . . .

My mind has drifted back to the Final Report. To the last 36 seconds.

Chris! Are you there? They turned on the stab cutout switches, right? And trimmed nose-up?

Yes. Two one-second bursts. And five seconds after that, MCAS trims nose-down for 9 seconds. The stab goes from 2.3 to 1.0. It's *game over*. Eighteen seconds later, they're dead.

§

Chapter Four

The DC-9 — Reflections on Past Loves

Powerful, Tough, and Sweet

How do we connect? People. Airplanes. People and airplanes?

I don't know. But we do. I have always felt that pilot and airplane are a relationship, and I feel that no less today, looking back.

There are some that have been there for me through thick and thin, through good times and hard times. With all their foibles. And mine.

How do we connect? Believe it or not in this digital age, with cables. Braided steel cables.

When I was cut loose on a new type, a *Crosby, Stills, and Nash* song would start in my head: *Love the one you're with*. It makes sense, after all. If pilot and airplane are cursing each other's little ways, it doesn't help the outcome.

So we try for harmony. But then – every once in a while – something happens, and you are, in some mysterious way, hitched for life. The DC-9, for me, is one of those connections.

Hold the yoke gently. Apply aileron for a roll to the left. Your crewmate is at the left wingtip doing the walkaround. What would he see?

The aileron would not move. But through a system of pulleys and steel cables, the yoke moves one of the two tabs on the aileron's trailing edge. Oddly, it moves down – what seems like the wrong direction. If your crewmate is tall, and there are no **NO PUSH** logos, he or she can move the aileron through its full travel. But it is not "hanging loose". Its movement is damped. It will stay where she puts it. Then, when you turn into a strong enough wind, or roll fast enough on takeoff, it will streamline.

If you are parked at the gate and there is a strong enough tailwind – especially a quartering tailwind – the elevators can move in opposite directions. If you try a *Controls Free Check*, the elevator will feel restricted, because the control tabs are against their stops.

There is a procedure for this:

First, face the aircraft into the wind. Then, pull the control column full aft – slowly. The pull force can be as much as 85 lb. Confirm that the ELEV PWR light is off. Then, push the control column full forward. Confirm that the ELEV PWR light is on. You're good to go.

What's going on here? Tab control.

The DC-9 ailerons and elevators are slipstream-powered. The pilot flies only a small tab on the trailing edge of the control surface. The tab "flies" the larger surface (aileron or elevator). The large surface flies the airplane.

The elevator also has a geared tab (the outboard tab). This is a *servo tab* which moves opposite to the control surface, reducing the *stick force per G* required at higher displacement.

For the pilot, the bottom line is that the DC-9 has a control harmony which is . . . well, beautiful. The pilot is directly connected to the airplane through braided steel cables and gently assisted by the slipstream. Hydraulics are not involved.

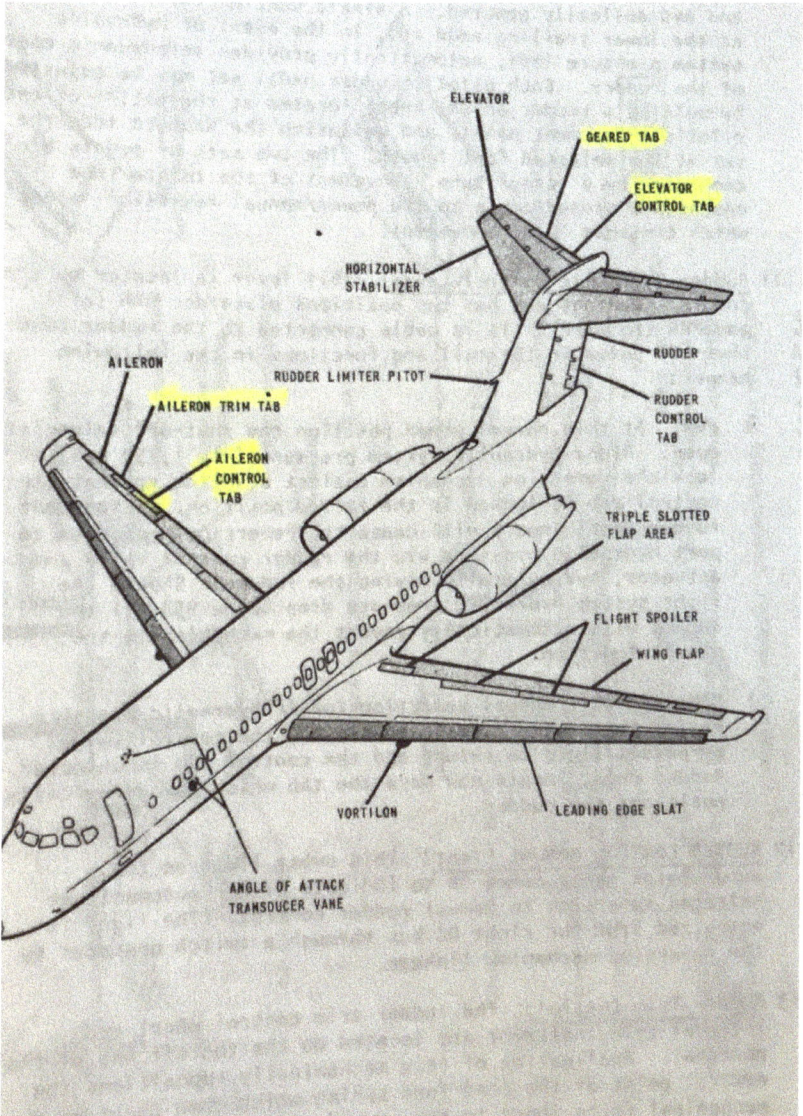

ELEVATOR

GEARED TAB

ELEVATOR
CONTROL TAB

HORIZONTAL
STABILIZER

RUDDER

AILERON

RUDDER LIMITER PITOT

RUDDER
CONTROL
TAB

AILERON TRIM TAB

AILERON
CONTROL
TAB

TRIPLE SLOTTED
FLAP AREA

FLIGHT SPOILER

WING FLAP

VORTILON

LEADING EDGE SLAT

ANGLE OF ATTACK
TRANSDUCER VANE

For those who want to see the flight control system in its entirety and have further questions, I offer these additional points:

- The ailerons are linked in their opposite movement by another cable system, independent of the controls

- The elevators can move in opposite directions because they are **not linked**. Each elevator **tab** is connected to its same-side yoke. The only connection between sides is at the yokes, and that can be overcome if one side jams.

- The outer tabs on the ailerons are trim tabs, actuated by the aileron trim knob on the pedestal

- The ailerons are damped by viscous dampers at the hinge points.

- The elevators are damped by allowing bleed in the hydraulic power servos, which in turn are there to ensure full-down-elevator can be achieved in a stall or approach to stall.

- The ailerons are assisted by spoilers at more than 5° deflection of the yoke.

- The rudder is hydraulically powered, but also has a control tab in case of hydraulic failure.

- There are two springs connected to the First Officer's column below the floor:

  - A load feel spring

  - A Mach Trim spring

- For comparison, many Piper airplanes have full-flying stabilizers. These also have geared tabs, which serve as both trim and as *anti-servo* tabs, *increasing* the *stick force per G.*

- Also for comparison, the Bonanza has a load feel *downspring*, which *increases* the *stick force per G.*

DC-9 and pilot are a tight act. Even the Sperry SP-50 doesn't get in the way. While primitive in comparison to today's autopilots – not digital! – the pilot interface is simple and well-designed.

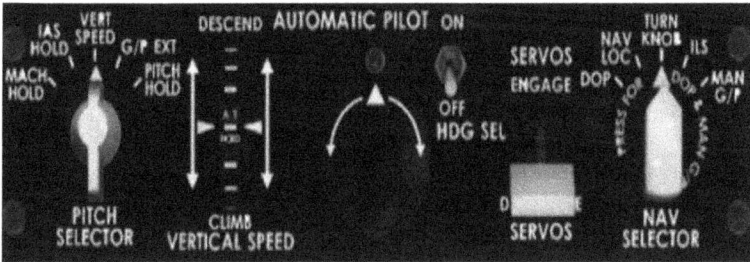

The control panel is on the pedestal behind the throttles (yes, we called them *throttles*, and the reversers were *buckets*), but you don't have to look. From the left seat, reach down to the centre of the pedestal and let your fingers find the *Turn Knob*. You hardly ever use it, but your hand fits it naturally. Your two middle fingers reach out and find the *Servos Engage* lever. Your fingers flip it up. It latches. Autopilot On!

Let's say you were just about to level at cruise. You were still climbing at 100 fpm. Your thumb reaches to the left and nestles in the central valley of the knurled *Vertical Speed Wheel*. Although your thumb covers it, that little valley is labelled (in very small letters) ALT HOLD. When your altimeter hundreds-pointer reaches zero, your thumb flips the *V/S Wheel* into its centre detent. You haven't looked down. There was no need to look.

Yes, we were a tight act. It was a late-1980's very junior December block. Halifax layovers. Christmas away from home. Same day every week. Christmas Eve arrival for the last cycle.

Four weeks running, it has been a broken record. A night CAT II ILS to runway 24. Weather W1X1/4F.

Again, no need to look. For vectors to final (or to fly a full approach with procedure turn) you have flipped the *HDG SEL* switch on and are steering with your heading bug. On intercept heading, your fingers find the *NAV SELECTOR* (a distinctive shape just to the right of the *Servos Engage* lever) and turn it to the right. It latches in *ILS*. You confirm selection in the little four-pane annunciator under the glareshield. At LOC capture, the *HDG SEL* switch unlatches to *off*. Electro-mechanical. Solenoid latches.

CAT II approaches on the DC-9 were flown on autopilot by the captain from the left seat. At *Decision* – 10-15 seconds before touchdown – it was like this:

- Autopilot off by 80 feet

- Do nothing but breathe in, then out

- Flare and land

At that hour of the night Grumpy (and his Chrysler with the 318 V8) were usually safe at home; instead, it was his boss who would greet us in his seedy old Cadillac. At some point – perhaps passing the *Inn on the Lake* as the fog eased a bit – he would reach under his seat for a mickey, and pass it back to us:

"Bars are closed, gentlemen. Perhaps you'd like a pull or two on this."

I have always been fascinated with clever electro-mechanical designs. I struck gold early. When I was twelve I got to know a Model T Ford. My great aunt, with whom I share a birthday, had won it at a raffle long before I was born. I think she never drove it. It had rested comfortably in the horse barn all those years. When I found it the horses were gone, but in the stalls stood the mint Model T.

She very generously agreed to let me get it running again. Grandpa (my great aunt's brother) helped me. He got fresh gas and found a battery somewhere. He explained what the pedals did. We got it out of the barn and into the driveway. He said, *Don't drive it on the road.*

What a gold mine of design! The ignition was four coils the size of small cigar boxes. They had vibrators to make DC square waves to allow induction to work. The distributor was a low-tension roller sending six volts to each coil in turn. If you cranked the engine with the ignition on, the coils sounded like a nest of rattlesnakes.

There was a parlor trick you could do with the Model T, especially if the engine was warm.

- Ignition off

- Spark retarded (left stalk on steering wheel)

- Throttle cracked (right stalk on steering wheel)

- Parking Brake set (essential – it also holds the transmission in neutral)

Now crank (yes, with the crank – there is no starter) through four Top Dead Centres. Carefully pull up to the fifth. Park as close to just beyond TDC as you can.

Get in. Turn the ignition on. It starts! And runs!

Now hold the left pedal as you release the handbrake. (The left pedal will try to spring back out of neutral into high gear. Don't let it.) Holding the left pedal midway down, push the middle pedal to engage reverse. Back out of your parking space. Release the reverse pedal. If the car is still rolling, press the right pedal to stop.

Now press the left pedal all the way down to engage low gear. Adjust spark advance and throttle. When you're rolling easily, take your left foot off that left pedal. That's high gear. Boy, did I have fun!

What's going on here? Planetary gears.

Sun gear, planet gear carrier, and ring gear are each connected to something. The trick is to stop the rotation of one and use the other two as input and output.

A modern car with an automatic transmission (not a Tesla or a Volt) uses sets of planetary gears in series, one for each gear. When a hydraulically operated band brakes one ring gear to a stop, that gear is engaged.

I learned about this great mechanical invention not from precept, but from experience. First was the Model T when I was twelve. Second was the 1958 Jaguar 3.4 Saloon I owned when I joined the airline. It had a regular four-on-the-floor, but also a *Laycock de Normanville* electro-hydraulic planetary overdrive. It was lovely. You didn't have to take your foot off the gas, like you did with a *Borg-Warner*. You flipped the switch on the glareshield and a band slowed a ring gear to a stop, smoothly changing the ratio.

What a pleasure! And now I have followed planetary gears through 65 years, to the geared turbofan in the A220.

But I should return to talking about the DC-9, which gave me pleasure in equal measure. It too would change pace with grace and with generous feedback.

Flap and slat speeds were high. You could take Slats Only, or Slats and Flap 5, at 280 knots. Take Slats Only, and as the slats move hold nose-up trim on the thumb switches for two beeps of the stabilizer. Time it right, and you need no elevator. The pitch attitude doesn't change. Sweet.

If you take Slats and Flap 5, the flaps partially balance the nose-down moment of the slats, and you need only one beep. Or wait a bit – if you have room and have planned ahead – until 240 knots and ask for Slats and Flap 15. Now you need no trim. Sweetest of all.

In my view the DC-9 had the best and safest stabilizer interface of any aircraft I have flown. The stab could be moved with either of two electric motors. The larger one – controlled by the suitcase handles on the pedestal or by the thumb switches on the yokes – moved the stab at 1/3 degree per second. The smaller motor, used by the autopilot (or by the pilot via two small sliders behind the throttles and between the HP Cocks) moved the stab more slowly, at 1/10 degree per second. That was great for fine-tuning.

For aural feedback, there was a beep for every ½ degree of stab movement.

The spoilers/speedbrake lever mechanism was another mechanical wonder. When used as intended it was robust and reliable. The problem was that it was a one-off. No one else did it that way. Well, almost no one. The DC-8 had a similar system, which gained instant infamy with the Air Canada 671 crash, some of which it deserved. That lever was on the right side of the pedestal, where the captain could not easily see whether it was armed. And it was twitchy. There is a note in the manual which begins, *to avoid personal injury* . . .

The DC-9 system, although similar, was better thought through.

The handle on the DC-9 was on the left side of the pedestal. The complicated linkages were more integrated and less hazardous. But the whole system was quite different from other, later systems.

The lever was spring-loaded to retract. Used as speedbrake the travel was restricted to about half, which yielded 35° of spoiler angle. If you squeezed the handle you raised a pawl, which you could latch into one of four notches, allowing you to continue using both hands for other tasks.

To get full travel for ground spoilers, you armed them by pulling the lever straight up, where it would latch – in a more verifiable way than the DC-8 equivalent. On a normal flight the spoilers are armed on the *Before Landing Check* and deploy with main wheel spinup – or, as a backup, with nosewheel strut compression. At deployment, the lever goes full aft and the spoiler panels extend to 60°. In the *After Landing Check* bumping the top of the lever stows the panels and returns the lever to the full-forward, unarmed position.

(These numbers ignore the effect of the aileron/spoiler mixer assemblies, which retain the ability to assist roll control even at 60° spoiler angle – by partially retracting one side.)

Ah, but there's a rub: a rejected takeoff. Full deployment of the spoilers is essential. This takes three very specific movements. As I recall, the captain's RTO Drill went like this:

- I will close the throttles, calling **REJECT – BUCK-**

ETS

- I will pull **UP, BACK,** and **UP** on the spoiler handle.

- I will apply maximum braking and reverse

On June 26, 1978, Flight 189 rejected takeoff on runway 23L at Toronto when the #3 tire failed. Spoilers were deployed and thrust reversers selected. After 2.5 seconds the spoilers started to retract, and the captain pulled back the lever again. Four and a half seconds after that, the spoilers retracted again.

The most likely scenario is that in the heat of the moment the captain didn't get that last **UP** movement to latch the spoilers at 60°.

The aircraft left the end of the runway at 70 knots and came to rest in a ravine.

On the *Aviation Safety Network* page under *Probable Cause*, there are two interesting statements:

- The aircraft accident investigation report by the Aircraft Accident Review Board Accident Report did not contain a "Probable cause".

- The company's RTO procedure did not call for immediate maximum braking.

In addition – and this is highly unusual – the page does not contain a link to the final report. Nor can I find such a report in the archives.

The DC-9 was B.I. – *Before Inertial.* Today's anti-skid systems can compare wheel speed to inertial groundspeed and control wheel skid with great accuracy.

The DC-9 antiskid system – very good for its time and extremely reliable – knew only wheel speed. It had to work with what it knew.

On a normal dry runway landing, wheel spinup takes about a

second, leaving behind a little puff of grey-black rubber smoke as the tires skid up to speed. The antiskid system uses that speed as a baseline and releases brake pressure to any wheel that slows too quickly.

On a contaminated runway, however, that wheel spinup can be a lot slower. If brakes are applied too early, when the wheel speed is still a fraction of the groundspeed, the braking available is in proportion to that speed difference. NASA tests with a DC-9-10 assembly of wheel, tire, brake, and antiskid transducer show that in the extreme case, where – on encountering a flooded runway – the braked wheel actually stops, the wheel speed will remain low even with the brake pressure near zero.

How did we deal with all that flying the line?

In a word, we knew we needed those wheels to spin up. So a firm landing didn't hurt. But we also knew that – in round numbers – if we slowed to below 100 knots with reverse thrust, we would be below hydroplaning speed and the wheels would be spinning up.

Then there was ice, snow, and crosswinds.

My experience in that area started young. In the last year of high school I got my driver's licence and bought my first car, a 1950 Austin A40. Like many British cars of the era, it had hydraulic front brakes and mechanically actuated rear brakes. The linkage to the rear brakes had long since rusted and seized.

That winter I would drive my friends home from school.

I had learned a trick. At moderate speed, in the middle of the block, I would brake the front wheels to a stop with my left foot, while keeping my right foot steady on the gas. Then I would turn the wheels for the next corner. The Austin would continue as if nothing had happened, sliding along through the snow. Then, approaching the corner, I would take my foot off the gas and, at the right moment, release the brakes. The front wheels would spin up, gaining traction as they did, and we would turn the corner. I got quite good at it.

Sure – I got some points with my friends. But what remained were healthy instincts about wheel speed and vehicle speed, and about how available traction could be used to brake or to turn, but not both. (More accurately, available traction has to be divided between those needs.)

So – landing on a snowy runway in a crosswind, it is best to touch down pointing where you are going. And when the downwind truck touches and you lose that into-wind lift vector, it is best to delay braking until you're sure you are not drifting toward those downwind runway lights.

The DC-9 was sometimes referred to as the *Diesel Nine*. I was uncomfortable with that – a lack of respect, maybe? – but I will admit it has a bit of poetic accuracy. She was powerful, tough, and sweet. And we can quietly forget (with a small inward smile) how incredibly noisy she was. And also forget that plume of black that followed her around – particulate carbon waiting to fall to earth as soot.

I haven't mentioned the DC-9-15: registrations CF-TON to CF-TOT. We called it *The Rocket*. It was gone when I came back to the DC-9 in the left seat, but that first winter on the line – 1973-74 – I flew it a lot. It would usually show up on the Quebec North Shore to Sept-Iles or on (as some called it) the *Road to Ruin*. That was the Rouyn/Noranda – Val d'Or triangle out of Dorval. Today the runway at Rouyn is 7500 feet long, but as I remember, that winter it was about 5000 feet. Landing on that runway was a bit of a dance. The *short nine* had a nose-down attitude on final, making it more scary yet. And the procedure, according to some captains, was:

I Will Hold Full Reverse Until the Cockpit Door Glows Red.

The DC-9-10 series had no leading-edge slats. The airfoil was a high-lift section to try to keep the runway speeds manageable. Even so, when the DC-9-30 series came out with full-span leading-edge slats, the speeds were six knots slower than the -10 even though the -30 was 5000 pounds heavier. The attitude on final in the DC-9-30 was a comforting zero degrees. And it handled better, too. But *The Rocket* sure was fun on a cold-day takeoff.

What about accidents?

Looking at them all is a project for another time. But for a quick overview, I will restrict the field to the two types with which I was familiar. As it happens, the very first hull loss, on October 1, 1966, was a DC-9-14.

That was the era – it seems so remote now – when experienced pilots had mostly multi-engine prop time. Reciprocating engine prop, at that. Jets – with their slipperiness and their greater vertical speed capabilities both up and down – were a novelty.

Three pilots were aboard this West Coast Airlines flight into Portland, OR – a First Officer, who was probably in the jump seat, and two experienced captains, one checking the other out on the airplane.

They were in IMC, being vectored for an ILS 28R at Portland. Their position was just to the west of Mt. Hood – elevation 11,300 MSL. From a North heading they were cleared for a right turn – a spiral all the way around to a 300° heading to intercept the ILS, and descend to 9000. They also read back a request to squawk 0400 – that was the transponder code for approach in those days. (This was before Mode C – the controllers could not see the aircraft's altitude.)

It is not clear whether the aircraft was equipped with an altitude alert, like our DC-9s were. In any case it kept descending, under control, on autopilot. It helps to remember that the Sperry SP-50 did not have altitude select or capture. To level off you had to roll that Vertical Speed Wheel into the centre detent. Still in the turn, they hit the east slope of a ridge at 3800 MSL on a heading of about 260°.

In all, the DC-9-10 had 25 hull losses. The DC-9-30 had 73.

What surprised me reading the Wikipedia summary was the number of collisions. DC-9s have had midair collisions with a Baron, a C-150, 2 Piper Cherokees, an F4, and a Convair 990. They have had ground encounters with a Convair 880 and two B-727's.

There were one or two bombs, two fires, one fuel exhaustion and ditching, and the usual number of CFIT – Controlled Flight Into Terrain. But for me the most interesting statistic is the number of LOC – Loss of Control accidents – the type that have unfortunately become common since Colgan 3407 in 2009. As far as I can see that number is *one*. And it was the most recent hull loss of a DC-9, on July 6, 2008.

The aircraft was a DC-9-15F, and the accident had eerie similarities to Colgan 3407: both aircraft entered 1.4 G accelerated stalls at low altitude.

USA Jet Flight 199 was on a LOC/DME RWY 17 approach into Saltillo, Mexico. The low visibility in haze seems to have surprised the pilots. The First Officer, who was flying, said something like "I can't see the airport". At the time the aircraft had left the localizer and was diverging east. Perhaps both pilots were looking out, where there was no valid information on either attitude or position. In quick succession the power went up to near maximum, and the aircraft was pulled sharply up. The stick shaker went off, and when the G load hit 1.4, the aircraft stalled and did a brief falling leaf maneuver (roll angle briefly greater than 90°) before impact.

Only **one** Loss Of Control accident seems amazing. Was it the airplane that was good, or the pilots? What changed between those two *short nine* accidents – between 1966 and 2008?

Well, everything. That, too, is a story for another time.

But in the end all stories are love stories in some way. Relationships. Between people. Between people and airplanes. I think what has changed is distance. We are not as close as we once were.

Braided steel cables have given way to electrical signals – most of them digital.

Apprenticeship has given way to training, where the goal is *train to standard*, rather than *teach to understanding*.

And I am an old man – desperate to teach, but without a class.

She was lovely. I miss her.

§

Chapter Five
Breaking the Chain of Experience

07 February 2023

Andy Grove's smile, from somewhere beyond the grave, is somewhere between *I told you* so and *miserere mei*. Pride in prophesy is not for the departed.

But I lapped up the news like a dog given scrambled eggs.

What's going on?

Just over a year ago, Boeing did not attend the annual meeting of the *Pacific Northwest Aerospace Alliance*. At issue was a sexual discrimination lawsuit. Then this year, at the end-of-January ceremony for the last B-747 off the line, The Boeing CEO said, about the company's commitment to innovation:

> "Our commitment as a leadership team at Boeing is to maintain this leadership culture forever. We're committed to it and will be forever."

Pointing at the final B-747, bound for Atlas Air, he went on:

> Boeing continues to have visions just like this one. The hangars are full of innovation."

But Boeing employees had already had enough. Through their largest unions, they commissioned a report by the same talking heads that were to appear at *this year's* PNAA annual meeting. The report was presented, with its authors present, at the Boeing Future of Flight Museum at Paine Field on February 7, the day before the PNAA meeting was to begin. This employee-initiated event made headlines. One read:

> **"What kind of vision is that? Industry analysts scorch Boeing and CEO . . ."**

The consensus among the speakers that day was that there was *No Vision*. Boeing's decision not to start another clean-sheet airplane until 2035, they said, leaves thirty years – a generation – between programs, and by 2035 Boeing will have forgotten how to do a clean-sheet airplane.

In 2022 more than ten percent of the Boeing engineers in the Seattle area took early retirement. About half of these retired in the last days of November, ahead of costly changes to the lump-sum retirement option.

Boeing thinks it can hire new young engineers to replace those who are leaving. That is true, but many of these young engineers will be joining Boeing specifically to pad their resumés. Then they plan to jump to one of the more interesting aerospace companies. That's why Andy Grove is groaning in his grave. His *Chain of Experience* is well and truly broken.

That was February 7th. On February 8th the NWAA annual meeting began, and the same aviation analysts detailed how Boeing has been stiffing its suppliers. The Tier 1 suppliers should be becoming risk-sharing partners, they said, but some have already left for other pastures. And all suppliers have already been bled dry. If they still want to ramp up production, they can't get the financing.

But even before the engineer annual turnover hit ten percent, the signs of broken links were there: a new variant – the cash cow – grounded for twenty months. And the cretinous piece of malware behind that grounding.

•

I was in California for the closing days of 2022, and experienced the phenomenon people are calling the *atmospheric river*. What we didn't know then was days before, when one of those *rivers* was passing Maui, an airliner had a ***very close call***.

It may have been a terrifying experience. You are flying into what looks like a wall. You have time to call for ***Gear Up***, and then the wall hits. Turbulence and rain, but rain like you have never experienced. What affects you most, though, is the noise. It is a roar, as if you were tearing through a heavy veil. What you did then remains to be seen. But you and the crew and the hundreds of passengers survived!

A win, right? A damn close thing, like Waterloo, but a win. Then, less than a month later, there was another, eerily similar incident during a takeoff out of Doha, Qatar. Still a win? Shouldn't we try to find out what's going on?

Yesterday an editor at one of the aviation journals opined that the Maui aircraft couldn't have pulled 2.7 G's in the pullout (as a different journal reported two days before that) because the aircraft, on arrival in SFO, stayed for only 2½ hours before departing for ORD. (Since the aircraft is certified for 2.2 G's, extensive checks would have had to be carried out before further flight.)

The editor's logic is interesting, if circular. He also said that if the aircraft had really pulled 2.7 G's, passengers' complaints would have long since been all over the media. Again, the 2.7 G pullout was unlikely to impossible.

Further, the editor reported that the pilots "filed the appropriate safety report", and that the incident was "not NTSB reportable."

Then today newspapers carried the story of one of the passengers on the Maui flight, who said the aircraft "pulled up at a very strong rate." Ten minutes after the pullup, when things had settled down, one of the pilots said on the intercom, "Well folks, you probably felt a couple of G's on that one . . ."

I understand that incidents like this one are something an airline would like to bury. But it seems to me that a careful analysis of what exactly happened is owed to the trade and to anyone who travels by air.

Two *safety experts* pointed this week to "the aggregate safety of the system" and to "the lack of commonality between each discrete incident." I'm not so sure about that, and I'm not alone in my doubt.

•

Thinking about these accidents and incidents hurts. In my distress I find I am thinking about myself and about the human pilot in general – wonderful creations who have limitations just like the airplanes we fly. In my discomfort I think about how our complacency can turn, in the blink of an eye, into raw fear. I know what happens to my performance in that situation and I worry about my brothers and sisters in cockpits everywhere.

In my compassion for those struck by fear on the flight deck, events cascade backwards in my mind from barely a month ago, when the ATR-72 crashed in Nepal, to October 2014, when the Virgin Space Ship *Enterprise* (not NCC-1701, but its namesake) broke up over the Mojave Desert.

This was supposed to be part of a later chapter, where I summed up our limitations: vestibular system, eyesight, perception, fatigue, and many more. *Human Factors*, the trade calls them. But sometimes the world speaks to us with a reality that gets us where we live. The way we like to think of things is suddenly shaken or is in pieces on the floor. We are hurt. We are at a loss. Our functionality is compromised or gone altogether. It happened to me over the last few days, trying to keep up with the rush of bad news.

But why are we surprised? That is what comes into my head today, as I recover my composure. After three generations, commercial aviation has become so smooth and polished that we believe the hype – passengers and pilots alike. Flying is *safer than driving a car* (True). The *On-Time Airline* (Sometimes). Your flight will be *stress-free* (Not since 9-11). We are *safer today because of automation* (False).

The fact is that you are sitting in an aluminum (or composite, these days) tube held aloft by a wing going fast enough to push down the weight of thin air needed to hold you up. You are breathing air that moments ago was sucked into an engine and compressed through a dozen or more compressor stages before being bled off for your breathing pleasure.

And the *Friendly Skies* have become a lot less friendly. I suspect that – at least until the multiple meltdowns of 2022 – even airline management was oblivious to the changes in the skies, notably the behaviour of the Jetstream. No longer, I hope.

Again, this was to be a later chapter. But worth noting here is how the moisture-holding capacity of air increases with temperature.

It is not a straight line.

One rule of thumb is that the water vapour capacity of air doubles with every 20° C. of warming. Actually, the curve gets steeper than that pretty quickly. And since water and its changes of state are what powers storms and violence in the atmosphere, it should come as no surprise that a warming of even a couple of degrees can radically change the weather.

When I was still working, Montreal to San Francisco was a six-hour trip; the return was about five hours. Today, depending on the crazy shapes taken by the Jetstream, that trip is often seven hours out and four-and-a half hours back.

Storms, which used to appear in a string along the Polar Front under the Jetstream and could occasionally merge near Boston along two different fronts to form the *Northeaster,* or *The Perfect Storm,* can now become one giant continent-deep storm system as the Polar Front and the Jetstream bulge south in one great sweep from Yellowknife to New Orleans. In these conditions, airline hubs can be shut down for hours, or even days, as we have seen.

The airlines have become victims of their own invention. Their hype has come back to bite them. No wonder they would rather not know.

Weather like we have never seen before. Pilots under pressure. Complacency turning to fear, and fear becoming *spatial disorientation.* The *Chain of Experience* broken and forgotten. Perhaps they are all part of the same puzzle. The events of the last few months certainly say so.

•

We'll begin in 2014, because that's where *complacency turning to fear* takes me.

Space Ship One won the $10 million Ansari X Prize in 2004, mirroring the accomplishment of Charles Lindbergh in his *Spirit of St. Louis* in 1927. Space Ship One and its mothership White Knight were two more innovative designs by Bert Rutan, who also designed and built the Model 76 Voyager, which flew nonstop around the world in December 1986, piloted by Bert's brother Dick and Jeana Yeager (no relation to Chuck).

Space Ship One, and its successor Space Ship Two, aka SS2 *Enterprise*, both have an imaginative articulation that radically changes the vehicle's shape. Along what would be, in a normal aircraft, the rear spar of the wing, is a (very robust) hinge which allows the tail and some of the wing to swivel up 60°. In the initial descent from the edge of space, the vehicle needs both drag and stability. So Rutan turns the plane into a badminton bird, and back to an airplane once the air is thicker. I still believe Rutan's design contains the seeds of great possibility.

The Rutan Space Ships do not have enough of a heat shield to survive a descent from orbital speeds. Nevertheless, they were a good solution for the mission, which was:

- Be flown to the stratosphere by the mothership

- Drop free, and ignite the rocket motor to climb almost vertically at supersonic speed

- In the thin air at the top of the trajectory, morph into a badminton bird and drop, fuselage almost horizontal

- Once subsonic at lower altitude, morph back into an airplane and glide to a landing

Space Ship One did that just enough times to win the prize, and then retired to the Smithsonian Air and Space Museum.

Space Ship One had one pilot.

Space Ship Two has two, so they operate as a crew.

In this mission, on October 31, 2014, Pilot One would fly. This is a demanding role in all phases of flight after the drop. He would establish a controlled glide, and then call for ignition of the rocket motor.

After ignition all hell breaks loose. The pilots are subjected to what must seem like raw violence unleashed – tremendous G, noise, and vibration. Pilot One now has to fly the *gamma turn*, pulling into a steep climb and balancing the tremendous thrust against gravity, but allowing the vehicle to accelerate to Mach 3.5.

Pilot Two would have to make two discrete control movements to get the tail up to 60° for the descent:

1. Unlock the hinge

2. Move the tail to 60° via the pneumatic actuators using a different control

But that's not the plan for today.

The plan is to wait until the ship has accelerated to Mach 1.4, and then unlock the feather locks and make sure that the *feather unlocked* lights are illuminated. Then, if they are not illuminated, to abort before Mach 1.8 by shutting down the rocket motor.

The problem is that all this goes by rather quickly. The planned burn for today is 38 seconds. We know that their speed was Mach 0.8 at 2 ½ seconds after ignition. We know that the G forces were 2.5 longitudinally (from the rocket motor) and approximately 2.5 G in the normal axis (from the pullup, or *gamma turn*). We know the target Mach was about 3.5.

In the event, the feather handles reached the unlock position two seconds after the vehicle accelerated through Mach 0.8. The feather section began to move two seconds after that.

We might remember the power of the all-flying stabilizer on to-day's jet transports. The feather on Space Ship Two has that beat by a mile. Imagine running a stab to full nose up in two seconds while being accelerated by a rocket. The G forces on SS2 must have been tremendous. They were, in fact, sufficient to break up the vehicle 2.2 seconds after the feather started to move. The elapsed time from rocket ignition to breakup was 8.34 seconds. The remaining burn time was to have been just under 30 seconds.

Pilot One survived because the ship broke up around him and left him flying solo in his seat. Before he lost consciousness from lack of oxygen he undid his seat belt. He was left with his parachute, which opened automatically at a lower altitude as programmed.

Pilot Two was programmed to unlock the feather: he did so a few seconds early, when SS2 was transonic. Realistically, how much time did he have between 1.4 and 1.8 Mach to unlock the feather and then evaluate and then abort – or to verify the abort with Pilot One?

We can figure it out. Let's simplify a bit and assume the ship is pointing straight up and the pilots feel 2.5 G acceleration in that direction from the rocket motor, so they are accelerating at 1.5 G, or 14.7 m/sec^2 (The pilots feel Earth's gravity plus the acceleration). The base line for our calculation is the drop altitude of 46,000 feet, or 14,000 metres, where their speed is Mach 1, or 295 m/sec. We assume a standard atmosphere.

It takes ten seconds to accelerate to Mach 1.4, and fifteen seconds to reach Mach 1.8. Pilot Two would have had a five second window to accomplish his tasks. But all this is moot, because with the noise, vibration, and G forces, he went from complacent to terrified in 1.5 seconds.

From a human point of view, the sequence of events is completely understandable.

But if we step back further from the fray, the question becomes *Why?*

The pilot's job is to manage risk. The mission is *never* risk-free. One risk must always be balanced against others.

Sure – there's a risk that at apogee the feather locks could jam, preventing deployment. There is a high likelihood of loss of vehicle in that scenario. But why do you want to test these locks during the burn, during a vanishingly small window of time, with high aerodynamic forces, vibration, and 2.5 G in at least one axis? And when you *know* that during the time the vehicle is transonic – 0.9 to 1.1 Mach – those aerodynamic forces **will** be strong enough to overcome the feather actuators and deploy the feather?

Why?

Let's say you are Toronto to San Francisco in your A320. Over the Front Range, you hit a mountain wave. Over Kansas a few minutes ago, you started to wonder – are those clouds lenticular? Now the thrust is almost back to idle as you surf the wave, and now you know. In a few minutes you will be using *Maximum Continuous Thrust* and perhaps be unable to hold altitude. Should you request a block now?

You are up-to-your-ears busy. Do you use the time to worry about whether the landing gear will really come down when you need it a few hours from now, over the San Mateo Bridge? Maybe you should try it right now, just to make sure it works? Never mind you're above V_{LO} and the gear doors will rip off. Never mind that with the gear down you'll need a much bigger altitude block than the two thousand feet you were going to ask for. Where are you going to land?

Why?

Space Ship Two was the accident that came into my head immediately when I thought about complacency turning to terror in an instant.

The transition to terror sometimes takes longer. With Fly Dubai at Rostov-on-Don, the fear began on the first go-around and gestated for two hours during the hold. With the very recent fatal crash of an ATR-72 in Nepal, fear took one very long minute to incapacitate both pilots.

The crew consisted of two captains. The left-seat pilot was Pilot Flying on this familiarization flight into the new Pokhara airport (VNPR). The right-seat pilot was Pilot Monitoring and the Training Captain for the flight.

The weather was CAVOK with light winds. After a straight-in

arrival for runway 30, the crew asked for and received a clearance to break off for a close left downwind and fairly tight left turn to base and final for runway 12. As it happened, the airplane had flown that sequence earlier in the day, with a different crew. Had the crews spoken?

You, the PF, call for *Flap 15* and *Gear Down*. You see and feel the familiar pitch changes and hear the familiar noises. All is good. You click off the autopilot and focus your attention outside. You call for *Flap 30*. The PM replies, *Flap 30 and descending*. You call for the *Before Landing Check*. Your right hand is on the thrust levers in anticipation, but your body says there is no need. The feeling is that there is less drag, not more. You are busy, flying a tight left turn with as much as 30° of bank. And there is a hint of doubt. As my late friend Larry would have said, "something doesn't smell right." You ask the PM, *continue the turn? Yes*, he says. You ask the PM, *keep descending? No, he says. Add some power.*

Now you do feel some drag. Something has just changed.

ATC gives you landing clearance. You say, *There's no power. There's no power coming from the engines.* You advance the thrust levers. You are at 368 AGL in the last turn to final. You are beginning to get very afraid. You push the thrust levers all the way forward.

You say to the PM *You have control.* Two seconds later, you say again, *There's no power.*

Four seconds after that, the stick shaker activates for the first time.

You have eight seconds left to live.

•

OK, you made your point!

Captain?

Yeah. You left me hanging. I couldn't stand the suspense . . .

Sorry – that's just where I left off writing for the day.

. . . so I went and found the Preliminary Report. A pretty quick read.

Yes – hey, I haven't heard from you in a while.

Sick. I got COVID.

Oh, I'm sorry.

It was the pits. But this morning I can taste my coffee. For the first time in a while. So that's something. I worry about long COVID, though.

Yes, me too . . .

I taste my own coffee, grateful that I am still COVID-free. Or pre-COVID. Who knows?

All I can say is that I'm grateful I got the shots. Had five of them. Last one was the Pfizer Bivalent. So it could have been worse. Even so I felt like shit for days. And I'm still tired.

What about going back to work?

I wait 'til I test negative, then go see the Doc a week later. I've got some time off. So I'll stop complaining. I'm going to use the time to catch up on some of that stuff you've been writing about. What a winter!

Yes. One thing after another. I have been overwhelmed.

Both engines in feather! What'd he do, reach too far left and miss the flap handle?

So it would seem. Have you seen an image of the pedestal?

Yeah. Condition levers next over. Just left of the flaps. But there are two of them! That had to feel different, right?

Maybe. But both flap handle and the condition levers have latches. You reach forward and under with your fingers. Similar.

So he reaches too far left. Unlatches. Pulls back to the next detent. That's feather. And it's not that much further back than the Flap 30 detent.

Right.

I've been studying the timeline. I see what you mean about *one very long minute*.

Yes. Exactly. He calls for *Flap 30* at 10:56:32. The recording ends at 10:57:32.

Yeah and the right-seat guy – looks like he did finally select Flap 30.

Yes. At 10:56:54.

And that was kind of like the nail in the coffin.

We both sigh. I find I am waiting for her to continue.

You know, she says, it unfolded like a nightmare.

I wait some more, thinking about bad dreams.

Only they didn't wake up, she says.

•

I am thinking about the scene in San Francisco Flight Operations that evening, December 18. Or perhaps it is the next morning, at Corporate Headquarters in Chicago, where the B-777 flew from KSFO. A hastily convened meeting with NTSB representatives, who order that the DFDR be pulled at once. It will be going with them, back to D.C.

But perhaps that scene never happened. Perhaps the DFDR, with its 25-hour capacity, has been completely overwritten. What data do we have left? DFDR data transmitted over ACARS for ASRS, the *Aviation*

Safety Reporting System? And ADS B Out data. Who has access? Will any of this ever come to light?

Another thought niggles sat the back of my mind. Last month a King Air crashed on takeoff from runway 18 out of Little Rock (KLIT) about noon local time. Here are the METARs that bracket the accident time:

> **METAR** KLIT 221753Z 21019G27KT 10SM BKN048 OVC060 24/14 A2962 RMK PK WND 22036/1721

> **METAR** KLIT 221802Z 30022G40KT 2SM -RA SCT036 OVC047 19/13 A2968 RMK A02 PK WND 300040/1759 WSH-FT 1748 RAB00 PRESRR

What happened at the surface between these reports is the passage of an unusually violent cold front. Here is a quote from a witness who was outside during the passage of that same front:

> *The rumble of the wind as (the front) came over the top of us and through our woods, will not be forgotten.*

I thought: *maybe that's Maui, too. I can go back in the archives and find the relevant METARs.*

The takeoff was at 2:49PM local time December 18. Kahalui Airport, Maui (OGG, or PHOG) is UTC-10, so the takeoff time from Runway 02 was 0049Z. Below are the METARs (2 before and 2 after the takeoff),

> **METAR** PHOG 182254Z 34010KT 4SM RA BR BKN009 BKN020 OVC100 21/19 A2977 RMK A02 TSB215E50 SLP085 TS OHD MOV NE

> **METAR** PHOG 182354Z 32010KT 3SM RA BR BKN009 OVC020 20/18 A2976 RMK A02 SLP081 TS OHD MOV NE

> Takeoff 0049Z

> **METAR** PHOG 190054Z 14009KT 3SM RA BR BKN009 OVC 020 19/18 A2977

> **METAR** PHOG 190158Z 18019G26KT 8SM -RA

SCT009 OVC 060 20/18 A2976

and the High Level Significant Weather chart valid 00 UTC 19 DEC 2022.

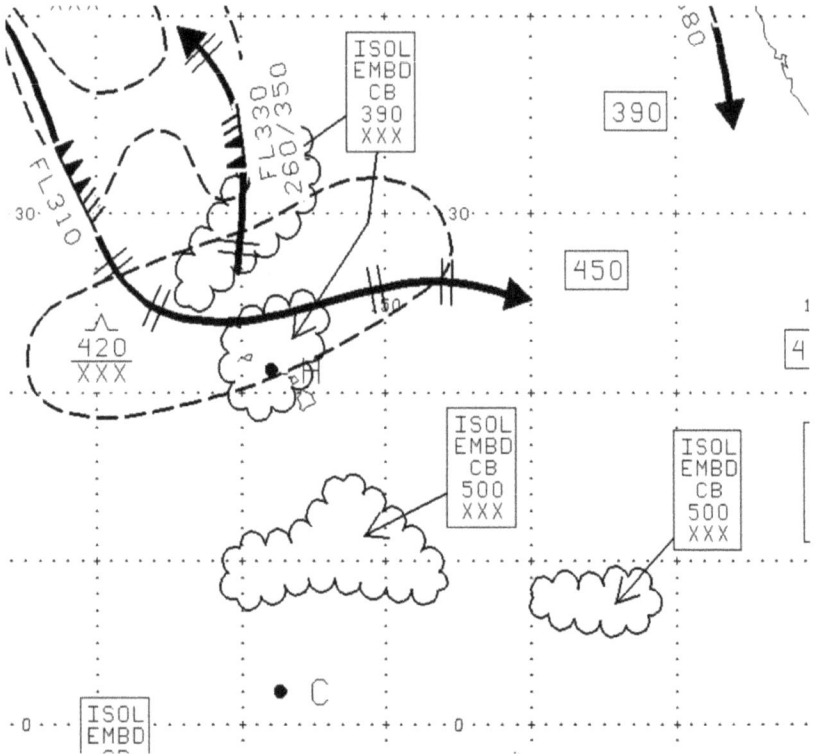

It is difficult to convey in words just how unusual and violent the weather depicted on this chart would be. It shows not one, but two Jetstreams. One is coming from top left, flowing SSE. Maximum speed of 180 knots is at Flight Level 310. Then it turns sharply East, slowing as it does so. The hashmarks are a slowing of 20 knots, so by the time it is passing just north of Maui (same position as that black dot at *21North/156.30West*) it has slowed to 140 knots.

The second Jetstream is shown starting north of Maui near the first, heading north and then curving northwest at 120 knots. Its maximum speed (the core) is found at FL330. The forecast is for ISOLated EMBeDded CumulonimBus (thunderstorms) from FL390 down to XXX, which is FL240, the lowest altitude for which the chart is valid.

The dashed oval predicts moderate turbulence from FL420 on down. It was more than moderate. An hour before the valid time for this chart, Hawaiian Airlines Flight 35 from Phoenix to Honolulu encountered severe turbulence in the area depicted. They were at FL410, about to start descent into HNL. Below them was a cirro-stratus layer between FL390 and FL380. Suddenly, a dark dome ("like a plume of smoke") rose out of the undercast in front of them. It happened so fast they could not turn to avoid it. Thirty-six people were injured, twenty of those were taken to hospital, and of those 11 were in critical condition.

But while isolated, embedded shafts of unstable, rising air existed as shown, the storm system was, I believe, another animal entirely. What we see on this chart is the genesis of a giant storm where the cyclone *is the Jetstream itself*. This same cyclone persisted for over a week, drifting east to California where it was announced, accurately, as an *atmospheric river*. It continued across the Rockies and into the plains, causing the infamous *airline meltdown* of the week after Christmas. And now, in early 2023, more such storms have followed. Today heavy rain is again hitting California, part of a giant plume that extends from Hawaii to the California Coast. Cyclone Freddy, presently in the vicinity of Madagascar, is about to beat the official record for *longest lasting cyclone in history*. Today is its thirtieth day.

So yes, these storms are something new. We haven't seen this before. And yes, they are a hazard to aviation.

So. What?

Just as the world continues on its course in the face of Climate Change, so do passengers buy tickets and airplanes fly, fully expecting to arrive intact at their destinations.

Most of them will do so, as will many people live out their lives – even in the present time – with only the vaguest notion of the existential threat facing Humanity.

At times like these it is soothing to step back, to get the big picture. Remember Earth, from geosynchronous orbit? How she is not down there, beneath our feet, but *over there*? How beautiful she is?

She is *Mother*. *Gaia*, to Greeks. *Prithvi*, the vast one, to Hindus. And Heaven knows she is not inert. If not God, she is certainly *Mother Nature*. She can take care of herself. Humanity, one of her many dear children, has heedlessly and in ignorance destroyed her harmony. She is a beautiful horse, shivering off flies and flicking them with her tail. There is no vengeance, just survival. Harmony must be restored.

Sometimes, at the end of the day, I feel I am one of those flies. I am on a flimsy raft, shooting rapids in a wild river. The cliffs above are unfamiliar, nor do I pay them much attention as I try to stay afloat. I am moving, but so is the world around me. It is also very much like I feel when I am suddenly overloaded while flying. On the verge of spatial disorientation. Terrified. Paralyzed. Struck dumb. Like the PC-12 pilot in Nevada two weeks ago.

I can't imagine greater stress. Single-pilot in a high-performance aircraft. Night. Bad weather. In an aircraft where the autopilot, by design, drops off in heavy turbulence.

But there you are. You have just levelled off at your cruising altitude of 19,000 feet. The turbulence hits like a wall. You probably have *eyeball bounce*, where G forces distort the eyeball enough so you can't keep a focus on the instruments. (At least that's what pilots call it, and how they think it works. But perhaps not exactly. See *Glossary: Semi-Circular* Canals) And how much recent time do you have flying by hand in these conditions? Perhaps there is icing as well, adding to the terror and making the handling more difficult and unpredictable. Perhaps you try the autopilot again but it won't stay engaged. It is as if you had help and now you have no one. And now you are pinned in your seat by the high G forces of the spiral dive as the aircraft begins to break apart.

I have flown in these conditions and I understand the challenge. I have mercifully survived to be able to analyze my performance after the fact. It is something I share with virtually every experienced professional pilot. There are perhaps a few pilots who still haven't experienced overload and spatial disorientation. But they will, any day now, as Mother Nature shrugs and ripples her horsehair coat.

Each of us might describe the experience in a slightly different way. For me, overload narrows my field of vision. That's the first symptom. Then I forget to breathe. I can see only one instrument, or just a portion of it. Perhaps colour vanishes, leaving black and white.

When this happens there is only one road to survival – follow aviation's number one commandment:

~ Pilot Commandment Number One ~
Aviate, Navigate, and Communicate. In that order.

But in true overload even the *Aviate* has to be broken down. *Attitude. Straight and level attitude.* Hang on to it like a drowning person, because that's what you are. *Breathe.* Slowly in and out, so you don't hyperventilate and get low carbon dioxide, which will further degrade your mental state.

Slow in and out. Straight and level. Breathe. Correct only attitude. Wait for the cone of vision to expand.

I am on that raft, hanging on, waiting. After a lifetime of navigation, am I lost? Or am I *temporarily unsure of my position*, because it is late in the day? Does anything I do make a difference?

●

You OK?

Captain?

The same. I got back from the Doc and was catching up. You were getting all philosophical on me. You down?

Not now. Sometimes at the end of the day. When everything seems corrupt and I lose sight of beauty.

I hear ya.

You too?

Sometimes.

But today's Friday.

What's that?

Martini night.

Whoah. All right. I'm down with that.

I know it doesn't help my REM sleep. But once a week . . .

Hey, yeah. I was a bit worried about you. But I also wanted to share something with you. Forgot, last time we talked. Probably COVID fog.

All ears.

Well, remember you told me about the hook? Last flight I did, I looked down, inside the FAF somewhere, and the bug was sitting on the hook. Almost.

How far?

1/16 inch, if that.

Oh oh.

Yeah. I pulled speed and dialed up ¼ inch. Landing was normal. But I didn't like it. I called Load Control and said *what the fuck?*

You said that?

No, but they got my drift anyway. Said they'd research it and let me know.

And?

Just got it this morning when I checked my email. There was a pallet in the Aft Cargo. Just over 1000 kg. They missed it, somehow. Didn't say how.

So – a metric ton overweight. Aft C of G.

And you can't tell much about handling in Normal Law, as you know. So it was probably my imagination . . .

. . . or your intuition . . .

. . . but I thought she felt twitchy.

I'm sure she was. Say, speaking of Load Control – did you hear about the two Alaska tailstrikes within six minutes of each other out of SeaTac?

No – where'd you see that?

Well, it was an *incident.* Took a while to come out. The incidents were January 26. The Seattle Times ran it February 17. Two B737's bound for Hawaiian destinations. A MAX-9 and an NG-900ER. Load sheets for both were 20,000 lb. light.

What the fuck?

Yeah. Got me thinking, I'll tell you. Press coverage praised it as a quick-thinking save, because Alaska Ops called a system-wide hold on takeoffs. Lasted 22 minutes. But they're talking about it as if it were just a Flex Thrust issue. 16 Left is 12,000 feet. No sweat.

Hmm. 20,000 lb. Tailstrikes, you say . . . any damage?

Not to speak of. They both came back and landed safely.

So who does their Load Control? In house?

No. Contracted out. A Swedish company.

So they get their load message via ACARS? Like we do?

Yes. It's called a NOTOC.

Pardon me, but what the hell is that?

Yeah. Made me laugh, too. *Notice to Captain.*

Jesus. And it – they – are 20 grand heavier and the C of G is wrong too, probably.

Probably.

But within the takeoff range, so . . .

. . . right . . .

. . . but that's not the issue. And neither is *Flex Thrust, Reduced Thrust,* or *Assumed Temperature,* or whatever they call it . . .

No.

They plug that NOTOC into the FMGC and get their speeds.

Yes.

And they're way low.

Yes.

So they make it off OK with two engines. Just a tailstrike. But if they'd had – Heaven help us – an engine failure after V1, they'd both be craters.

I am keeping a respectful silence. But in my head is the Jeppesen "wheel" I had in one of the breast pockets of my shirt for my entire time with the airline.

You're probably too young, I say, but have you ever used a slide rule?

I don't know about the young part, she says, but yes. I was an engineer, remember? I was fascinated with those logarithmic scales. Adding logs to multiply.

But you had to keep track of the powers of ten . . .

Of course. Some of it you're doing in your head.

Yeah, exactly. So what . . .

I don't know. My old Jeppesen wheel came into my head. Perhaps it's that reasonableness check.

You mean with the Alaska pilots.

Yes. I remembered that I always – or maybe always for high gross weight takeoffs – would do it in my head. You know, Empty Weight is 49,000 kg, 100 passengers is 10,000 kg, Zero Fuel Weight is 59,000 kg, Fuel is 18,000 kg, Takeoff Weight is 77,000 kg. Ball park. Reasonableness check. I think I told you about one captain on the 'nine. When we copied the load numbers he'd write it down on the hotel notepad he had clipped to the yoke. The Flight Number and the Zero Fuel Weight. I copied that. Did the same when I was in the left seat of the 'nine. 'Course on the 320 you enter it in the FMGC.

Yeah. It's good to get the right power of ten. How far off do you think the speed numbers were, with the 20,000 lb. error?

Well, manufacturers don't like revealing empty weights. Or payload. But to be fair, those can vary by Fin Number. So working from many sources, I get a speed error of 13 knots.

Wow. Craters for sure. Enjoy your martini!

§

Chapter Six

When the truth is found
To be – lies
And all the joy with-
In you – dies

. . . .

You better find somebody to love.

~ *Darby Slick – sung by Grace Slick with the Jefferson Airplane 1967* ~

Pushed around by the events of this past winter, I have been ignoring the hull loss in Halifax eight years ago. Now it is Spring, and it is time to look into it in detail. Amazingly, nobody died in that accident. But there are no congratulations in order. Nor is there blame to apportion. Rather, there is a lot to learn, and on many fronts.

The approach, that windy, snowy night, was a *Non-Precision Approach* conducted in conditions of low visibility and obscured, indefinite ceiling. That sounds like a *no-no*, and indeed it is. But this was also an approach conducted in rigorous adherence to the airline's SOP. It broke no regulations. Even the aircraft manufacturer was, for a time, on board with the procedures used. What could possibly go wrong?

To understand, we will have to go back and unpack forty years of slow, drop by drop change. Vast change, but change so stealthily accomplished that generations were led to believe that *standards* meant *status quo ante*. That passing on knowledge meant passing knowledge on exactly as it was. As it has been until now. But perhaps what we thought we knew, we really knew only incompletely. Perhaps there always has been more to it than that. After all, isn't that the history of science in a nutshell?

The *Non-Precision Approach* is an approach without a glideslope. It used to be the norm.

When I joined the airline, there were still some *Radio Ranges* transmitting. I think by then we had stopped doing Radio Range approaches, because we had higher-tech stuff available, like ADF, VOR and even ILS. Even so, I distinctly remember being allowed to fly, that first year, a *Ground Controlled Approach* at Sudbury in the DC-9.

The avionics suite necessary for using the Radio Range was a receiver and earphones. The range transmitted Morse *A* (._) and Morse *N* (_.) in alternate quadrants. Where the quadrants overlapped (the *beams*) you would hear the audio sum of the letters – a steady tone.

The *Ground Controlled Approach (GCA)* requires a similar avionics suite – a Comm radio and earphones. It was a *Precision Approach* because the runway had an associated *Precision Approach Radar (PAR)*. A controller dedicated to one aircraft – you – would talk you down. To 200 feet, in my experience – or all the way to touchdown, for an airplane and crew who have run out of options. In some areas the GCA is still in use today for such "saves".

Some of the stuff we used to do in those early days, when I look back, makes me shudder. Or gives me *frissons*, depending on my mood. In our Route Manuals we had plastic patterns with rotatable compass roses for calculating circling procedures in IMC. Well, not strictly IMC, because you had to have the ceiling. But with a ceiling of 600 feet, flying that timed pattern (I remember a teardrop) at 600 AGL and 160 knots, you didn't see much if you looked out. And you were *way* too busy to look out. But the DC-9 was completely capable of that stuff and I guess we were too. I can't remember any screw-ups.

Maybe there were some and I just don't know about them. Or maybe Transport Canada (the *MOT*, or *Ministry of Transport*, in those days) had something to say about it. In any case, when I returned to the DC-9 after a year of doing nothing but Toronto turns on the B727 as a **very** junior First Officer, these circling procedures were gone.

Fast-forward to the late eighties and early nineties. There was a new airplane – the fly-by-wire A320. It – and its big brother and sister, the A340 and A330 – were the subject of numerous pushes and pulls between the airline and Transport Canada, conflicts for which I, coming to the A320 in January 1995, had a front row seat. But at least one conflict was only marginally related to the new-technology aircraft – the *Non-Precision Approach.*

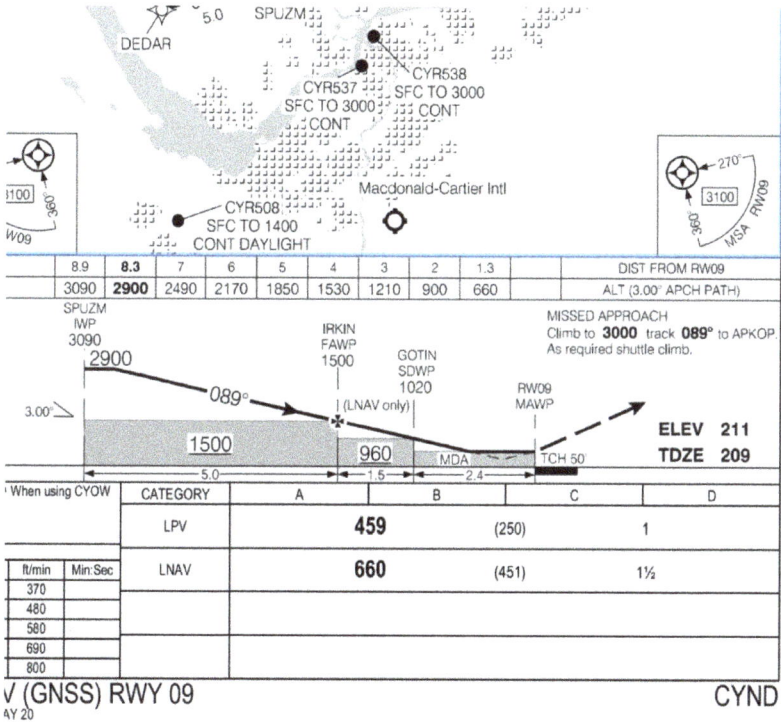

utical Data: © 2023 NAV CANADA All rights reserved

**Vertical Profile from the *Canada Air Pilot* Chart for the
RNAV RWY 09 at CYND**

To this day, Non-Precision Approaches are charted showing a minimum altitude for each segment. The altitude for the last segment – usually FAF to runway – is the MDA, the Minimum Descent Altitude. To simplify just a little, the approach is surveyed so that in theory, a helicopter could arrive at the FAF (*Final Approach Fix,* or FAWP, *Final Approach WayPoint,* on the chart) at the FAF crossing altitude, move ahead along the track so the tail rotor cleared the FAF, and then descend in a hover to the MDA. The airspace – with no simplification – would be safe for that.

But airplane pilots, who used to speak of these approaches as *drive and dive*, quietly adopted smoother techniques using a constant descent which would get them to the MDA at the appropriate point. Then, some years later, Transport Canada formalized the constant descent with the *Constant Descent Angle* technique, or CDA. In the above chart, the CDA numbers are found just above the vertical profile, and the rows labelled (at the right) as **DIST FROM RW9**, and **ALT (3.00° APCH PATH)**.

(As we proceed with unpacking what happened in Halifax that snowy night, we will come back to this CDA information, and also to the solid line in the vertical profile, which runs level from where it encounters MDA to the *Missed Approach WayPoint*, or MAWP. And we will also think more about the *appropriate point for arrival at the MDA*.)

The Non-Precision Approach, as I mentioned a page or so ago, was just one of a number of conflicts. These conflicts, in turn, were part of a larger dispute over Standard Operating Procedures, which began with the arrival of the A320 at the airline in 1988. Transport Canada's *modus operandi* was to apply pressure points, which usually involved failing the airline's pilots on rides. The Non-Precision Approach affair was one such pressure point. It went on for years, and had the unfortunate side effect of muddying the waters: just what is a Non-Precision Approach, anyway? And what is the difference among MDA, Minimum, DH, DA, and DP? SDWP? MAWP?

I chose the above image (**Vertical Profile from the Canada Air Pilot Chart for the RNAV RWY 09 at CYND**) because it is current as of today, and valid for both a precision and a non-precision approach. If your aircraft is equipped with WAAS GPS, you can do the LPV approach (Lateral Precision with Vertical) and descend to a Decision Height of 250 AGL – a Decision Altitude of 459 MSL. If you have an older, non-WAAS GPS, you cannot go lower than 451 AGL – a Minimum Descent Altitude of 660 MSL.

Of particular interest here is the solid bold line. Let's leave other considerations such as the *Approach Ban* aside, and assume your airplane is doing the Non-Precision Approach because your GPS is prehistoric, and the airport is actually W0X0F and that is a total surprise to you.

You have to follow the solid bold line. You level off at your MDA of 660 MSL, because you see absolutely nothing. Then, 40 seconds or so later (at 120 knots) you perform a missed approach. That is the dashed bold line with an arrowhead at the end.

Now take a look at the other dashed line – the non-bold one that continues below the MDA line, and then comes back up. That – with the same ignorance of the actual conditions – is what you would fly if you had a WAAS GPS. You would fly down to your Decision Height of 250 AGL, which is a Decision Altitude of 459 MSL, and then go around. Perform a missed approach. We used to refer to this DH, or DA, as a Decision Point, because that's what it is. It is a specific, and fully defined, *point in space*. To find where it is with a quick and dirty calculation, use the handy 1000 feet in 3 miles rule (for a 3° glideslope, 1000 feet altitude = 3 nm, so 250/333 = ¾ nm). This **DP** is on the localizer track 0.75 nm from the touchdown point and 250 feet above the **TDZE** of 209 MSL.

In the **CAP Gen** (Canada Air Pilot, General), **DP** these days means only **Departure Procedure**. But that *point in space* is important. It is on the glideslope. It is on your path to a successful landing.

OK. Do you feel lost in arcana? Me too.

It gets worse. A quarter-century ago, when Transport Canada was applying pressure points, it declared that the **DA** is frangible, but the **MDA** is not. So the pilot on a precision approach makes a decision at the **DA** to go around. She advances the thrust and raises the nose, etc. The airplane, being a physical object in the real world, is already below the **DA** and continues to descend for a few more seconds before climbing away. And no harm done whatsoever, because *its flight path is on or above the glideslope the whole way*.

The **MDA**, on the other hand, is the surveyed **Minimum** for that last segment of the approach. So the goal is **not to make a decision, but to level off**. That is important, as we shall see. But back in the days of conflict, Transport declared that a pilot who descended one foot below MDA would fail the ride. So for quite a few years our airline SOP's added 50 feet to all MDA's.

Ridiculous?

Absolutely. But the real and permanent damage – which persists to this day – was the muddying of the waters. The becoming lost in the arcana, the abstruse knowledge of the *great experts*. The great experts joining forces in ignorance. The pilots accepting as gospel what they did not understand. The Halifax flight, that March night, is flight-tested proof: the experts – airline, Transport Canada, aircraft manufacturer, and Transportation Safety Board – did not understand why a Non-Precision approach in obscuration and indefinite ceiling, is a *no-no*. Nor did they understand cold weather barometric altimetry or inertial navigation.

Back in Chapter Two I mentioned that it is sometimes difficult or impossible for a pilot to resolve a Flight Path Vector by looking outside, and that even when it is possible, you need the video, not the photo.

In the summer of 1999, I had a Boston layover with an early morning departure. The airplane was the A319, and the route was Boston to Vancouver. On the way to the airport our delightful driver told us, in her Boston twang, of JFK Jr.'s accident the night before. He had been on the way from New Jersey to Martha's Vineyard and had crashed into Long Island Sound.

After we settled down in cruise on the way to CYVR and were attacking our breakfasts, I thought again about the accident. I realized that although so far we had encountered no cloud, I could not see the ground.

I took off my sunglasses so I could press my head against the side window and look almost straight down. I saw a circle of farmland about a mile in diameter. Our altitude was about six miles. I checked the weather at multiple stations in New England, including Mahtha's Vinyid. They were all nearly identical: visibility 6 miles in haze.

Six miles seems like a lot, right?

The forecast for the Long Island Sound area last night was 4-6 miles visibility in haze, with the haze continuing up to 8000 feet. This morning we are in the same airmass and are not quite on top of the haze here in the Flight Levels.

I returned to my coffee and breakfast, but I found myself searching my aviation experience to try to imagine what JFK Jr. would have seen last night at 6000 feet.

He was inside a huge semi-transparent balloon, the center-point of a claustrophobic sphere. Outside was only darkness, but random spots of light were everywhere on the inside surface of the balloon. Stars and lights on the ground all looked the same. It was impossible to resolve a horizon, let alone a Flight Path Vector.

He had disconnected the autopilot to start his descent. What he could plainly see out the window held his attention as his uneasiness quickly grew into fear, panic, and spatial disorientation. His flight path, as reconstructed from radar returns, was consistent with complete disorientation ending in a spiral dive. There was nothing, looking out the window, that could have helped him. His only hope was to hold a *straight and level* attitude **on instruments** until his overload and spatial disorientation eased. But it can be difficult to believe there is no help in those lights out there. JFK Jr. was already following an instrument training course, but we teach instrument flying *under the hood* or in real IMC. What we don't often teach is how to evaluate what we see out there. Is it reliable, or is it a dangerous distraction?

The Mooney that wound up in the high-tension tower last winter is a case in point. Because for him the lights were only below, he had the additional problem of a powerful illusion – *if I can get just a little lower I will see more.* In obscured conditions, that is totally untrue. And deadly. Or, if you are really, really lucky – a mere hull loss. Which brings us back to Halifax.

When I was teaching instrument ground school, I had a slide showing a view of a runway and approach lights in the conditions we have been talking about – a classic *duck under* trap. The lights and the runway threshold are visible. I ask, *is it legal to continue the approach?* I cite chapter and verse, which in Canada are the Air Regulations and the CAP Gen. In the latter there is a list of ten references (runway markings and lights). **One** of these must be visible. In the slide, three or four of these are evident. So yes, you can continue to a landing, as per the regulations and the CAP Gen.

I ask, *is it safe?*

Then we have a discussion and talk about the history of these approaches and how they can safely be continued.

In a nutshell, there **must** be a glideslope, and someone **must** fly the airplane down to the flare **on instruments**, because there is insufficient – and confusing – visual reference.

In the 1980's, airlines decided that *Autoland* was the way to go. 100-foot approaches (CAT II) went from what we did on the DC-9 to **LAND 3** on the B767 and **LAND GREEN** on the A320.

It had not always been this way. The military used the *Pilot Monitored Approach* (PMA), where the PF stayed heads-down and flew instruments. The PM would look up at 100 above. Then at *Minimum* he would say either *Go Around*, or *I have control – Landing.*

I experienced one of those PMA's in 1979, sitting in the jump seat of a British European Airways *Trident*. The captain – P1, as he called himself – was of middle age and middle class. P2 and P3 would change seats (and identities) on alternate legs. They were children of about my age. It was P2's leg from Paris to London.

At top of descent, over what was a solid undercast down to 200 feet, P1 exclaimed:

"*I say, shall I perform an immaculate letdown?*"

Then, as flashes of ground contact turned into something more, the boy in the right seat said:

"***I have control. Landing.***"

As I recall, he did a nice job.

These stories – JFK Jr., The Mooney, the British European Airways Trident doing a PMA, and especially the A320 in Halifax, are all in service of a small but immensely important distinction: between a defined ceiling with good visibility below, and an indefinite ceiling with obscuration. The rules were written for the former. It is my task here to pass on some advice on the latter.

Obscuration comes in many guises. Fog is one. (The simple definition of fog is cloud which extends right down to the ground.) Snow is another. Moderate or heavy snow – especially combined with wind (blizzard conditions) can reduce both ceiling and visibility to zero. How do we know how much we are going to see, and whether we need a precision approach?

This was the weather at Halifax at the time of the accident:

SPECI   CYHZ   290313Z   35020G26KT   **1/2SM** R14/3500V4500FT/N SN DRSN **VV003** M06/M07 A2963 RMK SN8 SLP040

I would sum it up thus: A North Gale. Half-mile visibility in snow and drifting snow. And here is the clue: **Vertical Visibility 300 feet**. If there is a **VV** in the METAR, there is indefinite ceiling and obscuration, *and it is probably not safe to rely on a Non-Precision Approach.*

So what happened that night?

The crew left the autopilot engaged and continued descent below the MDA because they saw lights. They acted as if they were doing a Precision Approach.

Did they really believe they were doing a Precision Approach? Quite possibly. And if *they* did, so also did the *great experts.*

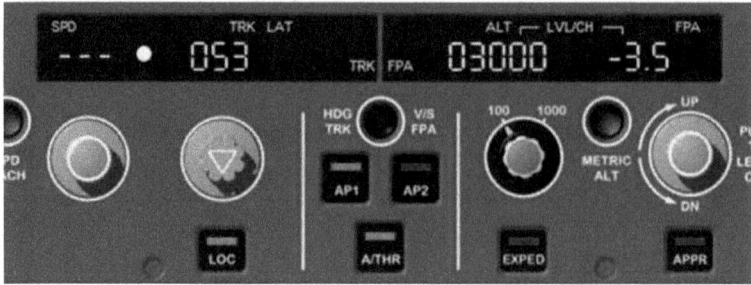

This is the FCU (Flight Control Unit) of the A320 during their approach. Note the black button in the centre, and (just above) that TRK FPA is selected. They are tracking the localizer (LOC button has a green bar) and the track is 053°. The selected altitude is 3000 feet, and the selected Flight Path Angle is -3.5. Autopilot 1 and Autothrust are engaged. The speed shows - - - because they are in *Managed Speed*.

Will the airplane fly the selected Flight Path Angle? **Yes**. Will it level off at the MDA? **No**, because the selected altitude is 3000 feet, which was set for the Missed Approach, and the airplane is now below that altitude. Were they using the Constant Descent Angle as published, which would have taken them to what we are calling the Decision Point? No. Their -3.5 FPA got them to the MDA a half-mile too soon. The time was 03:29:27.

In another universe they might have set the corrected MDA of 813 in the altitude window. The aircraft would have levelled off at MDA. A half-mile later, at the DP, the Precision Approach Path Indicator lights would have been visible, and the PF could have disconnected the A/P and flown the PAPI down to the flare. No harm done, and perfectly legal even with the FPA set to -3.5.

But airline SOP has forever been to set the Missed Approach Altitude as soon as the airplane is below that altitude. It makes sense most of the time. But nothing is foolproof – viz. the Asiana pilot, trying to get down to the PAPI glideslope, selecting FLCH and having the power go to climb thrust for the climb to 3000 feet.

I would bet setting the MAA this way is still SOP to this day. But it means that the A/P has no floor to refer to. The airplane is not going to level off.

The PF of AC 624 disconnected the A/P at 03:29:47, 20 seconds after descending through MDA. The autopilot disconnect was followed in quick succession by the

One Hundred

and the

Fifty

calls from *the German*. Then the PM said:

Pull Up!

They were at 30 AGL.

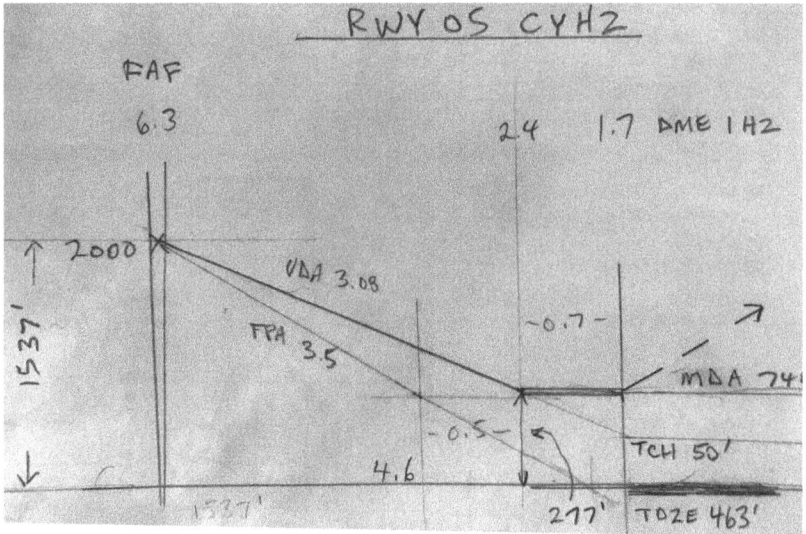

In my pencil drawing you can see where they were – just before the perimeter road, and low enough to snag the power lines.

Wait, you say. *Why have you used the uncorrected altitudes in your diagram? Shouldn't you have 2200 feet at the FAF and 813 as MDA?*

Good question. Because here we have a truly interesting apples and oranges problem. Or an intersection of frames of reference. Remember how we defined *Decision Point* a page or two back as a *point in space?*

Another way of saying *point in space* (at least here on Earth) is to say *position in reference to the surface of the Earth*. That frame of reference is what pilots use for navigation. In this case – the **LOC or NDB RWY 05 at CYHZ** – the DP is 0.7 nm before the runway threshold, and 277 feet above the TouchDown Zone Elevation (TDZE), at 740 MSL *in a standard atmosphere*. The FAF crossing is also a point in space and specifically, as above, in reference to the runway threshold.

The FAF crossing point is:

- On (above) the Localizer

- 4.6 nm from the runway threshold

- 1537 feet above the TDZE

- At 2000 MSL *in a standard atmosphere*

If you like, please go ahead and check my geometry. I hope you will arrive at a Vertical Descent Angle of 3.08° or thereabouts. The Jeppesen Chart the pilots used showed 3.08°. The Canada Air Pilot chart at the time showed 3.04°.

The desired flight path – the straight line between the FAF crossing point and the DP, can be flown by the A320 autopilot using Flight Path Angle (FPA) and selecting -3.1° (It is selectable only in 0.1° increments).

So where did the 3.5° FPA come from?

Well, I don't know for sure, but if you correct the FAF and MDA altitudes and look at the difference, you get 1387 feet, instead of the 1260 feet *actual difference* if you look at *points in space*. That calculation would yield a FPA of about a 3.4°. And the final report says that to be on a safe side, they rounded it up to 3.5°.

They had it backwards. That is making the slope even steeper.

•

I checked your math.

Captain?

Yah. Screwed it up at first. Plugged in the wrong numbers. Got just under 3.2°. Read your paragraph again. Duh – it's the difference. Not 1537 feet and 4.6 nm. 1260 and 3.9.

Right.

Then I got 3.08°.

Whew!

Got some questions for you.

OK.

You talk about the appropriate point for arrival at the MDA.

Yes.

The guys arrived at the MDA a half-mile early. But if they had put 813 in the FCU and levelled off . . .

Uh huh.

. . . they would have had plenty of time to look and decide, even before the DP, as you say, to get the PAPI and the video, while the airplane did its thing.

Right. Absolutely.

And they wouldn't have used up all that runway flying to the MAP, where the PAPI would be all white anyway.

I like it.

But in obscuration you really need the PAPI or VASIS.

Yes!

So if you are flying a Non-Precision approach and you do it by the book, you could be painting yourself into a corner. Especially with obscuration or a limiting runway. Or both.

Because . . .

Because if you decide to land at the MAP you're using up runway, and you've already lost the PAPI. So landing is not a good idea.

Wow. I like your analysis.

Bottom line: arriving at the MDA at the DP is a bad idea. The human pilot brain doesn't have enough time.

I agree. And if you use the CAP Gen CDA numbers, that's where they take you.

Wow. Yes! But another question. We use FPA all the time. Is that really Non-Precision? Seems pretty precise to me, if you use it right. I know it's inertial . . .

OK, good question. Hmmm. Remember I talked about flying an ILS with *Track Steering*?

Sure. And using your groundspeed to get a target Vertical Speed.

Right. So say you're doing that approach. And maybe it's VMC, and you decide to de-tune the ILS to see how well the inertial tracking does.

Ohhh. Point taken. You're untethered.

Uh huh.

And turn Track Steering on its side and you've got FPA.

Right.

And the only tether you've got is where your intercept altitude crosses that 3.08° slope at the FAF. Airbus says dial (minus 3.1° in this case) and then pull at 0.3 nm before the FAF. That way the software works as designed, in effect tethering the FPA to the FAF. So if you do it just like that, it's going to do a pretty good job.

Sure.

But it's like you turned off the ILS and you're still in IMC.

We wait. I am enjoying this. Watching another mind work is a wonderful experience.

By the way, she continues, that diagram – *Figure 15 in 1.18.2, Flight path angle guidance mode* – I'm glad I'm not the Airbus engineer who came up with that.

Amen, Sister. And while we're in the *Final Report*, turn the page. Page 49, section *1.18.3*. That's where they explain . . .

Wait – who's *they?*

The Board.

That's how they sign themselves?

Yeah.

OK – so they explain . . .

They start out well. Or OK. The first paragraph of the previous section – *1.18.2* – says *"the FPA is the angle between the horizontal and the total velocity vector of the aircraft."*

Yeah. The total velocity vector is the Flight Path Vector. That vector is in 3D. So it can have an angle to the surface. Duh.

And still in that first paragraph, *"Therefore the FPA guidance mode does not provide fixed vertical guidance with any reference to a ground-based aid, such as glideslope or ILS approach."*

OK. The FPA is *untethered*, as you call it.

Right. But then in the second paragraph we have *"When flying in the FPA guidance mode, external perturbations, such as wind variations or turbulence, can cause the aircraft to move away from the selected FPA initial approach path."* It goes on to describe what is going on in *Figure 15*.

Which is bullshit.

Well . . .

No, really. Hang on. Wait a sec. I've got *Figure 15* here. Notice how all these so-called perturbations all act in the same direction? They are demonstrating they don't understand what *inertial* is. And thanks to you and your Uncle Eric, I know enough to laugh.

I laugh, too. I can't help it. *Inertial can't work,* I say. *Because it doesn't take wind into account.*

Right. So it's just frickin' magic.

I take a breath. Where to start? *There is a guy of about my seniority,* I begin. He was mentored by one of the greatest and the craziest. Taken under the older guy's wing. Result was that if the young guy went on a new airplane, he got the manuals as early as he could. He studied his butt off. By the time he started course, he knew the airplane better than we did at the end of the course. I don't know if he knew D.P. Davies, but he followed Davies' advice, and minimized the distance between himself and the manufacturer. He trusted no one but the manual.

Smart guy.

Yeah. He knew his shit. So I just channelled him and dug out my manual. *AOM 2.34.10 P1:*

> Each ADIRU is divided in two parts, either of which can work separately in case of failure in the other:
>
> - The ADR part (Air Data Reference) which supplies barometric altitude, airspeed, mach, angle of attack, temperature and overspeed warnings.
>
> - The IR part (Inertial Reference) which supplies attitude, flight path vector, track, heading, accelerations, angular rates, ground speed and aircraft position.

You are an engineer. You took calculus. But there aren't too many people out there who actually understand how inertial works, let alone how a strapdown IRS works.

And now we have GPS. And that doesn't help either, because they are not the same thing.

No. And even though the details of GPS get complicated as hell, the concept is easier to understand. GPS computes a position – a *point in space* – about once per second.

And even my humble imagination can see that if I draw a line from one of those points to the next, I have a Flight Path Vector. With WAAS, the accuracy can be one metre spherical error. You could flare and land and have the nosewheel on the centreline.

Right. I've done it. Well, more or less.

OK, Chris. You'll have to tell me someday. But my point is that's differentiation. Two defined points in space, one second apart. Draw the line. That's the FPV. But integration – that's harder.

That was Uncle Eric's insight. That integrating accelerations could amount to navigation.

Integration has to be tethered. There has to be a starting point. And an end point, for that matter. And also an initial attitude, with IRS.

Yes. That's less intuitive. When I teach it – when I used to teach it – I called it the reverse of the GPS process. I had a diagram:

acceleration <> velocity <> position

Inertial goes left to right.

I see what you mean about reverse process. But the integration has to have that tether to that starting point.

Yes. And there's something else I wanted to bring up.

Shoot.

Actually two things. The accident was 29 March 2015. I first wrote about it when the report came out in May 2017. I finished my article in

June. This Final Report we're looking at was a *corrected version* released 26 September 2017.

There are differences?

Not entirely sure, but take look at *section 1.1 History of the flight*. It starts with three paragraphs in a box.

Gimme a couple of minutes . . .

Sure.

I wait. I am thinking, *don't forget the FCOM Temporary Revision and its history . . .*

Shit. Pilot privacy my ass. So you're telling me there's no CVR at all.

No DFDR, either.

So they – the fricken' Board – give us no raw data. Because they are "*respecting pilots' privacy*"?

Huh. Yeah. But they do give us some in the text.

But only what they want to, right? No one can come back to the report ten years – or a generation – later and come to a different insight.

That's true, I'm afraid. So it's hard for us to tell the story. But this is not the only report that has been sanitized. There's Atlas Air – where there is no DFDR data on the stab. And with the two MAX crashes, the only reason we have all the data is that the prangs were not in our political arena.

That sounds harsh.

Scusa. I'll stick to this Canada crash. Check this paragraph from *Section 1.18.3*:

In 2009, while working with Air Canada, TC identified a discrepancy involving all Airbus A320, A330, and A340 series aircraft when a non-precision approach was carried out in cold temperatures. When the cold temperature corrections were applied to the FAF altitude and the aircraft was flown with the FPA selected to the published vertical descent angle, the aircraft's position did not accurately correspond to the published distances and altitude. Since the Airbus FCOM did not include any applicable procedures, TC required Air Canada to work with Airbus to develop a procedure so that, when a cold temperature correction is applied to a FAF altitude, the FPA can be adjusted to compensate for the corrected altitude.

Yeah. But we know **why**, don't we?

Why Transport Canada required Air Canada to work with Airbus?

Well, that too, but no. We know why the *"aircraft's position did not accurately correspond"* as they put it in committee-speak.

We do?

Of course. Those CDA altitudes. Altitudes against distances from the runway.

OK . . .

Those altitudes are MSL ***in a standard atmosphere***. If you wanted to use them accurately in the cold, you would have to correct each one separately. Write out a chart before you started the approach.

I feel stupid. *Of course*, I say. *Of course you're right.* There is a silence while I digest the fact that I never thought of that. And *of course* that is the key to this whole crazy story. I sigh.

Thanks, Captain.

You agree?

Oh, a hundred percent. But I didn't see it until you said it. I guess I was so preoccupied with the craziness of **what** they did that I didn't see the craziness of **why** they did it in the first place.

Yeah. Pretty crazy, all right.

But you have given me the key. The **why** they did what they did.

For the **what**, let's just let the last paragraph of *Section 1.18.3* speak for itself. Then I've got a little sidebar for you.

> In April 2010, Airbus published a Temporary Revision to the FCOM *Standard Operating Procedures, Non-precision Approaches*. Although this revision, which introduced an FPA correction chart for cold weather operation, provided additional guidance, it did not take into account Air Canada's procedure for rounding up the correction altitudes. Therefore, Air Canada decided to develop its own procedures for adjusting the FPA when cold temperature corrections had been applied to the FAF altitude. This method was accepted by TC, and, in early 2011, Air Canada's Airbus A320 Quick Reference Handbook was revised to include the FPA and chart of approach altitude corrections for cold temperatures. The chart was designed to identify the applicable altitude correction (in 100-foot increments) to be added to the FAF and the degree correction to be added to the FPA based on the approach altitude height above the aerodrome and the temperature in degrees Celsius.

OK. That's quite a **what**. But what's the sidebar? Let me guess – does it have something to do with the Airbus *Temporary Revision*?

Bingo! Because, you see, Air Canada was not the only airline that had been mystified by FPA's behaviour in cold air. Looking back, I think that's why Airbus allowed itself to be dragged into this mess. That *Temporary Revision* was used as a basis for SOP's at a number of airlines. But it didn't last long. Perhaps wiser heads at Airbus – or wiser lawyers at Airbus – prevailed. In any case, queries to Airbus on the subject began to be met with obfuscation. And I learned from friends in the industry that the 2010 *Temporary Revision (TR FCOM 3 294-1)* had been deleted, and that all engineering and technical data concerning *Flight Path Angle* had been removed from the Airbus FCOM.

Wow. When?

Yeah. A long time ago. Certainly before 2015.

●

There is good news here. This is our trade. We can learn.

Our first reaction to not having access to the CVR and DFDR from AC 624 was anger, as you saw just above.

The Board, though, are people. They work within a system where both money and power have sway. And lack of learning will not kill them directly. If they stray into harm's way because of that lack of learning, it will be as passengers.

So Captain and I will let the anger pass, and recognize that learning something about our trade is a kindness. Passing it on to each other is also a kindness. That is good news.

I am about to put before you a man who exemplifies this kindness. He is one of us. He is a pilot. And I learned that he is a pilot only just now.

I knew of his contribution, but not much about the context and timing of his discoveries.

To see (and, I hope, to understand) we have to go back two generations to the two DC-8 crashes in 1963-64. At the time this man, the pilot, was forty-one years old. He had flown jets in the RAF in the 1950's.

I was still in college when the DC-8s crashed. I had not yet leaned to fly. In the airline world, aircraft with all-moving stabilizers were just entering service. These aircraft were jets that operated at high subsonic Mach numbers, so they had *Mach Trimmers*. Deep stall (see AF447) was a worry, so they had *Stick Shakers* and – eventually – *Stick Pushers* (Colgan 3407). *Jet Upset* – where the aircraft becomes uncontrollable in a dive – was also a worry, so there were a lot of flight test dives during certification. (Those test pilots discovered that at high speed in a dive, holding significant up elevator can jam the stabilizer drive. D.P. Davies also mentions this and outlines the necessary recovery process. That knowledge was lost to many writing in 2019 about the MAX crisis.)

The two DC-8 crashes happened within months of each other and both aircraft dove into the ground (Lake Pontchartrain in one of the cases) as a result of nose-down stabilizer – an eerie foreshadowing of the two MAX crashes 55 years later. The timeline looked like this:

29 Nov 1963	TCA 831	Ste-Thérèse, Quebec	DC-8
25 Feb 1964	EAL 304	Lake Pontchartrain	DC-8
08 AUG 1965	Published in Aerospace Medicine, Vol. 36	Theoretical Man-Machine Interaction Which Might Lead to Loss of Aircraft Control	J.F. Martin, and G. Melvill Jones

Eighteen months after the second crash, Geoffrey Melvill Jones had published the paper which – if it did not serve as an accident investigation (it was not intended to be one) – *did* prove the existence of a fundamental hazard.

The abstract of the article looks like this:

A theoretical model of a pilot-aircraft interaction wherein the pilot relies entirely upon his sense of the relative gravity vector for orientation information is developed. It is shown that the illusory effects arising from motions could cause him to operate the aircraft controls in a diametrically opposite manner to what would be appropriate. This model may serve as a basis to account for otherwise unexplained losses of control in jet transport aircraft. A series of recommendations for further investigations is proposed.

Geoffrey Melvill Jones retired in 2022 at the age of 99. As far as I can determine, he had his one hundred and first birthday recently: 14 January 2024.

I picture him celebrating in Calgary with his four children.

I am rewriting this section because my friend – the one I have known since kindergarten, and who is also a pilot, by the way – has just recently told me of flying with Geoffrey Melvill Jones out of the old Edmonton Municipal Airport (CYXD, closed in 2013) in a Fleet Canuck.

I knew that my friend had studied with Melvill Jones at McGill University in Montreal. Like GMJ, he had a Doctorate in Physiology before becoming a Medical Doctor and a pilot. What I didn't know was that they had flown together and that GMJ was a pilot.

After that conversation we both started researching Melvill Jones more thoroughly, and we shared the results. And my friend loaned me books and articles. In the last few days I have read:

- **Narrative Biographical Memoire of Geoffrey Melvill Jones**
  MA, MB, BCh (Cantab), FRCS, FRAeS, FRS, Written by Geoffrey Melvill Jones, 2014, and

-

Theoretical Man-Machine Interaction Which Might Lead to Loss of Aircraft Control

J. F. Martin, B.Sc., and G. Melvill Jones, M.A., M.B., B.Ch., FCASI, A.F.R.AeS.

There is a lot to digest. As I have done with books before, I recommend both of these to your library.

•

Well, maybe *you* let the anger pass.

Captain?

Yeah. I've got a bit of a temper on me.

I know. I love it!

I haven't found the article yet, but I've skimmed the *Memoire*. He seems like a really nice guy. I mean out-of-the-ordinary nice.

Yes. Did you see how after his wife dies in '91 he orchestrates a transfer to Calgary so he can be close to his kids?

Yeah. I think that did it for me. And buying a boat with his kids and sailing with his kids. And he's amazingly well-rounded. Sports galore. And music. Singing, the viola, learning piano at age 80. I wish. So can you tell me something about the article? Is this the *Somatogravic Illusion*?

Yes. He doesn't call it that yet, but yes. And I didn't find the article online. Not yet anyway. My friend razored it out of the journal. Obviously ages ago. I scanned it. I'll email it to you.

Please. Thank you. Then give me a half-hour.

OK.

I get up and make myself an espresso. Probably shouldn't but at my age it doesn't hurt to be a bit wired when considering complex subjects. I put the cup down on our lovely four-foot-square oak kitchen table, and notice the spot in front of me where the nice finish has been etched away and not repaired. That was where I overhauled a master cylinder. Forty years ago, at least.

Chris?

That was quick. Did you read it?

Yes. Amazing. Amazing mostly because the knowledge has been there all this time.

I sigh.

Yeah, me too. But do you have any idea why?

Why it's still not understood?

Yeah.

Well, talking to you I think I'm beginning to. Think *Inertial*.

> During flight maneuvers the direction of the apparent gravity vector changes continually, since it is the resultant of the actual gravity vector and those force vectors acting upon the airplane as the result of its aerodynamic interaction with the relative velocity vector (the flight speed and path). It is well known that this motion of the apparent gravity vector can lead to illusory changes in attitude, particularly if the resultant gravity vector is identified, in the mind of a subject within its influence, with the actual gravity vector.[1,2] It is for this reason, of course, that instruments which indicate attitude to the pilot are necessary for flight out of visual contact with the ground.

That's paragraph three in the article.

It kind of says it all. You call it *Local G*. I call it coffee on my tray table.

Or gin.

Yeah.

But it's non-obvious, especially so back then. It would be another decade before INS would be installed in an airliner. And I don't know about *It is well known that this motion of the apparent gravity vector can lead to illusory changes of attitude*. Maybe he should have said *illusory changes of **perceived** attitude*. Anyway, at that time GMJ was in the RAF. I think he saved a number of pilots lives. Some of them believed his briefings.

I think I can see where you're going. Our bodies sense G inertially. I mean, how else are they going to sense it? And few people understood inertial then. Few people understand it today, and that's a problem. Because so much in our airplanes is based on inertial sensing. And so much in us, as you say. Semi-circular canals. Otoliths. But wait – Melvill Jones had that covered, too. Where is it?

Yes. Hang on. Second page, last paragraph :

In this connection it is important to note that the impression of tumbling due to this rotating gravity vector will not be supported by corresponding information from the semi-circular canals, which in this particular circumstance would signal a small nose-down angular velocity (average of 3°/sec. over first three sec.). However, in view of recent experimental demonstrations that a rotating (g)-vector alone can induce marked compensatory nystagmus[3,4] it may well be that the illusion of pitching up would be strengthened substantially by a visual illusion akin to the oculogyral illusion[5] but induced by otolithic rather than semicircular canal stimulation. Backward rotation of the gravity

vector, as in Figures 2 and 3, would be expected to induce vertical nystagmus with slow phase downwards, which would give rise to a visual impression of upward cockpit rotation.

The pilot's immediate and natural reaction to this supposed situation will be to push forward upon the longitudinal control element in order to check the apparent nose up motion. Not having recognized that the pitch up sensation has arisen from a nose down change in aircraft attitude his action will be entirely the reverse of that appropriate to the situation and will lead to a further deterioration, in that larger and more negative acceleration will be imposed upon the airplane.

A theoretical mechanism for a pitch-up disorientation in the presence of what is in fact a pitch-down out of a steady climb has been established. How far this mechanism may be realized in actual practice will be discussed subsequently.

It's longitudinal acceleration that gives the illusion. So it's the otoliths, the linear accelerometers, that sense it.

Yeah. And I love how he proves it. It's a *reductio ad absurdum*. By pushing forward and accelerating he feels he has done half a loop!

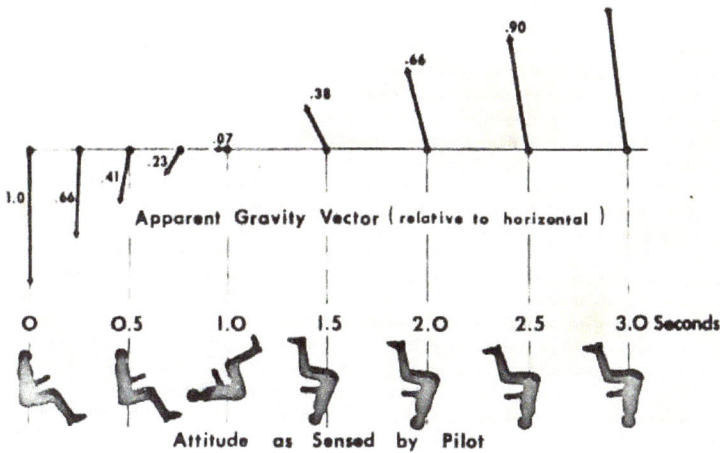

Fig. 3. Pilot's concept of attitude during pushover.

I see what you mean. Already, at one second into the pushover, he feels like he is lying on his back.

Then he discusses the **Why**. What are the necessary conditions for the illusion to take over? And he knows and we know that our vision is our tether for integration of the forces. That resolving a horizon – by whatever means – is the only way to survival.

A theoretical man-machine interaction has been presented which would lead a pilot, relying solely upon his sense of the apparent gravity vector for orientation, to so maneuver his aircraft as to worsen a "push-over" situation. The question now arises, "under what conditions would a pilot be compelled to rely solely upon the apparent gravity vector for orientation?"

Two conditions are obviously essential, the first being that the pilot should have no external reference to the ground and the second that he should be unable to determine his attitude from instrument indications. The first of these conditions is easily satisfied by flight in

(The above paragraph continues . . . *by flight cloud at night*. See *GLOSSARY: EYEBALL BOUNCE*)

But *unable to determine his attitude from instrument indications?*

Well, apparently the early DC-8s had a small A/H with a black background. No *blue side up.* No arrows pointing the way to sanity like we're used to today. Here are two bullet points from the probable causes of EA 304:

- The attitude indicator, which was small with a solid black background, was difficult to interpret at night.

- The pitch indication of the attitude indicator was "geared down" but not indexed as to degrees.

Jesus. Does "geared down" mean real fine control around *straight and level* but *who the fuck knows* in an unusual attitude?

Huh. Don't know. Sounds plausible. Yuck.

Yeah, yuck. Check out the second recommendation:

(b) A program be established to determine to what extent even experienced transport pilots (particularly those not possessing considerable aerobatics experience) may make use of their sense of the apparent gravity vector as an attitude indicator during normal flight maneuvers;

And by the way, Chris – from my present experience on the line I'd say that could be half of the people I fly with. Entirely possible they *may make use of the apparent gravity vector as an attitude indicator.* Of course they would deny it, but they might do it.

So. The *Somatogravic Illusion* was clearly defined two generations ago. But the accidents are still happening. That means that **never heard of it** and **it couldn't happen to me** are still very much out there. The bottom line appears to be that if you are a pilot and you have experienced severe spatial disorientation, you believe in it. If you haven't yet, you do not.

•

To pass certification, an airplane must have *Longitudinal Stability*. This is sometimes referred to as *speed stability*, but it can be more accurately thought of as *Angle of Attack Stability*. Left to its own devices, an airplane will eventually return to its trimmed AoA when it is disturbed – either by turbulence or by a push and release (or a pull and release) of the yoke. It is acceptable that the return overshoots the mark, as long as the oscillations get smaller. That oscillating behavior looks like a sine wave of diminishing amplitude and is known as a *phugoid*. An airplane demonstrating that behavior is said to have *positive* **dynamic** *longitudinal stability*. If the airplane doesn't do a phugoid but rather just diverges further from its initial AoA, it is said to have *negative* **static** *longitudinal stability*. That, of course, is a no-no.

In general, designers build in positive stability by placing the *Center of Gravity* ahead of the *Center of Lift*. This creates a nose-down moment which is balanced by negative lift produced by the horizontal tail surfaces. If a disturbance leaves the airplane in a more nose-down attitude, the airspeed will increase (decreasing the AoA) but the negative lift of the tail will also increase, raising the nose and transitioning back to the original airspeed and AoA.

Also, at higher subsonic Mach numbers, the *Center of Lift* moves aft because of shock waves forming on the wing. To compensate, a *Mach Trimmer* applies a pull force to the yoke which increases with Mach number. To the pilot, the airplane seems to fly normally at high Mach. A spring force has moved the neutral point of the yoke back, but the pilot doesn't feel that. (On the DC-8 and DC-9, a rod will extend a few millimetres from a tube on the side of the yoke, mechanically indicating that the spring pressure is being applied.)

Similarly, large fan engines placed on pylons under and ahead of the wing create more lift at high AoA and can reverse that stability moment. An example is the B767. If you were slowing – pulling the yoke to increase AoA – the stick force would initially increase with G, but at a higher AoA the stick force required would decrease and even reverse. That is *negative static longitudinal stability,* a no-no. So once again a spring force on the elevator (a *push*, this time) can re-introduce static stability by moving the neutral point of the yoke ahead.

I know all this is Too Much Information, but the point is that we have made it into the 1980's and things are still OK. Airplanes are certificated with springs, and the *stick force per G* is made predictable and acceptable over the whole speed range of the airplane. Perhaps most importantly, we protect the airplane from the stall by *warning the pilot.*

My Bonanza has a downspring on the elevator. Its purpose in to *increase* the stick force per G, because otherwise the elevator would be too twitchy. On the ground you notice it because you have to pull against the spring to hold neutral elevator. But once airborne you notice nothing but lovely control harmony. There is a tiny (½-inch square) spring-loaded vane under the leading edge of the wing. At high AoA the airflow pushes the vane up against the spring and sets off the *stall warning*, a red light and a horn. In the DC-8 and the DC-9, the warning is a *Stick Shaker*. A motor turning an eccentric is attached to the yoke, and it literally *shakes the stick*. In each case the pilot is warned, but *control is not taken away*.

Then, somehow, we lose context. Some of that **TMI** is forgotten. Or perhaps, with automation taking over as a solution, the human pilot is left out of the loop, and the fix – to allow the aircraft to be certificated – *takes control away from the pilot.*

We have seen this in the Dash-8 Q400, the Colgan airplane. It has a *stick shaker* which warns the pilot. But if the AoA increases still further, there is a *Stick Pusher* which pulls the yoke forward. It is **very evident** to the pilot. If he tries to counteract it he will need to pull with more than 60 pounds of force, as the Colgan pilot did. It is true that the airplane is only trying to survive. But to the panicked pilot, the airplane appears to be suicidal.

This is a watershed development which crept up on us. I think perhaps we pilots unconsciously accepted that *stick pushers are stick pushers*. Or maybe – when they were benign, as on the B767 – we didn't notice. (I flew as First Officer on the B767 for four years in the 1980's, *and I didn't know it had a stick pusher*.) After the B767 I flew the DC-9 again, this time in the left seat, and its beautiful control harmony and its stabilizer feedback – beeps for each ½-degree of movement – lulled me into contentment and perhaps complacency.

Then in 1995 learning the fly-by-wire A320 took my full attention. I thought a lot about having silicon chips as my only connection to the aircraft. But I was impressed by the Airbus design – much of it inspired by Bernard Ziegler. Remember, this was the late 1980's, and processors were largely either Intel or Motorola. The *Flight Control Computers* each had two channels with different processors, one of each make. The software in the two channels was different right down to assembly language. The channels had to agree, or the Flight Control Computer would declare itself unserviceable. That took care of my worry about a stray cosmic ray changing the state of one memory location, effectively severing what used to be a braided steel cable.

So you worried about losing your connection to the airplane.

Captain?

Yeah, sorry to butt in, but I'm having some reactions to what you're saying. I don't even understand them. My reactions, I mean.

I hear you. I have reactions too. Emotions – I'm beginning to think you never understand them. At least not while you're feeling them. Maybe later. To some extent.

I wait. Maybe she needs some time. Maybe we're both doing the same thing. Sorting out our feelings about this stuff.

Chris?

I'm here. Take your time.

That's me, sighing. I was thinking, believe it or not, the Bus is my first big airplane. Flew it, stayed on it, got promoted on it. Now they're asking me to do LITC.

Great! Good for you! I did it for eight years and enjoyed it very much. They still call it that – *Line Indoctrination Training Captain*?

Yeah. I think it's just to distinguish it from *Check Airman*. Or *Check Pilot*. Or *Check Airperson*. You're not checking. Just teaching.

I am smiling in recognition. Trying not to laugh or react, because she is going somewhere.

What I am trying to say, she goes on, *is I have never known anything different*. And maybe I think the Bus is beyond all that nonsense. You know, *full envelope protection* and all that.

She has stopped again. If we could see each other, I would just nod. I nod anyway.

Yeah. But if I felt any airplane was trying to take control from me, I would be pissed. Some pissed. I mean, really, really pissed.

I nod. It seems to be working.

But I don't feel that way about the Bus. She feels like she's helping me. We can be partners. I know she's not perfect, but I'm getting to know her pretty well . . .

I decide not to worry. She knows I'm listening. I'm not going to think of *ALT** and rain on her parade.

. . . and no one's perfect. We all have out little ways. They're part of us. *ALT Star*, for example. I've just been reading about the A330 crash in Toulouse where, as you might say, they inadvertently flight-tested *ALT**. At least I think so. In the Wikipedia article, one of the causes is listed as:

- Absence of attitude protection in the autopilot's altitude capture mode

I feel a tug in my guts, pulling me to January 1995.

Chris, what do you think?

Yeah. It's pretty close to home.

You had an ALT* incident?

Well, it was in the Sim. The A330 accident was 30 June 1994. Seven people died. Sure – there was distraction and overconfidence. But yes – it was an inadvertent flight test of ALT*. And the next winter I did my initial ride on the Bus. With Transport looking over our shoulders. Me and Rob, the F/O. He was great. He was Toronto based, but he would stay long enough to have a beer with me before driving home. Or a Coke. It was during the time Transport was pressuring the company. And Transport had a point: our SOP's on the Bus were bullshit.

How so?

OK – you know how an engine fire presents on the Bus . . .

Sure – ECAM.

So, since 1988, our SOP was do the drill. Do the whole ECAM from memory.

You're – *kidding?*

No, 'fraid not. Anyway, one pressure point was – *OK, if you want to have the A340 and A330 as a common type for training purposes, you have to base your procedures on the Airbus FCOM.* Otherwise, no go. The other pressure point was failing pilots in the Sim. That was me and Rob.

They failed you?

No, as it happened. We had talked about it that week. *What would they do to us?* We thought about ALT*. We'd get it in a go-around on one engine. Where the Missed had a low level-off altitude. That night I looked at Montreal, Toronto, and Ottawa . . .

And?

Bingo. Ottawa Runway 25. Missed Approach Altitude 2200. After the rehearsal ride, Rob and I briefed it. I think he even had a beer that night.

So, you got the engine failure . . .

And the approach on 25. So we were expecting it. I disconnected and pushed the nose down to – I don't know, plus 8° or something.

Couldn't you just *Push to Level Off?*

No – *Push to Level Off* didn't exist then. It came later with a software revision in the FCU.

OK – I'll bet that was after the early accidents. We learned some important stuff from them, didn't we?

Boy, did we:

- 26 June 1988 – Mulhouse – IDLE OPEN is IDLE OPEN. There is a spool-up time.

- 14 February 1990 – Bangalore – if you don't get **BOTH** Flight Directors off, you'll still be in IDLE OPEN.

- 20 January 1992 – Strasbourg – minus 3.3 means FPA -3.3°, but only if you're in TRK/FPA. If you're in HDG/VS, which they were, minus 3.3 means –3300 feet per minute.

Yeah – that's the one. That's why they did that FCU change.

Right.

And FPA -3.3° is about 800 feet per minute.

Yes. But since they were in HDG/VS they descended at 3300 feet per minute. Right into a ridge.

That was an ergonomics mistake and Airbus fixed it. And we learned from that. And from the other two we learned that it's never just *Autopilot Off*. It's *Autopilot Off, Flight Directors Off*. Both of them.

STILL LEARNING TO FLY

I nod.

That's how you get the *Autothrust* out of IDLE and into SPD. We learned to read our *Flight Mode Annunciator* and call it out.

I have been smiling and nodding, but keeping my mouth shut.

And that *Push to Level Off.* That's a one-touch way to exit ALT*. It's what you didn't have in '95. So you had to go *Autopilot Off.* Hit the button. Get *the Cricket.*

I think so.

What else could you have done?

I don't know.

Well, if there *was* a way to exit ALT*, it wasn't one-touch.

No.

So you and Rob passed.

Yes.

And Airbus fixed the ergonomics.

Yes.

And we all learned.

There is a long pause while she digests all of this. She knows her airplane. Knows her stuff. But she doesn't know the whole story about how we got here.

I can't believe – did you really do a fire drill from memory and ignore the ECAM?

Well, Rob and I didn't. We were strictly FCOM.

FCOM. The Airbus *Flight Crew Operating Manual.* But you were on course. What were they doing on the line?

The SOP since 1988.

Fire drill from memory?

Yup.

So Transport . . .

I think about Rob and me on course. Panic in the ground school. They have to push us through, but the old SOP is off-limits and they haven't written a new one.

. . . Transport says no old SOP. You're on course, and what? There's no new SOP?

Exactly. But there's FCOM.

But – let me guess – it's not a full airline SOP, with the verbal calls and whatnot.

That's right.

So you and Rob . . .

. . . and Lionel. Head of the ground school. He was briefing us day-by-day on what was going on. Near the end of the *learn the aircraft systems* part of the course, he got us a copy of the FCOM. Just the Normal Ops. And how to handle Abnormals and EMERs. It was a bunch of 8 ½ by 11 sheets of paper. Stapled together.

Holy shit! What'd you do?

It wasn't so bad. In retrospect, it was great experience. We took the FCOM to the beer place and talked. We were due to start in the Sim the next week.

So – you . . .

We made our own SOP. Bare bones. As simple as possible. Verbal calls – what we would say to each other. We used the mechanical checklists. They were OK. But starting with the cockpit check . . .

Ooh. I think I see this coming. Your instructor has been doing this for a while. On the old SOP. Has anyone briefed him?

To this day I don't know. But from what we experienced, I don't think so. We got in our seats, strapped in, and he pulled out one of those extensible car antenna pointers, tapped the thrust levers, and said:

"What I like to see, right away, when you sit down, is . . ."

. . . is what?

I don't remember, but it wasn't *the Flow*.

Ah! The *Flow* was from the FCOM!

Yes.

Like we still do today? Left to right, top to bottom. Turn out all the lights in the switch/lights. 'Till you're left with the green EXT PWR light.

That's the one.

So. Your instructor . . .

Yes. We – I – explained to him that we weren't going to pass the ride unless we did it *this way*. I handed him the FCOM sheets. I told him Rob and I were going to work as a team with an SOP based on those sheets, because there was nothing else.

Wow. How'd he take it?

He was still breathing.

I can feel her piecing this together.

Actually, I think his biggest concern was the number of sim sessions. Management had just cut two out of the course. 14 to 12, or 12 to 10 – I can't remember.

Yeah. He's got to get you through the syllabus. He wants you to pass, but he's pressed. He doesn't even know what the FCOM says.

Yes. It was a bit stiff with him for a while. But at the end of the first week I met Dave in the hall of the Sim Building.

Dave?

Good guy. My seniority, more or less. Always did well. By then he was in management, God help him. He said, Chris, I know what you're going through. You and Rob are the first crew through, and the Sim sked is too tight. I can't do much, but if you guys need a couple of extra sessions before the ride, that I can manage.

Did you take him up on it?

I was grateful. I think it eased our anxiety. And it was close – the instructor and I had a few words . . .

Tell!

It was near the end of my two hours as PF. We were on approach with an engine out and some extra system failures. I forget what. On short final he said,

OK, new airplane, new day. Go Around.

I said,

No, I want to land off this one.

He was quiet until we turned off into the taxiway. Then he said,

OK – stop. Set the brakes.

Then he started a lively, heart-felt rant. Lasted a while. Minutes. Then he stopped. Went back to his panel. Set us up at the gate. Then he said,

You guys OK to keep going without a break? Or just a quick pee?

Things went fine after that, including the rehearsal ride the next day.

I guess he got it off his chest.

Yes.

And then Transport gave you ALT* on the ride.

Yes.

And you and Rob were using an SOP that was only yours.

Yeah, and looking back I think that was the best part. We had given a lot of thought to what makes a good SOP. I think about that to this day.

There are – here and there – bits and pieces in the SOP that strike me as someone in the head shed marking a fire hydrant.

We share a laugh. It feels good. A silly cockpit moment floats into my head.

Years ago. I forget what airplane. I was an F/O on Reserve. Caught day two of a three-day trip. First day had been a Route Check for the Captain. I couldn't tell if he was venting or satirizing. Probably both. That whole day, every time we passed 18,000 feet in the climb, he would say,

29.92 inches – set. POINT!

But he wouldn't point.

Let me guess. The SOP said, say *29.92 inches, set*, and *point at the altimeter.*

Yup. I think it even said, *point at the altimeter setting window in the altimeter.*

•

We have already spoken about the two early DC-8 crashes. As we have seen, they are the beginning of a long and sad saga of learning and forgetting which is still going on to this day.

Recall that they happened just months apart:

- 29 November 1963 – Trans Canada Airlines Flight 831 – CF-TJN

- 25 February 1964 – Eastern Air Lines Flight 304 – N-8607

In both cases the horizontal stabilizer was found. In both cases the horizontal stabilizer was full nose-down at impact.

Dear Reader – a treat awaits you. You can immerse yourself in the ethos of 1964, the year I was a sophomore at college. You can go back to the historical sources and read the Final Reports on these crashes. Both reports were written on typewriters. Both are, if anything, more relevant today than they have ever been.

As an historical researcher – and I urge young pilots and aeronautical engineers to do that research – you can read the documents and come to your own conclusions. But you will see that the issues I address in this book are all there. A small sampling:

- The paramount importance of **attitude**

- The **power of the horizontal stabilizer**

- The importance of **longitudinal stability** and *stick force per G*

- The direct **relationship between stabilizer position and Angle of Attack**

- The effect of **pitch and roll moment** on pilot technique

I might as well admit it. This year I read the Final Report on EAL 304 for the first time.

My detailed study of TCA 831 was in 2019. I discussed that accident with my friend Mark Goodrich, and he told me about EAL 304. At the time I thought, *similar accidents, close together – interesting*, but I didn't pursue EAL 304 in any level of detail.

My bad. But perhaps it was meant to be that way, because reading the Final Report *now* has been an eye-opener for me. For a start, the two accidents were **similar** but **not identical**. And second, my assertion, a few pages back, that *we have made it into the 1980's and things are still OK* was premature at best. Even my last bullet point just above should be modified to include the yaw axis.

It has been a week. I write a page or two and get stuck. I start over. I go from what I think is understanding to doubt and confusion. But – mostly in dreams – powerful echoes and connections are emerging.

Reading about EAL 304, I come across a lovely description of **Pitch Moment**, and of the dangerous reaction a pilot can have to it – **Pilot-Induced Oscillation**. From page 23 of the report:

> In further attempts to assess the combination of turbulence and handling characteristic elements of the man-machine-environment triangle, the Board found two other discussions by the research pilot significantly important   "In our experience we find that slightly positive static margin .   . is an area where pilots get into more difficulty than zero static margin, or even considering slightly unstable.   What happens is that, especially in large aircraft, we have these slow response characteristics . . . as long as you fly an airplane and don't try to force it – you allow the airplane to respond well within its capa- bilities – you don't have any difficulty   If you, however, try to force the air- plane to respond faster than it wants to, then you can get into what we call a low frequency pilot-induced oscillation.   It is nothing more, really, than over- controlling.   You don't see the airplane respond immediately so you have the tendency to put a little more elevator in, and by this time the airplane has started to respond and you suddenly find the response is more than you wanted. So the tendency is to reverse the process. . . . I can see this situation can be quite critical in turbulence or possibly under IFR conditions plus turbulence where, let's say, you do have some large gusts which change your attitude appreci- ably   If the pilot attempts to . . . maintain his attitude tightly, there is a possibility that he can get himself involved in a PIO."   As amplification of this thought and in answer to a question concerning pilot comments, the witness, citing

from a particular case, stated, "Here is a configuration in the short period, 0.2
cps and a damping ratio of 0.5. This particular pilot rated the aircraft a nine
on the Cooper scale, which would be completely unacceptable. He says (quoting
from the report) 'Trim ability extremely poor. Stick forces light initially,
causes immediate response, wants to overshoot . . . The general feel is very bad,
almost dangerous.' I think that comment is fairly respresentative."

The Board discusses the effect of an inoperative (or an inoper-
ative-extended) PTC on the speed stability during climb at various
speeds. They conclude that while it could worsen the situation, *it is not
a necessary prerequisite to a PIO situation.*

One element, however, common to almost all PIO occurrences has been the
application of nosedown stabilizer trim at some point during the oscillatory
cycles. The Board sees in this the results of forcing the aircraft, as described
by the research pilot. In other words, the pilot, finding his aircraft in an
excessively nose-high attitude, pushes the column forward and, when the aircraft
does not respond to his satisfaction, he also actuates the trim switch. He then
suddenly finds the aircraft responding more rapidly then he anticipated, and this
motion could also have been aggravated by a gust reversal which becomes additive
to the elevator and stabilizer inputs. At this point, in all probability, the
PIO conditions have ended for all practical purposes, and the aircraft is in a
dive The problem now becomes one of dive recovery.

I dream about springs in the elevator system. I have echoes of
PIT, *Pilot-Induced Turbulence.* I have watched pilots describing rough
air approaches, demonstrating what they **had to do** with the yoke. The
rough use of the controls they act out is the diametric opposite of the
technique of that Class I Aerobatic Instructor I flew with, who exem-
plified *Attitude Flying.*

These echoes mingle in my dreams and turn into a nightmare:
American Airlines Flight 587, climbing out of JFK on November 12,
2001. This accident is a nightmare or worse for any pilot who has studied accidents. It is the second-deadliest accident in US history. Climbing through 2000 feet, the flight experienced two wake turbulence
encounters, fifteen seconds apart. During the second encounter, the
control movements were as follows:

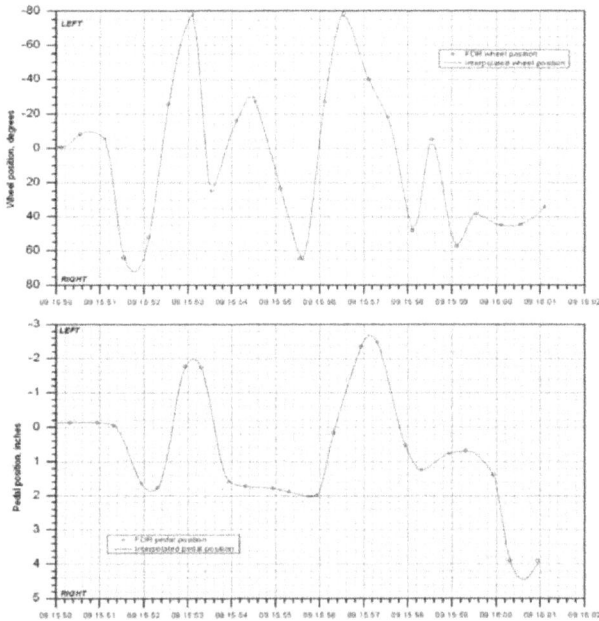

Figure 1. Control Wheel and Rudder Pedal Movements During the Second Wake
ncounter

The rudder goes:

1. Right (09:15:52)

2. Left (09:15:53)

3. Right (09:15:54)

4. Left (09:15:57), and immediately

5. Right (09:15:58)

Less than one second later (09:15:58.4) the vertical fin separates
from the aircraft, along with both engines and their pylons. This Airbus
A300-600, with 260 souls on board, is in an unrecoverable flat spin.

•

It might be instructive to discuss what would happen with these inputs if the airplane was an Extra 300 and not an A300-600. Since the Extra is rated at +/- 12G, its airframe probably would have survived. I will leave that discussion to someone who knows the airplane better than I do. But I have a limited experience in the Extra, during a *Pilot Confidence Course* I took some years back. I wanted to experience a snap roll – *but not too violent*, I asked my instructor. *Sure*, he said. *We'll do them at 90 knots. Smoothly, over a second or so, apply full rudder and full up elevator.*

It was ballet. It was one of the most beautiful moments I have experienced in an airplane. The roll took about one second – maybe two – and was smooth as silk. But the recovery was *return the controls to neutral.* We were moving horizontally while the aircraft was in a spin – one wing largely stalled. If we neutralize the controls the airplane returns to level flight at nearly 90 knots, as it was before the maneuver. But to try to work *against* the airplane, to *"try to force the airplane to respond faster than it wants to"*, as the report says, would be counter-productive.

•

Now you got me scared.

Captain? Why?

The Bus. You can't see what the other guy is doing. I mean you can't feel it.

Tell me about it.

It's the thing I like least about the Bus. And doing Line Indoc – that's going to be a dog's breakfast.

Yeah. I sigh. I think she can feel me sigh.

Chris – you? In Line Indoc?

Yeah. It was the closest I ever came to bending something.

Ooh boy. Tell!

I'm in the right seat, coaching a new captain. Montreal, Runway 28. Night. Wind 320 at something gusting to something. I'm talking him through the crosswind landing. It's going OK, but at the flare he's a bit right of centreline . . .

And?

. . . and suddenly the right wing is coming up. Fast. The upwind wing. My hand is on the sidestick. I slap it full right.

Ouch!

Yeah. We hit hard, but we're lined up with the runway axis and the wings are level.

Take that, Earth!

The In-Charge comes up when we get to the gate. *Chris, what the hell was that?* she says.

Red faces. What about damage?

I'm worried. I call maintenance to do a walkaround and I request a hard landing check. I tell the left-seat guy to wait for me upstairs.

She's waiting for me to go on. Not much you can say.

I did the walkaround with the maintenance guys. Wing tips, nacelles, stab tips, tail skid, outer flap corners. All OK.

Whew!

Yes, now I'm less worried. He had it lined up OK with rudder, and we hit mains first, thank goodness. So I'm thinking, *no dings, no damage.* Or I hope not. But now it's **Why?** Why in God's name would he use left aileron?

You debriefed him . . .

Yeah. Turns out he's a helicopter pilot. Just wanted to translate left a bit.

I can feel her intake of breath, feel her arrive at the *why*. Why someone would pull this incredible no-no. And how, on the Bus, you can see the airplane react, but you can't see what the other pilot just did.

You're scaring me, Chris. And all this talk of PIT and PIO and overcontrolling. And just plain being rough with the airplane. And that goddamn crash. I haven't read the report yet. Any indication *why* the F/O snapped off the vertical stab and the engines in less than seven seconds?

Yeah. He had a history of being rough. And rash. Two incidents in the B727 in 1997. Both related to wake turbulence. In the first he was "very aggressive" with rudder, and according to the captain, did not use aileron.

> An American Airlines captain who flew several times with the first officer on the 727 (when they were a junior captain and junior first officer, respectively) told Safety Board investigators that, during one flight sometime in 1997,[28] the first officer had been "very aggressive" on the rudder pedals after a wake turbulence encounter. Specifically, the captain indicated that, when the airplane was at an altitude of between 1,000 and 1,500 feet, the first officer "stroked the rudder pedals 1-2-3, about that fast." The captain thought that the airplane had lost an engine and was thus focused on the engine instruments. The captain stated that he then asked the first officer what he was doing and that the first officer replied that he was "leveling the wings due to wake turbulence." The captain, who had his feet on the rudder pedals, thought that the first officer had pushed the rudder to its full stops.
>
> The captain did not recall what type of airplane the 727 was following. He thought that the wake turbulence encounter required only aileron[29] inputs to level the wings but did not think that the first officer had made any such inputs during the encounter. The captain recalled being startled by the first officer's rudder inputs and indicated that they did not level the wings but created left and right yawing moments and heavy side loads[30] on the airplane. He further indicated that the first officer did not need to be so aggressive because the 727 was "a very stable airplane."
>
> According to the captain, he and the first officer discussed this event later in the flight. The captain pointed out to the first officer that his use of the rudder pedals was "quite aggressive," but the first officer insisted that the American Airlines Advanced Aircraft Maneuvering Program (AAMP)[31] directed him to use the rudder pedals in that manner. The captain disagreed with the first officer and told him that the AAMP directed that the rudder was to be used at lower airspeeds. The captain told the first officer to review the AAMP when he returned home and to be less aggressive on the rudder pedals when they flew together. The captain indicated that, during a wake turbulence encounter

Factual Information   page 13   AA
587   Aircraft Accident Report

on a subsequent flight, the first officer modified his wake turbulence maneuver; specifically, the first officer used the rudder during the encounter but did not push the rudder to its full stop. The captain added that the first officer was still "very quick" on the rudder.

The captain stated that he did not document or report this event at the time that it occurred. The captain further stated that he remembered the event with such clarity because he had never seen any pilot other than the first officer perform this maneuver.

In the second incident, in IMC, a B737 ahead of them did a go-around. The first officer – it sounds like he did not consult the captain – made a "fast" decision to go around because of the wake turbulence.

AAMP, huh?

Yup.

In their fucking trainingness, you'd think they'd learn . . .

I don't know what to say. She's upset. I concentrate on my breathing. In, out. With each breath a thought floats by. *I get like this too. It's when you think of a fatal accident not as a statistic but as people dying.* Of course it hurts. But we have to keep breathing and learn something. Really learn. Own, home at heart.

That second B727 incident, she goes on. Pretty evident that our rough guy seriously mis-handled the airplane. Pulled hard on the go-around. Maybe almost stood it on its tail. Recovered. *One of the more memorable ones of his career.* Well, I guess so.

I nod.

Maybe the fucker was trying to give himself a pilot confidence course. With a hundred passengers on board. And he thinks he's a pilot?

Haah, I sigh.

If he had pushed full rudder as well, as he did in the first incident, we would have had a flight test of a B727 doing a snap roll.

I am glad I was not trying to swallow. I manage not to choke on my intake of breath. I think of Colgan and the Dear Dead Girl. I think of the slowly panicking captain at Rostov-on Don.

And he doesn't learn, the asshole. Oh, no. *He* knows better. Captain tells him, *go back and study AAMP. And if you're going to fly with me, you better be less aggressive on the rudder.*

I can feel her think about herself. How she might handle a person like this.

I let you get away with it one time, and we survive. My bad. But if you so much as make a nod at doing it again it's **I have control, Motherfucker.** And don't you ever bid to fly with me again. Ever. In your life.

I can feel it. Now she's thinking about how *rough guy* died, taking 259 people with him.

What is it? Power? Control? Domination? It sure as hell isn't love. Don't you love your trade? Don't you love to fly airplanes? Don't you want to feel them? To get to know them? To be partners with them? To love them?

Well, you did it, you cunt. You broke a big one into four pieces, which floated separately to the ground.

Why couldn't you be gentle?

§

Chapter Seven

Clue: Thoughtless Mode
*Answer: **Autopilot***
~ From The New York Times crossword puzzle, 14 May 2023 ~

*Th*oughtless – an apt name for an autopilot. Who, exactly, is doing the thinking when the autopilot is engaged?

On the other hand, how much thinking was taking place when that huge, rudderless glider fell in pieces from the sky?

Just what is the pilot's job, anyway? Has it morphed, as some believe, into a management position?

In the meantime, braided steel cables have been replaced by co-ax, twisted pairs, or just plain wires. Or glass fibre, with its light weight and huge bandwidth.

Even the word *autopilot* is now a misnomer. Where does autopilot end and fly-by-wire begin? Or vice-versa?

Behind these questions is a larger question: Why is there a human pilot on board at all? As a last resort? As an underwriting requirement?

At least for now, I am going to ignore that larger question, because I know there are young people out there who want to fly. They are drawn to the beauty and the mystery of it. They want to learn. They want to be pilots. And fly-by-wire is here to stay. So we had better take a close look at *flight control laws*.

The C* Law

The first question to ask about flight control is: *What is the feedback loop?* Some sort of feedback loop is essential for any pilot, human or otherwise. The previous chapter explored what happens when the putative pilot does not have one: Pilot-Induced Turbulence, Pilot-Induced Oscillation, and sadly, aircraft disassembly. Without feedback, a pilot is fooled by moment in a control axis. He is rough. He over-controls. He is surprised by what the airplane is doing. Feedback – being a *closed-loop pilot* – is essential.

As engineers thought about what pilots do, they came up with two different possibilities for feedback in pitch:

- Attitude (the obvious one), and

- G

This in turn bears further exploration.

Rather than get into equations (because I am not very good at it) let's think about things that we, as pilots, already know in some sort of *"fundamental or simple sense"* as Richard Feynman would say. We want to understand them – and flight control laws – in *"a more physical way."* And maybe we can get there proceeding via analogy.

> **Navigation:** A moving point in 3D space which makes a line, which can be described as a vector. *Equilibrium*, where that vector is a constant. The application of a force to that vector, causing it to change in length, direction, or both.

> **The Airplane:** To counter the force of gravity, the wing pushes air down by meeting it at a small angle. This *lift* balances gravity and holds the aircraft in equilibrium. The pilot can control lift by changing that small angle – the AoA. The pilot can also "steer" that lift (a vector) by banking or pitching.

In this familiar mix we have:

- First-order parameters – snapshots – like position, attitude, or altitude

- Second-order parameters that describe movement and change – like velocity or pitch rate, and

- Third-order parameters, like G

My only experience with true fly-by-wire is on the Airbus A320 family. In these aircraft – the A319, A320, and A321 – if you click off the autopilot and take your hand off the sidestick, the aircraft will *continue in one-G flight*.

It is instructive to take a moment to think about what **being held at 1 G** means:

> If the wings are level and the Angle of Attack is such that lift balances aircraft weight, the airplane will remain in equilibrium. *Thrust = drag* is the other necessary condition for equilibrium. However, if drag somehow becomes greater than thrust the airplane will slow down, *and the nose will **not** drop to maintain the initial speed*. The reverse is also true. Thus the aircraft is not speed stable (AoA stable) and must have *envelope protection*.

Using *local G* as a control feedback parameter goes back to the 1960's. In May 1966, a paper was presented at the Aerospace Electronics Conference in Dayton, Ohio: *A New Longitudinal Handling Qualities Criterion*. The criterion was called C^*, and it forms the basis of most fly-by-wire implementations, including that of the A320 family. The 1966 proposal uses *pitch rate* at lower speeds and *local G* at higher speeds, fading from one to the other above and below a *crossover speed*.

G is useful because it is almost synonymous with flight control. Inside an aircraft in equilibrium, all objects experience one G, as they would if the aircraft was parked. But a flying aircraft also experiences *local G*. Any longitudinal control movement will change local G. If the pilot is skilful, she can execute a turn keeping local G vertical with respect to the airplane, so as not to spill the martini. Even though the gin weighs more, it is not sloshing in the glass. So it is not surprising that G – specifically *local G* – is used for feedback in fly-by-wire flight control systems.

The system in the A320 family uses mostly *local G*. The exceptions are takeoff and initial climb, where the sidestick controls the control surfaces more or less directly, and flare and landing, where the software mimics the qualities of an airplane with braided steel cables.

Although my last Airbus flight (it was an A321) was nearly twenty years ago, I can still clearly remember the handling described above.

The aircraft is in *Direct Law* for the takeoff roll and liftoff, so in a crosswind you hold into-wind aileron and you need opposite rudder to hold the centreline, just as in conventional aircraft. The blending from *Direct Law* to *Normal Law* takes just a few seconds and begins 5 seconds after liftoff. Liftoff, in turn, is defined by extended oleos and pitch attitude > 8° nose-up. There is a backup at 50 feet Radio Altimeter height. It feels quite natural to take a breath after liftoff and let the controls slowly return to neutral. If you don't, you'll be reminded by a roll into the wind.

We would fly approaches by hand often. My policy – which I know was shared by many or most – was to aim for at least one flown-by-hand approach for each pilot on each trip. Of course that was not always possible, but it was a goal, and we stayed in practice. If the two of us were flying the whole month together, as was often the case, we would each try to fly one *everything off* approach – i.e. by hand with auto thrust off. That was more challenging, but if you had a target thrust in mind for the flap setting, and didn't over-control in either attitude or thrust, it was quite doable. And it was satisfying and confidence-building as well.

Still, if a cold front was coming through we would leave A/T engaged and use *Ground Speed Mini*, as described in a previous chapter.

While we're on the topic of keeping in practice, I'd like to pass on comments I read in an aviation publication a few months back. So as not to infringe on this airline pilot's privacy, I will paraphrase his advice.

> Jetlag is a real hazard, especially eastbound. What can you do to *get with it* at *Top of Descent* after a long haul? Start with a good pull on the oxygen mask. Make sure you're awake and get your blood oxy back into the green band after who knows how many hours at 8000 feet cabin altitude. Then hand fly at least part of the descent and approach. Maybe all of it. In any case, be aware that we humans are very poor at monitoring automation, especially if we're tired.
>
> If you haven't flown for a month, you're not really current, so start by hand flying *at cruise*. See if you can hold altitude to +/- 50 feet. Then try for +/- 20 feet. Turn off the *Flight Director*. Hold course by track steering. If you can do that for minutes at

a time and enjoy it, you're current enough to hand fly up to and down from 18,000 feet. Maybe not every leg, but often enough so it feels natural to you.

Fly your light aircraft, if you're lucky enough to have one, single-pilot, no-autopilot IFR as often as you can.

He adds a comment on his comments, saying *these days most of this is probably illegal*, or words to that effect. Perhaps, but the bottom line is that we can't stay current with just SOP's and recurrent training. We are responsible for our own currency.

Back to landing the A320.

With the tweaks Airbus added to their version of the C* Law, flare and landing felt quite conventional. *Normal Law* goes into *Flare Mode* at 50 feet Radio Altitude. It memorizes the pitch attitude at that point and uses it as a datum for what follows. Starting at 30 feet RA it blends in a 2° nose-down command over 8 seconds.

To the pilot, it feels like a normal airplane. You memorize the attitude as well, and you pull gently as necessary to keep the nose from dropping. Then you obey *the German* when he says *RETARD* (close the throttles) and wait until the green arrows appear above the spoiler panels on the *Wheels Page*.

The C*U Law

C*U was developed by Boeing for its last great success story – the B777, which entered service with United Air Lines in June 1995.

The new term in the equation – U – is calibrated airspeed. The idea is to make the control algorithm mimic a conventional airplane more closely by re-introducing *"trim feel."* Pilots have come to unconsciously rely on *trim feel*. The traditional airplane's nose will drop if the airspeed drops. If you get slow on approach, for example, the nose will feel *heavy*, prompting the pilot to add power. (The **lack** of this characteristic is quite noticeable when flying an *everything off* approach in the

A320 family.) The Bombardier C-Series – now the A220 series – also uses C*U. Test pilots on that airplane pointed out that during the "*startle factor*" phase of a threat, the pilot is more likely to react quickly and correctly if that *trim feel* is still there.

So far, at least, it appears that C*U is indeed an improvement on C*. But that's not the whole story. Just as with C*, it is instructive to dig deeper and look at what this *conventional response* means in terms of our *conventional understanding* of aircraft function.

For example, we pilots have come to assume that the thumb switches on the yoke control the position of the stabilizer. That is no longer the case on the B777. Instead, use of the thumb switches changes the trim speed reference **in software**. This reference speed is used in turn to generate the control feedback term U_{ERR}, which is the difference between the trim speed reference and the actual calibrated airspeed. This time I will include the equation for C*U:

$$C^*U = C^* - K_V\, U_{ERR}$$

K_V is the *speed stability gain*, or how fast the airplane will respond to a speed error. As one article puts it:

> The feedback of the airspeed error re-establishes in principle the conventional **lowly** damped phugoid behavior. (My emphasis)

K_V reminds me of Langewiesche's airplane changing pace behind the curtain on the proscenium stage. Of that behavior after a pitch change which is *so airplane*. Increase the AoA, and it zooms. Then, as it returns to equilibrium, it resumes the glide at the new AoA. Short and long term response.

K_V damps down the long-term response so it doesn't fight the short-term feedback – pitch rate and local G. Yes, it re-establishes dynamic pitch stability. And yes – on the B777 you can control the stab directly with the *Alternate Pitch Trim Levers* on the pedestal.

There have been tweaks to that airplane's Auto-thrust software – notably after the Asiana crash. However, the changes did not prevent

Emirates Flight 521 from attempting a go-around at Dubai with idle thrust.

By all accounts, the flight control software on the B777 is some of the best in service. But software is not God. It is never infallible. And auto-thrust logic is at times quite illogical.

Having said that, it is hard to fault that logic in the case of Emirates Flight 521.

It is August 3, 2016. Two of the four preceding flights have performed go-arounds at Dubai. When UAE 521 receives its landing clearance for runway 12L, the tower reports the wind as 340/11.

The captain hand-flies the last part of the approach with the A/T engaged. During the flare, the A/T reduces thrust to idle as programmed at 25 feet RA.

The touchdown is 1090 meters past the runway threshold and so soft that neither pilot is aware they have touched down. But the right main landing gear truck tilts, triggering the Weight on Wheels signal, which – also as programmed – disables the TOGA palm switches.

Meanwhile, with the rear wheels of the right MLG truck spinning, and the left MLG touching down, the wind changes direction from a 10-knot tailwind to a 5-knot headwind, keeping the airplane flying.

The captain presses the left TOGA switch and calls Go Around. Immediately thereafter there is an audio annunciation *Long Landing*. The captain begins raising the nose for the go-around, but despite this the airspeed continues to increase for another ten seconds. Both MLG trucks go through a couple of tilt cycles, and the Speedbrake Handle starts to move back and then retracts. The aircraft becomes airborne again at 1590 metres from the threshold, and uses its kinetic energy to climb to a maximum RA of 83 feet.

During the climb the normal calls are made: the flaps retracted to 20, and the gear selected up. The airplane touches down again 2530 meters from the threshold with the gear partially retracted. Just under 2000 meters of runway remain.

That's what ya get for greasin' one on.

Captain?

Yeah. Big airplane. Jesus.

Yes.

Lotta momentum.

Sure.

But very well behaved.

Absolutely. Can't fault it.

If the gear hadn't been up, it would have landed again. All by itself.

You're probably right.

Save a hull. But they survived.

Yes. Everyone on the airplane. But a firefighter got killed. Falling debris when a fuel tank exploded.

I can tell that we have both come to the end of *what happened*. Now we are considering the *why?*

Asiana got slower than he did, she says.

Yup.

And the airplane might have landed that one herself, too . . .

Most likely.

. . . if he hadn't pulled so hard and rotated the tail into the sea wall.

We sit and contemplate together. I am getting used to it. I like it. It is that feeling I used to get in the classroom.

Very big ship. Handling qualities so good that no one notices the engines are at idle.

I sigh.

So what about *Alpha Floor*? Doesn't the triple have something like that?

Not exactly. It'll let you stall it but you'd have to fight it.

Thrust?

Yeah, but I think only if the A/T is active.

And here – I mean Emirates – it's off.

Yes.

And Asiana, it's stuck in **HOLD**.

Yeah. I think that hole may have been plugged since. Not sure how. Maybe I can find out.

I'm going back in time – Bangalore. Mode was **IDLE OPEN**, but what about *Alpha Floor*?

Maybe they never got slow enough. Just timing. I'd have to check.

And Mulhouse?

Alpha Floor worked. That's why they settled gently into the trees as the engines spooled up.

We are back in contemplation mode. The airplanes, even with their foibles, have passed. Now we are thinking about pilots. But not just pilots. Pilots caught in a web of SOP's and regulations. Caught out by a less-than-complete intimacy with their airplane and its limitations. Friends, but not lovers.

We sit.

Maybe it's the reverse, she says. *In the first flush of infatuation the love object has no faults.*

You're right. I have a friend I have known since kindergarten. Seventy-four years and counting. And we are quite aware of each other's foibles.

She laughs. I laugh.

I'm glad you're not against fly-by-wire, she says.

Heavens no.

I probably won't fly anything else.

We are comfortable. Free-associating on the subject at hand.

So I want to know all I can absorb, she goes on. *This chapter helps. Could you send me some links to those articles you've found?*

Of course. I'll reference them in the book, too.

Thanks. Ever notice how you think you know what you're doing, and then you learn more? And then you feel stupid for thinking that you knew?

Yes I do. And I'm grateful.

Grateful for feeling stupid?

Yes. Grateful for feeling stupid. Because it means we're moving. Seeking. Still learning.

•

I am thinking of how I left it with Captain yesterday. How **we** left it, of course. But she's probably working today, so I'd better keep working too. Where does my understanding fall short in this fly-by-wire era?

Envelope Protection. You have to have it with C* because there is no long-term speed stability. No phugoid, no certification. What about C*U with artificially induced phugoid behavior? It feels like an airplane. The handling is good. Is that enough?

The rub is the failure cases. With fly-by-wire, you have to go down the chain of failure possibilities and work out the options. You have to be able to control the airplane somehow, even with multiple failures.

And then there's progress. Once you have implemented envelope protection – and looked at its history in service – what's not to like?

OK, we know from the accident history that envelope protection is not perfect, but we also know that it has saved many lives.

We also know, thanks to the various implementations of envelope protection, that there are different philosophies about how it should interact with the pilot. We have had this discussion before, on the subject of Mach Trimmers and Stick Pushers. Do they work in the background, improving the handling and smoothing out the *stick force per G*, making the airplane feel better than it actually is aerodynamically? Or do they – in extremis – take control away from the pilot?

The short answer is – *I don't know. Both?* And what I said to Captain the other day is nagging at me. *What about Alpha Floor?* she asked. *Alpha Floor worked*, I said. Did I mean Alpha Floor or Alpha Prot? In which accident? Memory – with its associative structure – can be tricky. Better go back to the books.

So I have. Back to the early days of fly-by-wire in line service. To look at the first two A320 accidents in detail. To see what stuff in the design got flight-tested.

Bangalore. I went to the second accident first. I don't know why. I read something there that scared me. It was only tangentially related to that crash, but I started to sweat. Boy, was that close! A one-touch way out of ALT*?

Another memory. It must have been in 1995, my first year on the line in the A320. Boston. On the curb, waiting for our ride. There was also an Aer Lingus crew. I shot the breeze for a few minutes with the captain. He was on the A330. *Fockin' ALT Star*, he said. *Give me my beautiful Boeing any day*. He had been flying the B747, and he missed it.

ALT*, the Airbus altitude capture mode, works a charm. Where it begins, and how long it lasts, is dependent on the Vertical Speed. When triggered, the software calculates a path – an asymptotic curve to intercept the selected altitude. It is a path in space which approaches that altitude as a limit. It is very smooth. It is calculated **once**. It doesn't like to be interrupted. It memorizes the *Flight path Vector* at the trigger point and works from there. The only thing that will force a recalculation is changing the selected altitude. It knows nothing about engine failure. Hence the A330. The one in Toulouse.

What was it in the Bangalore accident report? A discussion about ALT*. Specifically, what would the pilot have to do to exit ALT* and select a vertical speed?

Now, of course, she could push the V/S knob to level off. One touch. And while she was there, turn the knob to the vertical speed she needed.

But before the FPU change? In 1995, when Rob and I had our ride?

There is a lively argument transcribed in the Bangalore report, where pilots being consulted offer an opinion along with evidence to the contrary, while Airbus remains silent. But the bottom line is this: there is only one way to exit ALT* early (that is, before it finishes its intercept and becomes ALT), and that is to **select a different altitude**.

But the terror is this: with that early software you could select a V/S, or pull the knob to sync to the aircraft's V/S, and it would show V/S in the window. **But only for a few seconds**. Then it would revert to ALT*. And that would remain true for as long as the altitude capture was in process, no matter how many times you did it.

That is a disaster. Literally. In a tight situation, where seconds count, you turn or pull or both and get your feedback, and then look away. While your back is turned, it switches back to ALT*. No wonder Airbus has no comment.

It is my first year flying as LITC. I like to speak of the airplane as *Fifi*, as many of my colleagues do. *She's mute*, I say. *She can't speak. But what about the German?* they might ask. *You know, Thirty, Twenty, RETARD?*

Sure, I say. *But sometimes she won't say what she's doing, so we have to speak for her.* I talk about how we have to be constantly aware of the *Flight Mode Annunciator* (FMA) along the top the *PFD* (Primary Flight Display). How we have to announce the changes there to make sure the three of us are all aware of them. Well, Fifi is aware because she put it up there, but one of us has to say IDLE OPEN or **Vertical Speed : minus 1000**. And here is the reason behind that last challenge and response on the *Before Landing Check:* AUTOTHRUST. How the only acceptable responses are **SPD**, or **OFF**. And what do we do if it says IDLE? The PM reaches up to the glareshield with both arms, hands two feet or so apart, pushes the two switch/lights, and says **Flight Directors Off**. Then both of us look at the left end of our FMA to make sure they both say **SPD**. Believe it or not, this is the only one-touch way to get the Autothrust back into **SPD**.

Also, we keep it simple: if we have briefed a visual approach, we will fly most of it with the autopilot off. And when the PF clicks the A/P off and hears the cricket, he says **AUTOPILOT OFF, FLIGHT DIRECTORS OFF**. It is always one neat package, always the same.

And what about Visual Approaches? There are many traps for the unwary: night, parallel runways, and use of approach aids, especially for staying on a safe glideslope – even if that means using distance to the runway and the old *3 miles is 1000 feet* rule. And we start with the definition of *Visual Approach* in TC-AIM RAC 9.6.2 or the equivalent in the USA or other locale.

But the upside is doing Visual Approaches by hand is good for your currency and competence. It's also a lot of fun. And since Visual

Approaches increase landings per hour, you will essentially be forced into doing them sooner or later. Might as well be good at them.

The memories continue. Watsonville, where I got my first job in aviation, teaching ground school. Two men, day and night but birds of a feather. Each with his Stearman duster, poised nose-high in that stinking paddock near the ramp. San Miguel Canyon. Strawberry Canyon. Dusting strawberries. Spraying strawberries. On the slopes beside the winding canyon roads. Often in a slip to parallel the slope as the roads wind along in S curves. The lovely rumble of those radial engines. The snort and spit as they came to life, again and again after a new load of poison is on board. Then as the sun becomes a red shape somewhere off the Santa Cruz Pier they jump into that fake-wood station wagon and go somewhere to get pissed. Sometimes disorderly. The growly stubble moon-faced former captain of Martin 404's. The tall mute indigenous man wearing his pride like a shield.

But they would *walk the fields*. Every detail memorized. There is no time to learn new shit in a 30° bank at 30 AGL with full spray tanks.

Then there was my friend and student Ron. Learned his electronics in the army at Ft. Ord. After evening ground school he would gaze at the Stearman biplanes sitting in the paddock with their noses in the air. He came to worship them and their pilots.

He learned fast in the airplane. Great hands and feet. I tried to steer him into instrument flying, my own great love. But no. A year or two later he was in a Piper Pawnee. Dusting not in the canyons, but the flat fields between Pajaro Dunes and the Elkhorn Slough. He hit a wire at 20 AGL and nosed in. Alive because of the five-point harness. Hands thrown forward to the panel. Every bone broken. The delicate bones between the wrist and the knuckles. Fingers. Thumbs. Two years later, re-located to Montana, he did it again. There was no doubt about his dedication.

CSY3. Sorel, Quebec. Runway 03/21, 4000x75, asphalt with grass growing through. *CAUTION: Hi trees W of rwy*. Yeah, and everywhere else as well. The cut for the runway is perhaps 4400x125, so for that last 100 feet you are in a box. It was great for teaching how to watch those trees: if they are rising, you're going to hit them. If they're steady, you'll drag your gear through them. On approach, you gotta keep them descending in your field of vision. But what about if the box was open at the approach end, as it is for Mulhouse/Habsheim Runway 34? What about if you had never been there before? Never walked the field?

And what about spool-up time? Jet engines are reluctant to come off idle. The geared turbofan on the A220 howls, perhaps in displeasure. The sound reminds me of the CF-104 exercising the afterburner nozzle before takeoff. In the latter case it is more in menace than unwillingness, although for me the CF-104 sound was simply otherworldly.

On the DC-9 we would *stand up the throttles*, although in the book it was *select 1.1 EPR*. It was SOP. If anti-ice was selected. If flaps and gear were down. It was simple common sense. It is also an essential part of every *visual approach*.

When you are cut loose – *Cleared for the Visual Approach Runway 24 Right* – you almost always have too much energy. You have to have a strategy, and idle thrust is almost always part of that strategy. That, in turn, means that the spool-up point also has to be part of the plan. In the interest of crew co-ordination, it should also be verbalized.

The moment, for me, is also beautiful. It is part of the very-well-executed (and lucky) descent and approach. The thrust goes to idle at *Top of Descent* and stays there until you "catch V_{APP}". When traffic and skill permit, that is a lovely moment.

•

The Second A320 Accident

Bangalore, India

14 February 1990

An Indian Airlines A320 is doing a visual approach at Bangalore after flying from Bombay. Coming from the north, it is being vectored for a long left base and final to Runway 09. The runway is 10,850 feet long. The airport elevation is 2914 feet MSL. The wind is light from the north. There is a tailwind on this long base leg.

In the left seat is Captain Fernandez, who is PF. He is new to the A320, and is on a Line Check with Captain Gopujkar, who is PIC but PM on this flight. Captain Fernandez does overshoot the runway centerline slightly, so by the time he lines up the final leg is shorter than planned. The thrust has been at idle since 4600 MSL.

Jeppesen Chart for Bangalore VOR 09 with VOR Track and Actual Track

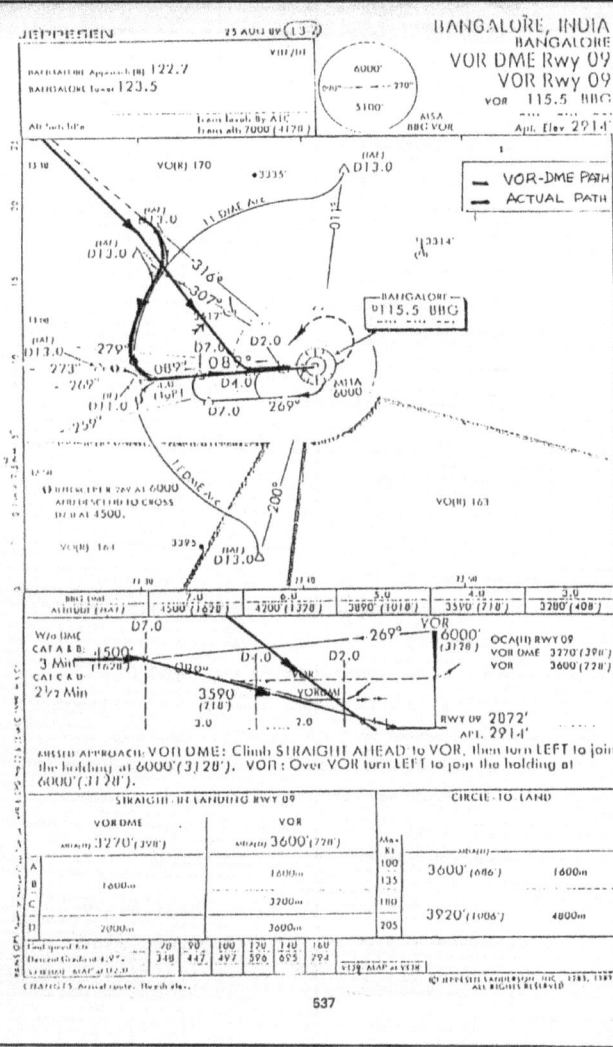

The Final Report comprises 581 typewritten pages in pale repro-duction. Its length stems from the system in place (at least at the time) for accident investigation. Instead of a Commission of Inquiry, it is a High Court of Enquiry. The Chief Judge is tasked with assembling ex-perts in various fields and lawyers who will argue the experts' points of view. Point by point, the Chief Judge will make a ruling.

Getting facts from those pages and assembling them into a timeline is like pulling teeth or finding needles in a haystack. Nevertheless, the High Court does come to a factually correct conclusion: *Down to 100 AGL or thereabouts, the thrust was in IDLE.*

The High Court concludes that the pilots were late in recognizing the seriousness of their situation. That also is factually true. By the time the pilots moved the thrust levers to TOGA, *Alpha Floor* had triggered, but had not activated because the aircraft was descending through 100 AGL, **below which Alpha Floor is inhibited.**

FMA/ V/S	Speaker	Event	A/S Alt	Time	page
		FLAP 2		13:00:19	
		GEAR DOWN		13:00:22	
		FLAP 3		13:00:38	
		RWY in sight, A/P disconnect		13:00:42	
		FLAP 4		13:00:48	
V/S	CM1 (Capt. Fernandez)	Land Check?		13:01:20	
	CM1 (Capt. Fernandez)	1400 AGL(?)		13:01:30	
ALT*		(4600 MSL)		13:01:36	228
	CM2	ALT*		13:01:40	232
		4 mile final, about 400 feet above CDA slope			234
IDLE OPEN		Selection of MDA (3280 MSL) or 1500 MSL (below ground level)			235
-2000 fpm	CM1	*Vertical Speed -1000*	148 KT		247
SP-D|VS temporarily?	CM2	Sets V/S -1000			
	CM2	Landing Clearance . . .			260
	CM1	*MA Alt?*			
		CM2 : *Short Final,* TWR : *Cleared to Land*	1000 AGL		265
V/S avg. 1200 fpm		**For time period from ALT* 4600 at DFDR second 228**			

	Capt Fernan-dez	OK, 700 ft. rate of descent Note: A/P was off Aircraft crossing CDA slope	c. 500 AGL		
IDLE OPEN	CM2	Missed Approach is . . .			295
	CM2	You are descending on **idle open descent** ah all this time . . .	300 AGL		306
	CM2	You want the FD's off now?			307
	Capt Fernan-dez	Yeah!			
	CM2	OK, I already put it off			312
IDLE OPEN 1 FD –	Capt Fernan-dez	But you did not put off mine			313
	CM2	You are on the autopilot still?			321
	CM1	No.			
	CM2	It's off			
	Capt Fernan-dez	Hey, we are going down			323
		Alpha Floor triggers. NOTE: Alpha Floor inhibited below 100AGL			
	CM2	Oh shit			324
		SINK RATE			325
		SINK RATE **30**			327
		SINK RATE **10**			328
		First Impact			329
		End of crash sounds			332

The cockpit door is open, held against the wall by its magnetic latch. A Flight Attendant is singing *Qué Sera Sera*. Was she singing to herself, or loudly enough so the pilots could hear her? Was she pretty? Did she know Runway 09 has an upslope?

The first touchdown – the tail on grass – is smooth. In the next one the engines are removed as they hit a berm. The force is enough to pull the cockpit door from its magnetic latch. It slams shut.

·

The First A320 Accident

Mulhouse/Habsheim

26 June 1988

It is Sunday. There is to be a flyover for the airshow at Mulhouse/ Habsheim, a general aviation airport. Runway 02-20 is asphalt, 1120x80 metres (3675x260 feet). Runway 34 is grass, 785x100 metres (2575x328 feet). Neither runway can support an A320.

The plan is to do two flyovers – one in landing configuration, demonstrating the airplane at slow speed, and another in clean configuration.

The flight was arranged by Air Charter as a passenger sightseeing flight: planned first to the Vosges region, then to the Alps, and then – because of weather and a request of the Mulhouse Flying Club – flyovers of the Mulhouse/Habsheim airport.

The crew flew the airplane and passengers first from Paris-Charles de Gaulle to Basle-Mulhouse. After a short stop, they took off again for Mulhouse/Habsheim. Captain Michel Asseline was an enthusiast for the Airbus design, and planned to do what he had done before on several occasions. He would turn the Auto Thrust off and then fly down to 100 AGL and get the PM to set just enough thrust to spool up the engines and stabilize ("catch") the speed at Alpha Prot. At the appropriate time he would push the thrust up to TOGA and zoom away. Very impressive.

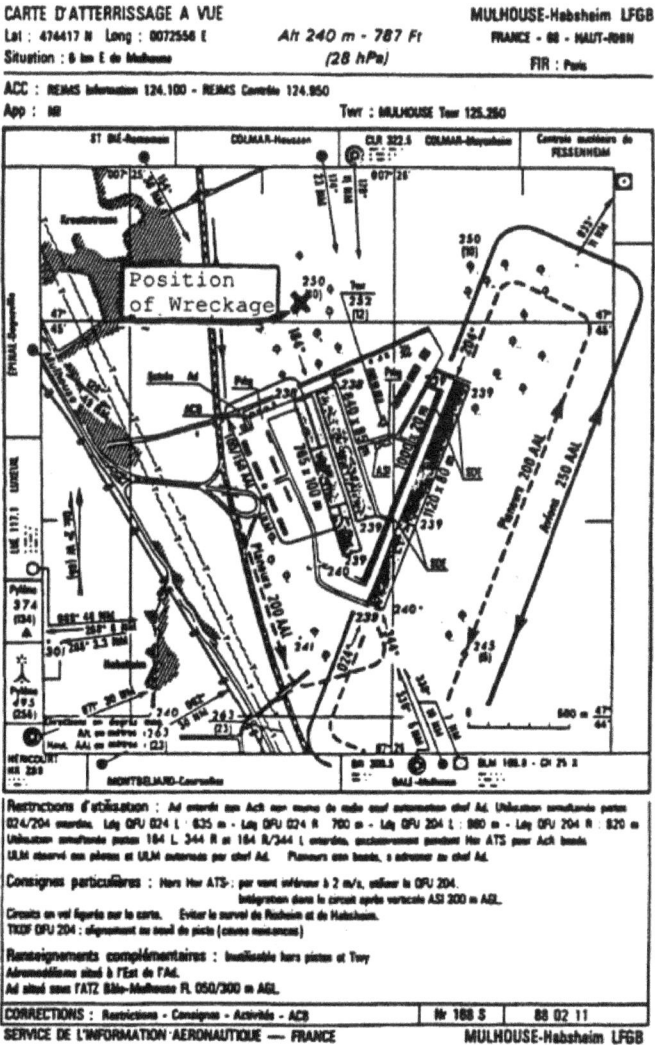

However, these performances had been on 10,000-foot runways with wide open approaches. At 120 knots, he could fly at 100 AGL for 30 seconds and use up 6000 feet of runway. At Mulhouse/Habsheim, when he overflew a clump of trees (just before the threshold of runway

34) at 100 AGL, the Flight Control Law briefly went from C* to **FLARE**. Twelve seconds later, at 30 AGL over the grass runway, the **AoA** was at **Alpha Max** and the engines were at idle. Although the airplane was fully controllable because of the AoA protection, it was too late. There was no extra energy. The airplane *could not zoom* to convert kinetic energy to altitude. A climb could come only with thrust. And at low airspeed, IDLE to TOGA thrust could take 6-7 seconds.

It seems that at about 6 seconds before impact, the captain realized that the different shade of green up ahead wasn't a different type of grass. It was a forest. A second later, he had the thrust up to TOGA. A second before hitting the trees, the N_1s were up to 83%. The engines continued to accelerate to over 90% and became giant lawnmowers, chewing up the treetops. But that didn't last long. The combustors rapidly filled with charred wood chips, and the engines shut themselves down in an orderly manner.

Ctrl Law/ V/S			RA/ N_1%	Clock	Time to Impact
		Takeoff from Basle/Mulhouse		12:41	
		Climb to 2000 MSL/ 1000 AGL			
		Follow motorway north to Mulhouse/ Habsheim			
		Thrust Idle, Gear Down, Flaps Down		12:44	
600 fpm		Confirmation of Airport	450 AGL	12:44:30?	
		TOO LOW - TERRAIN		12:44:55	
		TWO HUNDRED		12:45:06	
C*		**TWO HUNDRED** (interrupted by personal remark)		12:45:11	
	F/O	P........ G........!		12:45:11	
	F/O	G... ... is going to .... eh!		12:45:12	
600 FPM	F/O	OK, you're at one hundred feet there, watch, watch		12:45:14	
				12:45:15.3	
descent rate Decreasing		**ONE HUNDRED**			
FLARE		Aircraft flies over clump of trees		12:45:19	20
C*		**FORTY**		12:45:19.1	19.9
		Lower descent rate	50 AGL	12:45:22	17
		FIFTY		12:45:23.6	15.4
	Capt	OK. I'm there. Disconnect Autothrottle		12:45:26	13
		FORTY		12:45:27.5	11.5
-600 fpm	F/O	Watch out for the pylons ahead eh See them?		12:45:32	7
	Capt	Yeah, yeah. Don't worry . . .		12:45:33	6

Capt	Sudden awareness of danger	30	12:45:33.5	5.5
	TOGA Thrust	30	12:45:34	5
		29%	12:45:35	4
	Sidestick Full Back			2
		83%	12:45:38	1
	Increase in engine speed, Contact with trees		12:45:39	0
Capt	*Sh. . . . .!*		12:45:39.9	-0.9
	END OF TAPE		12:45:41.5	-1.5

You made me laugh.

Captain? Why?

I liked *shutdown in an orderly manner*. Does that have any basis in fact?

Yes. The position of various bleed valves.

OK. Good for the old CFM-56. But I guess wood didn't work out as an alternate green fuel.

We laugh. It feels good.

When I got home yesterday I saw you were into the first two accidents, so I had a pretty good look at them myself. First of all, I think your observation sums it up. *Software may be ace, but it can't change the laws of physics.*

Thanks. But you were the one who put it that way. And you pointed out, back in Halifax, the reason all that FPA correction stuff got going in the first place.

OK, so we're even. What's next?

Well, what did you think about their flight planning and crew co-ordination?

One on five and one on five. The one is because they actually discussed stuff. Sort of. But then they didn't really act on any of it. So perhaps zero-point-five on five. And it looks to me as though they were unfamiliar with the Habsheim airport. Did they just assume they were going to have a 10,000-foot runway?

Well, I think there were a number of assumptions. To be fair, though, there could have been an illusion of scale. The report points it out. The Habsheim tower is 40 feet high instead of a hundred. Scale up the Habsheim long runway, and you get the illusion of 9200 feet.

But it's really a toy airport.

Yes.

So he has ten seconds, not thirty.

Right.

And the right-seat dude did not understand that the captain wanted the thrust levers stood up for the overflight.

No. The captain referred to it on the ground in Basle, but obliquely.

There was no readback. No real communication.

No. And then things started happening very fast.

Did they ever discuss which runway they would overfly? I didn't see it.

No.

So – why did they decide to overfly the shorter runway? The grass runway?

Yeah. Good question. Know what? I think they – or he – didn't decide. They just did it.

There was something about seeing the grandstands . . .

Yeah. That's when he committed, I think. And they were already heading about 340°. You can see that on the radar trace form Basle.

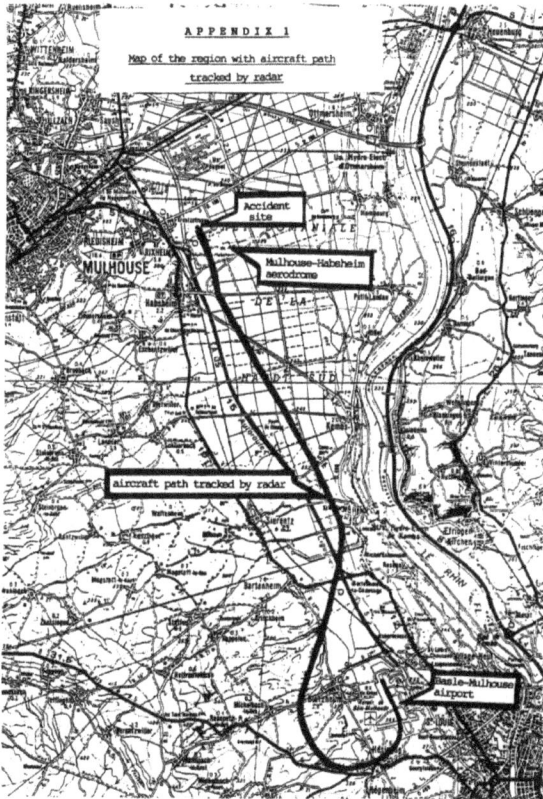

APPENDIX 1

Map of the region with aircraft path tracked by radar

They were lined up with the grass runway.

Yes.

And the right-seat dude didn't like it. He was not on board with it.

That's right. But he, too, was oblique. All he did was refer to the Air France Safety Officer.

Given as just initials on the CVR . . .

Yeah. But he referred to him by name. The guy apparently had a bit of a rep.

Well, so did Captain A. The report says *he had a strong personality.*

Uh huh. *Yeah yeah, don't worry.*

And that was how many seconds before impact?

Six. It was after impact when he said, Shit!

We share a private chuckle. It doesn't last.

Chris, wait . . .

Yeah?

You spoke of Asseline's intent – to disable Alpha Floor and turn Auto-Thrust off. What does that mean? What did Asseline actually say in that 0.5 out of 5 briefing?

He said:

> . . . we extend the flaps to 3, landing gear extended, and then you leave it to me. I'll give it alpha max, I'll disengage the alpha floor and then, if I tell you it is hard you help me and you hold the power to keep zero vertical rate . . .
>
> Zero vertical rate and me I'll hold it at alpha max. At the signal you give me TOGA and I'll pull the stick and if you're there I bank away . . .
>
> That. I've done it twenty times, that one.

That sounds like bullshit to me.

Yeah. I know. Makes no sense. Let's go back to the book . . .

HIGH ANGLE OF ATTACK PROTECTION

Under normal law, when the angle of attack becomes greater than αprot, the system switches elevator control from normal mode to a protection mode in which angle of attack is proportional to sidestick deflection. That is, in the αprot range, from αprot to αmax, the sidestick commands α directly. However, the angle of attack will not exceed αmax, even if the pilot gently pulls the sidestick all the way back. If the pilot releases the sidestick, the angle of attack returns to αprot and stays there.

This protection against stall and windshear has priority over all other protections. The autopilot disconnects at α prot + 1°.

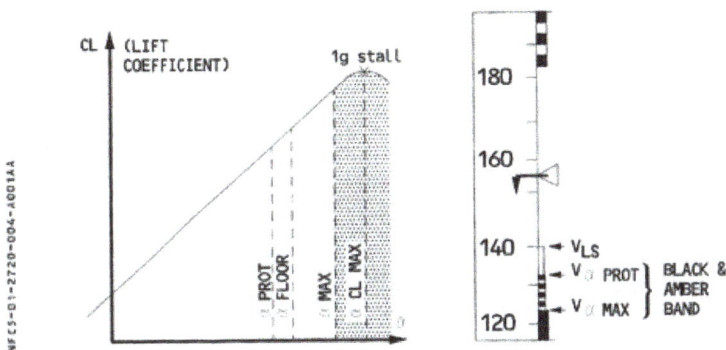

Vα prot, Vα floor, Vα max vary according to the weight and the configuration.
To deactivate the angle of attack protection, the pilot must pushed the sidestick :
– More than 8° forward, or,
– More than 0.5° forward for at least 0.5 second when α < α max.

Note : 1. At take off αprot is equal to αmax for 5 seconds.
2. αfloor is activated through A/THR system when :
– α > α floor (9.5° in configuration 0; 15° in configuration 1, 2; 14° in configuration 3 ; 13° in configuration FULL), or,
– sidestick deflection > 14° nose up with either pitch attitude or angle of attack protection active.
αfloor function is available from lift-off to 100 feet RA before landing.

So – bottom line. He **did** turn off alpha floor. But it was by going below 100 RA.

Right.

And autothrust was off, and the engines were at idle.

Yup.

And what was the F/O's feedback in the briefing?

Zero vertical rate and me I'll hold it at alpha max. At the signal you give me TOGA and I'll pull the stick and if you're there I bank away . . .

    You want to get off there then?

    That. I've done it twenty times, that one.

    OK, we're agreed!

And he doesn't put the power up.

No.

And Asseline doesn't realize . . .

No.

Jesus.

§

Chapter Eight

The Whale, the Exotic, and the Kluge

My time with the TriStar was too short – less than a year in 1980-81. So was the airplane's production run – 1972 to 1984. Lockheed's break-even number was 500 aircraft, but the last one off the line was number 250.

Looking back, it seems like the blink of an eye. Why was the L-1011 so memorable?

I wasn't going to talk about the B-747 because I never flew it. But it is the elephant in the room in this story and cannot be ignored. It was the first "jumbo jet". The first "widebody". The two three-engine wide-bodies – the L-1011 and the DC-10 – were responses to it. Although they were both 3-engine twin aisle jumbos, they were very different airplanes.

The Whale and Lockheed's short-lived Exotic had this in common:

- Pilots loved them

- Passengers loved them

- They had four hydraulic systems

It's odd looking back through the decades. Similar events occur in sequence, giving the (perhaps erroneous) impression of cause and effect. Boeing's last successful airplane (the B-777) first flew in 1995. In 1997, Boeing was forced to swallow a wallowing McDonnell Douglas. The merger came with a poison pill: a passion for profit.

Twenty-five years earlier, Douglas and Lockheed each wanted to mount – if not the equivalent, at least an answer to the B-747. As I mentioned, the conceptions could not have been more different. Mc-

Donnell had just swallowed Douglas, bearing the same poison pill they would bring Boeing a generation later. McDonnell's direction for the project was:

> "Cost overruns (are) unacceptable – even at the expense of safety."

The subsequent history of the DC-10 speaks for itself.

Lockheed, with its proud history of innovation in aviation, had the opposite directive. We will, they said:

> "Take the most advanced technology of the day and when that technology is lacking, Lockheed will create it."

Perhaps that vision is naïve. Perhaps profit has to be a goal. Or if not profit, at least that break-even number that Airbus is struggling toward today with the A220. And that in turn is not helped by the on-wing time of the engines (the Geared Turbo Fans) being well short of promise. Shades of the RB-211. There is nothing new, it would seem, under the sun. And today the Leap engine is facing difficulties similar to the GTF and giving airlines big headaches and big downtimes.

Back in 1971, Lockheed had no sooner committed to the diameter of its S-duct for the centre engine, when Rolls-Royce went bankrupt.

Like the airplane it was promised for, the RB-211 was a pioneering vision, ahead of its time. It was a three-spool design with carbon fibre fan blades. These blades, in their first iteration, failed bird impact tests.

The $350 million fixed price contract for Rolls-Royce to supply 540 RB-211 engines to Lockheed by the middle of 1971 proved to be an impossibility, putting both companies in danger. Rolls-Royce succumbed first, declaring bankruptcy on February 4, 1971. At that date the L-1011 development and that of the RB-211 were equal partners in imperilled progress. In both cases governments helped. Rolls-Royce was nationalized, and the US Government gave Lockheed $250 million in loan guarantees. The impossible timelines were stretched out, and both developments continued. Although ambitious, both visionary designs came to fruition. But not without a lot of heartburn for the bean counters.

Perhaps in a panic, Lockheed bribed the Prime Minister of Japan to get a foot in the door in Asia. There was a leak and a scandal. The Japanese Prime Minister resigned and was charged and convicted, although not for accepting bribes. Lockheed, as a result, lost a huge slice of market. Perhaps Lockheed management was just not very good at criminality.

Pioneering vision? Technological advance? Naivety? Greed?

Sure. But that's just the background to the short-lived wonder that was the L-1011, the TriStar.

•

A winter engine start was something to behold.

Like most engines, the RB-211 has more burner cans than igniters. The starter turns only the N_3 shaft. The other spools follow with airflow through the engine. Occasionally, the igniter will not succeed in lighting its burner can within the 30 second limit. It is acceptable to turn off fuel and ignition, keep the starter engaged, and after an additional 30 seconds to try again. And whether it's no light on the first try, or a slow light-around of all the burner cans, by that time there is a lot of raw fuel back in the turbines which burns at low pressure and creates a lot of smoke. Watching three engines start on a winter morning was five minutes of entertainment, especially if you had a good vantage point, such as the cockpit of a sister aircraft which had already starred in the same show.

Then if there was a long taxi-out and the temperature and the dew point were right, those carbon fibre fan blades, turning at near idle, could pick up ice. These blades are not de-iced and rely on centrifugal force on the ice/blade bond to shed the ice. During acceleration to the N_1 that will shed the ice, the blades could be out of balance, producing more than acceptable vibration for too long a time. This situation complicates the acceleration phase of the takeoff and potentially compromises the distance required. All this in addition to another complication the L-1011 shares with the B727 (also an aircraft with an S-duct): the center engine is more susceptible to compressor stall at low airspeeds. Balancing risks in certain conditions, many captains elected to advance thrust to, say, 60% N_1 before brake release, and then advance engines one and three to Takeoff Power, following with engine two so that it reached T/O power at 60 knots.

FCOM Insert 533, *Engine Fan Blade Ice Removal – Ground Operation* formalized what at least one crew had already done: a run-up before taking position for takeoff. It separated the risks, formalizing a procedure for shedding ice on the fan blades:

- Find a sticky piece of asphalt

- Turn into the wind

- Run up the engines, watching the vibration gauges

- Observe various limits

Success would see the vibration suddenly disappear. Then the takeoff could be started with no ice on the blades.

•

The TriStar neatly occupied a cusp in aviation technology, especially in flight control design. True *fly-by-wire* was a decade in the future, but on May 25, 1972, the L-1011 was the first airplane to demonstrate a fully automated flight, from the takeoff roll in Palmdale to the Autoland at Dulles. The L-1011 was also my first experience with CWS (Control Wheel Steering), which itself was a cusp between hand-flying and autopilot modes, between auto flight and hands-off fly-by-wire behaviour, such as C* or C*U. I confess I didn't use it much. The airplane flew so nicely I didn't see the point.

The TriStar was quiet. Inside, I mean. Perhaps it was the famous dolphin nose, but the cockpit had, in my memory, the lowest white noise component of any airplane I flew. Vibration was also almost non-existent. Whereas in the DC-9 you could hear the altimeter vibrators through the white noise, in the L-1011 the vibrators, with their higher frequency than those of the DC-9, were practically all you could hear. It was a peaceful flight deck – so large and open you could picture your-

self outdoors. And the noise that remained, paradoxically, was soothing, like wind in the trees or surf on a beach. Maybe it was even soporif-
ic, but I was young then. Maybe too young to need a nap now and then.

I had heard rumours. There had been stall incidents over the
North Atlantic. Several TriStars had lost four or five thousand feet
before regaining control. I found that hard to believe. Then I found
myself as Pilot Flying at cruise altitude somewhere north of Lake
Superior.

There were backups on the approach to Toronto, our destination.
We were asked to slow from our cruise Mach – 0.83 or 0.84 – to Mach
0.78. The latter was normal cruise for the DC-9, but I had never before experienced that as a cruise speed in the L-1011. I reduced power
enough to start slowing, watching carefully. It was hard because the
changes were in slo-mo. I was thinking I had better be ready to "catch"
Mach 0.78 as I would "catch" V_{APP} on approach. So maybe I had *backside of the power curve* in my head somewhere.

As we reached Mach 0.78 I brought the power up to where it
had been at Mach 0.83. And I watched. This was really slo-mo. I began
to involve the clock in my scan. Yes, five minutes have gone by, and
the Mach is unmistakably 0.775 or less. I added power. Another five
minutes. Mach 0.77. I told the captain what I was doing as I advanced
the thrust levers to Maximum Continuous Thrust. Now we were both
watching. Mach 0.76. The captain gave ATC the option: a descent, or
Mach 0.82. As I recall, we descended.

I think it was that day that gave me an awareness of the drag
curve – whether at approach speed or at high-level cruise. *Am I on
the frontside or the backside? Where, approximately, is minimum drag?
How flat is the curve?* Because the flatter the curve, the longer the timeline for change. So I achieved a bit more awareness. But decades later
that bit was not enough the first time I tried to slow a Mooney to approach speed.

We thought of the L-1011 as a "pilot's airplane". Why? Well, as
I mentioned, it flew nicely. Flying it by hand was a joy. But there was
more, and much of it had to do with DLC.

The TriStar's pitch attitude on approach was higher than most types. Some captains I flew with would joke that the airplane flew on final at "87° Nose-Up". It didn't, of course, but it was high enough to bring the cockpit eye-height at the flare well above the thirty feet or so which is the limit of where a pilot can use binocular vision to judge height above the runway. I am sure the B-747 is similar. In Lockheed's case they programmed the Radio Altimeters to produce audio, so you could know where you were without looking inside.

At 100 feet RA you would start to hear beeps in your headset. As you descended toward the flare, the beeps would get faster in a parabola, like the graph of $y = x^2$, and stop at the design flare height of 50 feet RA. If you have heard the sound of two black holes in a death spiral – as recorded in the first discovery of gravity waves by LIGO in 2015 – it was like that. The moment the black holes swallow each other was the signal to flare. It was very effective. It was not just a **NOW** bolt out of the blue. It was like a conductor breathing in and raising her eyebrows as well as her baton, and with the exactly right comic pause, giving the downbeat.

I got through my checkout just fine, but on one flight soon after – I remember it was on runway 24R at CYUL – I crunched one. The captain laughed. As we slowed to taxi speed and turned off at the LIMA (that is as I remember it – today that taxiway is called the BRAVO 4) he raised his eyebrows and said, *Mr. Brown – was that one of your* **DC-8** *landings?*

But I was going to tell you about DLC – *Direct Lift Control.* I learned only much later that one of the reasons for DLC was to lower the flare height – from sixty-something to fifty feet RA. At the time we just saw it as a way to avoid large pitch changes while holding a glide-slope. Here is how it worked:

> When landing flap is selected, the spoilers extend to 11°. Small control wheel movements don't move the all-flying stabilizers (more on that later) but instead move the spoilers in the range 0° to 22°, so small changes in vertical speed can be achieved without stabilizer movement or pitch change, giving at least the illusion of a very-well-flown approach.

I am sure the passengers appreciated this as much as we did.

But there is more. Let's say there is a crosswind. As in any airplane, you use rudder to keep the airplane aligned with the runway, and gently lower the upwind wing to steer the lift vector so the airplane doesn't drift downwind from the centreline.

Now comes the good part: if you brush on the rear wheels of that upwind Main Landing Gear truck enough to tilt the truck, the spoilers extend to the DLC limit of 22°. That is just enough to smoothly land the front wheels of that truck and the whole of the other MLG truck. With truck tilt on both sides, the spoilers then extend fully. It was beautiful.

The B-727, on the other hand, was a bit of a pain in that situation. Of course the Seven-Two had two-wheel MLG struts, so there were no trucks to tilt. The spoiler signal was strut compression, sensed by magnetic pickups. But those pickups (and the associated air-ground switch) *were only on the left main landing gear.*

The bottom line was that the airplane's behavior depended on whether it was a left crosswind or a right crosswind. The spoilers would only extend if the **left** main gear strut compressed. As a result pilots would develop a preference, and that preference might vary from pilot to pilot. I preferred a left crosswind, but rarely got one. At my home base of Montreal Dorval, the usual crosswind situation was Runway 24 after a cold front. A right crosswind.

I don't know why this is, but often when I start musing about a point of piloting technique, something happens out in the world as an illustration. In this case, thank goodness, it is only an incident:

> It is a training flight – a line indoctrination with passengers. It is the Pilot Flying's first flight in a large airplane – a B-767. He has been properly briefed, and does very well until the mainwheels touch. Then, as the spoilers deploy, he relaxes his vigilance. He hasn't understood that *it's not over, now you have to land the nosewheel . . .*

And that's just for a start.

In a tailwheel aircraft, all this is glaringly obvious. In the ubiquitous C-172, not so much.

. . . the nosewheel hits the ground so hard that the top of the fuselage buckles over the First Class cabin. There are no injuries, but the airplane is a write-off.

So it **is** an accident, after all – and an accident that points to yet another case where there has been training, but not learning. The relevant Pilot Proverb is:

Having wheels on the ground does not mean you can stop flying the airplane.

In taildraggers we actually felt and learned the *why* of this proverb. *Why* we hold the stick away from the wind while taxiing. In the C-172 it was a rote thing to pass the test. And then it is perhaps forgotten, because we don't see the point of it. Flying clubs solve the resulting safety problem by setting crosswind limits for their students, reasoning – usually correctly – that sloppy flying within those limits will not result in aircraft damage. But it also means that their students can graduate without learning to fly with precision. Since this proverb is just as true for big airplanes as it is for trainers, occasionally this lack of learning can be expensive.

In their limitations section, aircraft Flight Manuals and FCOMs do not generally have crosswind component limits. Instead they have **demonstrated crosswinds**, where a test pilot has successfully landed the airplane with such and such a crosswind component. It doesn't mean that every pilot has the skill to do so. And large airplanes add another complication: most of the airplane is behind you, so you can't see it. You have to internalize its size and shape. In the **very** big airplanes you are sitting not over the nosewheel, but well ahead of it. In tight turns on taxiways the cockpit has to overshoot to keep the nosewheel on the line. If that internalization hasn't happened, you are at risk of dropping a main truck into the mud. It has happened more often than anyone would like to admit.

There is more to having all that airplane behind you where you can't see it. Engine nacelles. Wing tips. Flap trailing edges. Stabilizer ends. And the tail skid. For all of these there is an attitude in pitch and roll where they touch the ground at the same time as the wheels. All this is in your FCOM. Memorize it. It is a vital part of your internalization. Who knows? Maybe those two Alaskan Seven-Threes could have avoided tail strikes and become aware that something was wrong with the takeoff numbers before the Flight Attendants at the rear doors called and told them.

There is also spoiler logic, as we were beginning to see a few pages back.

The DC-9, as we saw in Chapter Four, was a lovely design for the time (before inertial). It used mainwheel spin up for both anti-skid and spoiler control. It worked a treat, and I loved it.

The B-767 ground spoilers extend when both main trucks tilt.

The Airbus A320 series, taking advantage of computer logic and IRS and wheel spin, uses a logic diagram for both anti-skid and ground spoilers. They too work a treat. For most landings the operative condition is ***main wheels spun up to 72 knots***. Whereas on the DC-9 you had to guess where the wheels were in their spin up, on the A320 you knew. If you greased one on in wet conditions (as I miraculously did on my very last landing) you can sneak a peek inside at the bottom of the Wheels Page and see 10 little green arrows pointing up from ten little lines: the five spoilers on each wing.

The A320 even manages to imitate the L-1011, using logic instead of clever mechanical/hydraulic/electrical design. If you are still on one wheel in a strong crosswind, and you nick a reverser into idle, the spoilers will extend to 10° – enough to settle the airplane on both main landing gear. Hooray!

Boys and girls, the bottom line is:

~ Pilot Commandment Number Two ~
Know thy Airplane

You will probably change types a number of times in your careers, perhaps moving from the right seat to the left onto an airplane you have never flown. Don't assume that following the type course as designed is sufficient. Ask yourself questions. Do your own research in the FCOM. The answers are probably there if you look for them.

First and foremost, look at automation. It is never perfect, and neither are you, but acting as a team you and the computers have a good chance of survival. What is the communication and the feedback between you? Where do you look – and when – to see what the automation thinks it is doing?

And that's in the heat of the moment. The real work is at your kitchen table as you ask *how* this particular system works. Good examples are today's antiskid and ground spoiler systems. Here is the logic diagram for the A320 ground spoilers:

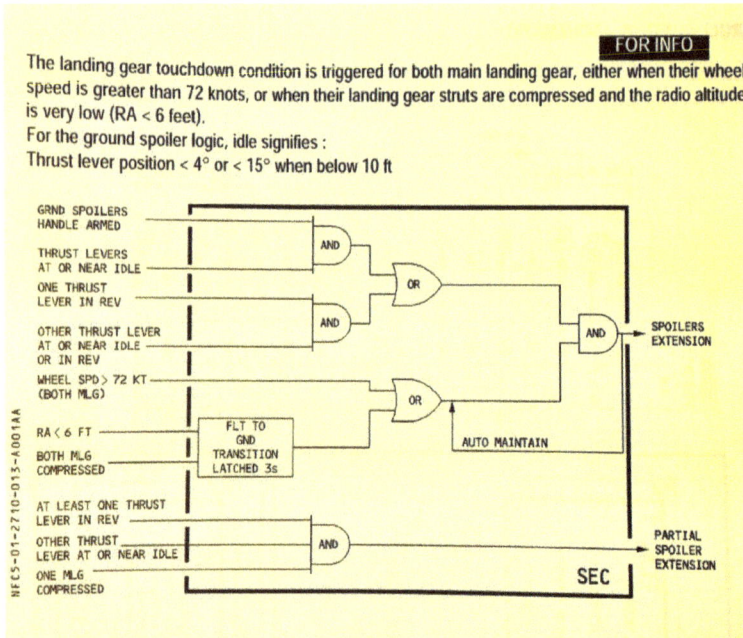

FOR INFO

The landing gear touchdown condition is triggered for both main landing gear, either when their wheel speed is greater than 72 knots, or when their landing gear struts are compressed and the radio altitude is very low (RA < 6 feet).
For the ground spoiler logic, idle signifies :
Thrust lever position < 4° or < 15° when below 10 ft

Using the diagram, run through various scenarios, starting with a normal landing on a dry runway. Look at all the ANDs and the ORs. What happened to extend the spoilers? Then get as zany as you like. What if you grease it on to wet ice and the wheels are barely turning? Will the spoilers deploy? If so, is there a delay?

If you change types between two fly-by-wire airplanes, do they have different control laws? Have you changed from C* to C*U, or vice versa? Are you unconsciously making the assumption that they will behave in the same way? Once again, it will pay dividends to ask yourself questions.

In most of the previous chapters we have been following up on D.P. Davies' prescient warnings about the power of the stabilizer. We have seen how it is involved in many fatal accidents. Where does the L-1011 fit in that history?

I have written elsewhere about one of the mechanisms of classical tragedy – hubris and nemesis. The protagonist has a tragic fate not because of weakness, but – paradoxically – because of his strengths. An example is the A320 and subsequent models. Bernard Ziegler, who inspired much of the design, was an engineer and a decorated fighter pilot. He joined Airbus in 1972 as Chief Test Pilot. He was a visionary, a pioneer of fly-by-wire and envelope protection. He believed he had made an airplane that was "pilot-proof" and "unstallable". That was until Air France 447 zoomed ballistically out of the flight envelope at 37,924 feet and hit the ocean four minutes later in a deep stall.

The Cherokee 140, the airplane in which I first soloed, has an *all-flying stabilizer.* That is, the entire horizontal tail surface moves, hinged near the front spar. What looks like a trim tab at the trailing edge is an anti-servo tab, which increases the stick force per G, like the elevator down-spring in my Bonanza.

Like the Cherokee, the L-1011 has an *all-flying stabilizer.* Actually, there are two, one on each side. They are not mechanically connected. They too have a tab, geared to the stabilizer as a *servo tab.* Lockheed calls it an *elevator which effectively changes the camber of the stabilizer/ elevator airfoil.* Lockheed says of this configuration:

The flying tail provides direct and positive insurance against jet upset and runaway trim.

Like the B-747, the L-1011 has four hydraulic systems. Each stabilizer is operated by a *dual hydraulic servo unit.* Hydraulic systems A and B operate the left stabilizer, and systems C and D operate the right stabilizer. As Lockheed says:

Thus, two servo control paths and four hydraulic actuation paths back each other up to provide maximum protection against system failures.

Then on April 12, 1977, Delta Airlines Fight 1080 lost pitch control after takeoff from San Diego in night IMC. The left stabilizer had jammed in the full nose-up position during the controls check. *At the time there was no cockpit indication of the stabilizer position.*

The save is a hair-raising story, and well worth looking up.

Yesterday I did. I read Captain Jack McMahan's account of the incident at https://www.tristar500.net/library/flight1080.pdf. The airspace of it hung around me all evening. It appeared in my dreams. I know that airspace off Playa del Rey Beach. I know it from when KLAX is landing east. It is the same airspace where Alaska Airlines Flight 261 went down on January 31, 2000:

This photo is from the Final Report on Alaska Airlines Flight 261. It is the stabilizer jackscrew.

Picture the workings of a Variable Incidence Tailplane (we have been calling it the *stab*; Airbus calls it the *Plan Horizontal, or THS – Trimmable Horizontal Stabilizer*). The whole horizontal surface can move about its lateral axis. The axle, if you like, is set about one-third of the way back from the leading edge, near the centre of lift. The leading edge is moved up and down and held in place by a jackscrew, which is in effect a very large bolt. This bolt is turned by the trim motor(s), which are fixed to the fuselage. Inside the leading edge of the stabilizer surface is a nut – the female part of the nut-and-bolt assembly. It is known as the **acme nut**. The jackscrew is made of steel. The acme nut is made of a softer aluminum-bronze alloy. Like crankshaft bearings in a car, the acme nut is the sacrificial element. These softer parts are designed to wear and be replaced at intervals, leaving the larger and more expensive parts (jackscrew and crankshaft) intact. In this way, with periodic maintenance, the assembly can have a long and useful life.

The photo above shows plainly what went wrong. The periodic maintenance schedule requires both lubrication and a check of the end play between the jackscrew and the acme nut. Alaska Airlines failed to perform these checks. The curls of material clinging to the jackscrew are threads from the acme nut. A mechanic would say that the threads of the nut are *stripped*. Eventually, as happened here, aerodynamic forces on the stabilizer could move the acme nut along the jackscrew – even if the latter were not turning. During the fatal flight, it moved in this way to the full nose-down position. The pilots even tried flying inverted, so the stab would be in effect full nose-up. It didn't work. The aircraft was still uncontrollable.

A great save, and a great attempt at a save. May that lovely beach-front airspace remain a celebration and a memorial for pilots faced with the second-deadliest threat – flight control failure. (I would put fire in the number one position). And may we all – and pilots especially – work to retain a humility in the face of the challenges that will come our way.

•

Today I read an article about the plight of the German railroad – the Deutsche Bahn. It was set up after German reunification. All debt was forgiven. It has a company structure, but the sole shareholder is the German State. The company's debt is growing at €5 million per day. The on-time performance is tanking. The president of Germany's federal audit office commented, "We have all the disadvantages of this company structure, without the benefits."

I was immediately reminded of Canada's own national entity which was spun off to be a non-profit in charge of our airspace infrastructure.

That in turn took me to ADS-B out, and then to what is called *distributed processing.*

In the early 1980's I was a project pilot, working on the implementation of an air-ground datalink.

ARINC of Annapolis, MD (now part of Rockwell Collins) was first off the mark in 1978 with *ACARS*, the **Aircraft Communication and Reporting System,** which began as a way to detect and report OOOI times: Out, Off, On, and In. It doesn't sound like much, but when I recall *The Captain will determine the times*, and the 4 by 4 inch green sheet he had to fill out for every flight and the radio reports to the company that (usually the F/O) had to make, it was a very useful advance. Of course over time *ACARS* came to be much more than that, with global coverage via satellite.

Our implementation team saw the possibilities for a major streamlining of cockpit duties, and proposed, among many other things, transmission of ATIS, Weight & Balance, Fuel Uplift checks, and a complete Flight Profile. We also proposed a **distributed processing** communication system, where the aircraft avionics unit kept track of which ground units it could "see" and made the decision to connect to the station with the strongest signal. Our ground stations emitted a regular **squitter**, saying, in effect, **here I am.** At the time, ARINC's system was centrally controlled.

By the late 1980's our version was operating successfully system-wide, and was even licenced in Japan for time. Then in the great disassembly, merger, and bankruptcy mania of the late 1990's, our datalink was decommissioned in favor of an ARINC contract.

If you are thinking of today's ubiquitous cell phone, you are right. It is exactly the same technology, albeit with different radio frequencies and a more limited application.

Why do I return to that wrinkle of yesteryear?

Because it reminds me of where we are today with ADS-B Out.

Stateside, ADS-B Out is mandatory for most controlled airspace. But for General Aviation there is a sweetener: 978 MHz UAT. In exchange for requiring ADS-B out transmission, small aircraft can keep to just their bottom-mounted transponder antennas and receive FIS-B (weather and NEXRAD radar, among other things) information at no charge. This is a *huge* advantage. In Canada, I have to have a separate satellite receiver (and costly subscription) to see the same data. And here in Canada with our vast and thinly populated North, a network of ground stations like those in the USA would be impractical. So far so good. And NAV Canada has already invested in satellite coverage. Again, so far so good. But our local Experimental Aircraft Association Chapter is up in arms, and for good reason.

NAV Canada's mission is to "ensure the safe, orderly, and expeditious flow of air traffic in Canadian airspace." But their vision is of a top-down, centrally controlled system, like Air Traffic Control in today's controlled airspace. But Experimental Aircraft – and light aircraft in general – fly in uncontrolled airspace much of the time. And that airspace is increasingly busy – dangerously so. There is only so much the *see and be seen* mantra can accomplish with human vision alone. For one thing, there is more than vision involved in spotting traffic. There is also perception. Our peripheral vision, especially, can be aware of motion before our brains do the extra work to construct a picture or to direct the eye to look more directly at what is moving. The problem for pilots is that *if the other aircraft is moving in your frame of vision, it is not on a collision course with you*. The dot that is not moving – just getting bigger – is harder to detect.

There is no technical reason why Automatic Dependent Surveillance cannot provide traffic information from aircraft to aircraft in uncontrolled airspace, independently of NAV Canada's centralized control. In two words, think *distributed processing*. In a word, think *cellphone*. And it wouldn't need a new top antenna.

•

But back to our dreamy exotic, the TriStar. By 1980 the shorter, longer-range version – the L-1011-500 – was entering service. For all of us, this was our first exposure to a Flight Management System. But my first flight on a *dash 500* was memorable not for the FMS – it was a primitive one from the ergonomics standpoint – but for the captain, a prince of a man now some years deceased. It was my Line Check on the -500. He spent the entire cruise portion of the flight to KLAX learning and teaching. Together we found our way through the annoying interface. It was like using a touch-tone phone to write a novel (touch this key three times to get a C). My Check Captain was a model of humanity, humility, and patience. To this day I think of him with affection.

●

Of all the landings of my career, one stands out as the most immensely pleasurable. I wasn't the PF. But it **was** the TriStar.

I don't remember the exact lead-in, or I would start the story earlier. But it was winter, and Dorval was opening up after a snowstorm. The landing itself I remember as if it were yesterday.

We would be landing east, perhaps even the first landing after the storm. Were there men and equipment on Runway 06L, and snow removal in progress? Were we going to have to hold?

In any case, the captain asked for a runway report for 06R. The report came back: *four inches of fresh powder*. A could feel a light bulb go off as the captain paused. It was not for long. *Requesting 06R*, he said.

Forty-some years later I have found the page: *LIMITATIONS: 01.30.01.*

> **A take-off must not be attempted from a runway which has an appreciable area of its surface covered with:**
>
> **a)   More than 10cm (4 in) of light dry snow . . .**

I knew it was right on the limit. It is only now I see that the limitation is for takeoff. But beautiful?

Oh, yeah. It was like a perfect powder day on skis or snowboard. You are briefly airborne, perhaps off a mogul. The landing is on that steep but smooth section ahead. You only know you have landed because your board is throwing powder again.

In my imagination now we all have huge grins and the Second Officer is mouthing

Whoaa!

§

Chapter Nine

To everything there is a season
~ Ecclesiastes 3 ~

I have had the same dream three nights running. One morning (was it after the first night?) I shared it with my spouse, but this morning I find myself longing for Captain's voice.

It is not a bad dream. Because I love its subject matter so much, it is almost erotic. I am hand-flying a descent in instrument conditions (in this case it is smoke and rain showers that make it impossible to resolve a horizon looking through the windshield).

I have just switched to Terminal Control, and I recognize the controller's voice from my airline days. He was young then and always pleasant and kind, a nice layer on top of his professional competence. He must be nearing retirement himself now. I wonder if he knows how much I love this. This descent. These many, many descents. This life of mine.

But you can't *drink and drive.* It is my father speaking to me. Lecturing. Explaining. Being practical. I should leave this descent alone. Let it go.

Perhaps.

Not long ago I was in the kitchen making spaghetti sauce.

OK, I think. I'll need to chop two onions. I open the drawer at my knees and select one. The others are all small. OK, three onions.

I place the first one on the cutting board, which was a wedding present. Fifty-five years of slicing and dicing later, the surface is shaped like a saddle. I set aside the white, shiny medium onion I have just peeled. I pick up the brown onion skin to throw into the compost bin, which sits behind the cutting board. My situational awareness does a jump-cut. The brown mass is too heavy. It contains the two smaller, unpeeled onions. *Shit*, I think. How could that happen?

I know I have that problem of old age – writing to short-term memory. The *What did I come in here for?* syndrome. But this seems different, somehow. My immediate awareness space dropped a term. My visual field perception lost a couple of objects and was surprised when fingers added them back.

•

Hey, Chris. Remember you were going to discuss crosswind landings?

I do now.

She brings me back. Rescues me from my dreams.

That was back in Chapter Two. Don't leave me hanging, OK? Some people I'm flying with just don't get it. Really don't get it.

OK, I'm on it.

I'm grateful she's still there. I can get back to the business at hand.

And that *Visual Approach* you activated in the GTN 650. Tell me more.

OK.

And take care of yourself. You're not off the hook yet.

She doesn't know about my dreams. Not yet. But I know she will before long.

•

The NTSB Final Report on the Maui B-777 is out. Did the NTSB stop the airplane in Chicago, as I imagined all those months ago?

It doesn't matter. The incident, which was *"not NTSB reportable"*, got noticed by the NTSB. The data from the dive after takeoff and close call has not been erased. We have the data.

Of course we do not have the CVR data. That had been overwritten before UA 1722 landed in KSFO. But we do have the pilots' written reports. Between these and the DFDR data, we can put together a timeline. We know what happened. And as usual, the real question is not the *what*, but the *why*? Why do the two human pilots do what they do? And what pressures, assumptions, training, and experience are behind that behavior?

New facts have come to light. In all likelihood it will take a few days for me to absorb them, awake and in dreams. What I thought I knew will change. I know the pilots better now, for one thing. I know about their concerns and briefings before takeoff, and about their decisions on takeoff flap and power. I will try to find compassion as I imagine myself in their situation.

Fly Dubai is in my head, as is C*U. Also *fly by feel* and *fly by trim*. Heck, the whole of this book so far is echoing. Maybe it's just that I'm old and memories are floating in my head. But it all feels relevant – essential, somehow, to understanding.

So – what's new?

The pilots were very much aware of the potential for windshear – the same picture I got from archived weather reports back in Chapter Five. Just as KSFO lands on runways 28L and 28R 90% of the time, so Kahului, Maui (OGG, PHOG) uses runway 02. But today there have been landings on runway 20. Unusual. And for the Triple Seven, this is also a short runway – just under 7000 feet. With the surface wind now 320/10 knots, they will use runway 02, but with Flap 20 instead of the usual Flap 15. In view of the potential for windshear, they will skip Flex Thrust and use full power.

They briefed all this, as well as the possibility they might have to use the *Windshear Escape Maneuver* (shades of Fly Dubai), except in this case the pilots carefully briefed the maneuver beforehand. They also spent three minutes in position on Runway 02 getting separation from an A321 departing ahead, so they had time to study the radar returns on the departure path. And – as I imagined back in Chapter Five – it was raining hard. The captain elected to put his wipers on *High* for the takeoff.

. . .

No! Wait a minute! This is all wrong! We don't have the data!

So that story about the NTSB catching up with the DFDR at O'Hare in time to save the data? Didn't happen. In fact nothing much happened for quite a while. No hull loss. No loss of life. So it was an *Incident*, not an *Accident*. And not only was the NTSB slow on the up-take – so was I. My usual path to *Final Reports* is through the *Aviation Safety Network* database. That doesn't work the same way here, because UAL1722 was not an accident. But it was awfully close:

	Time	V/S	Pitch Att	RA
Takeoff	14:49			
	14:50:51	-8536fpm	-16.74°	1386 AGL
Lowest RA	14:50:57	Pullout G	2.66 G	748 AGL

So how do we know? Where did we get this data?

We knew something the day after the incident through ADS-B out. Anyone who becomes aware of an incident by whatever means can go to FlightAware and look at enough data to get a good idea of what happened. As we saw in Chapter Five, several aviation journals did just that, but soft-pedalled their comments until a passenger account appeared in the newspapers a day later, supplying a piece of data that ADS-B didn't have – G. It could be inferred from the ADS-B flight path, but now we had a witness.

There is another source: ASRS, the *Aviation Safety Reporting System*. Live data is transmitted back to the airline's computers via ACARS, the datalink that originally used VHF but now is also transmitted via satellite, giving it worldwide coverage:

The captain of MH370 (also a B-777) pulled the ACARS breakers before he deviated from the planned route. Military primary radar tracked the flight for a while as it reversed course. Then MH370 climbed again, heading for the world's furthest point from land – in the Great Southern Ocean.

The captain, on oxygen, had turned off the *Air Conditioning Packs*, de-pressurizing the aircraft and putting everyone but him to sleep. He continued the flight until he ran out of fuel. Several pieces – including a flap fragment – washed ashore in the Western Indian Ocean years later.

When ASRS data *does* reach the airline, computers flag any exceedance of normal parameters and save the data. Pilots are very aware of this. If they bust a limit, they are going to have to write a report, so they had better get their story straight. In this case (as with Fly Dubai) the first exceedance was flap speeds.

I mentioned I had a heck of a time finding this *Aviation Investigation Final Report*. I knew it existed through Juan Browne's Blancolirio channel. Shoutout to Juan Browne for among other things, showing me about *Dockets* at the NTSB. These are virtual file folders that contain files relevant to an investigation. Once I got the code for the investigation right – DCA23LA172 – I could access the (name redacted) pilot reports.

But the *Doh!* Moment for me was the *Memorandum for Record*. It describes how the NTSB only became aware of the incident in late February. They contacted the airline, which sent the requested data in an email on March 8. What data did they send? What had been flagged in ASRS. That's all there is. The DFDR data is long gone.

•

I'm sorry, Chris. You *did* talk about crosswinds. In the L-1011 spoiler logic.

Yeah. A bit.

Enough to get me thinking. The way you look at it. *Steering the lift vector.* How did you teach it?

I think I failed at teaching it. I think all I did was scare the Beejasus out of the poor student.

But wait – you're consistent. Attitude as feedback for control movement. Rudder to stay aligned. Not aileron, but *bank angle* to steer lift.

Yeah, exactly.

You're sounding discouraged.

Huh. I guess I am, a bit.

So there are times you didn't get through. I know all about that, too. *I'm* listening. Teach *me*.

Well . . .

I want to know. You can get through to me.

I sigh. Yeah. Well, I would find a longish runway, preferably with not too much traffic.

How long?

For a C-172 or similar, 4000 feet is plenty.

OK. And then?

Instead of flaring, add just enough power so you can fly down the runway in ground effect.

Within a wingspan.

Yes.

Aha! Now I see why you scared the crap out of them. They have to keep flying. With precision.

Yes.

You talked about that guy who didn't, and trashed a perfectly good B-767.

Yes.

You know, it's sad, but I see that all the time. They flare, and then they think they're done. It's like they want to look away. I think they really are afraid of low flying.

Should get some float flying.

Huh! Yeah. But go on. If you can get them to do a low pass at approach speed, what then?

Then we practice using bank angle to displace sideways. Both upwind and down. And back to hold the centreline. All while holding altitude and speed and staying aligned with the runway. Bank planned and held precisely. Strictly limited between level and a few degrees into wind.

Ya flunk if that upwind wing comes up.

Yup.

Like that helicopter pilot.

Yup.

She has gone somewhere. But I'm not worried. She's thinking about the problem. How is she going to use any of this while flying the line in the A320?

It's the timeline, she says. How are you going to get all that done in Flare Mode?

In the Bonanza, I would cheat.

How?

Use 10° Flap for landing.

Prolonging the flare and hold-off.

Yes. Say you get a big gust that lifts you and moves you downwind

. . .

You've still got the energy to slide back to the centreline. And feel for the ground with the upwind wheel.

Yes, exactly.

She is quiet again. But I can feel her mind going.

There's an awful lot going on in those last seconds, she says.

Yup.

So maybe – just maybe – I talk myself through one. Demonstration, with commentary.

I like it.

But mid-trip. If we're on a wavelength. Maybe we have been discussing the subject.

Sure.

Then if I fuck it up we both get a laugh.

She has gone silent again. I can feel the laughter glow slowly morphing into *miserere nobis*.

That airspace off Playa del Rey. I know it, too.

Of course.

A respectful silence. As in church. I give her space.

It's probably raining. October, maybe. And we won't have to do the LAXX ONE Departure.

Do a U-Turn over the ocean? Used to be called the LOOP.

That's the one. Oh boy. You talked about the second-deadliest threat. The next-to-greatest threat.

Uh huh.

I don't want to even *think* about fire.

She is going somewhere. I say nothing. I try to stay with her.

All I know is **get it down NOW**. Don't give up.

Yes.

Air Canada taught us about that, for sure. And never reset a breaker more than once.

I do a double-take. And some math.

How come you know about that? AC 797 was before you were born.

Stan Rogers. He died in that . . . *thing*.

You're a fan?

Totally. If I'm down I play *The Mary Ellen Carter*. Brings back hope.

Well, me too. And my kids as well. When we get together, we sing along.

He sings about real people. The fisherman. The Newfie working on an oil rig in Alberta, yearning to get back to *The Rock*. The ageing ranch wife.

I sigh. *Yeah.*

We're not heroes either. Just fucking pilots.

I let that echo around our shared space.

And those pilots. In the LOOP airspace. They just dealt with what they had. As best they could. One amazing save, one not.

Sounds like you've read the Delta 1080.

Yes, and the Alaska 261. *Requiescat in pace.*

She is silent again for a while. So am I.

Chris, did the L10 really not have a control position indicator?

Well, I couldn't tell you from memory. But I found this:

L-1011 OPERATING

INSERT 438

ISSUED: JUN 16/80

SUBJECT: ELEVATOR JAM WARNING MODIFICATION

The airplane is tolerant to a jam of an elevator at any deflection angle normally encountered in flight, but a jam during the pre-flight control check could create serious control problems. On unmodified aircraft, the elevator positions are not monitored and if a pre-flight elevator jam occurred, there would be no indication or warning to the flight crew prior to takeoff . . . therefore, an indicating system is being added to provide a means for alerting the flight crew to an elevator jam condition prior to takeoff.

Jesus. I see what you mean about *hubris* and *nemesis*. Shit. Now, when I say . . .

Elevator Up, Elevator Down, Neutral

. . . on every flight, I'm going to mean it. Not just Up and Down.

Neutral!

•

United 1722 at Maui is still inhabiting my dreams. There is something that doesn't add up.

STILL LEARNING TO FLY

I have spent a few days, off and on, studying the dockets for UA1722. First I put together a timeline, using the *Flight Data Derived Strip Chart* from the *Memo for Record*, the *Narrative description of flight data*, and the pilots' statements.

In most cases a timeline (by merging pilot actions and statements with known events – usually from the DFDR) can yield insights about a rapid and complex sequence, and this timeline was no exception. But I hadn't yet read the *Flight Crew Debrief Narrative*, which is at the end of the First Officer's statement.

Where to begin? Let's start with the incontrovertible.

The usual flap setting for takeoff is 15. The decision to use 20 Flap for takeoff turned out to be a trigger to what followed:

- The available positions on the way to Flaps UP are 15, 5, and 1. At the first flap retraction, the captain called for flap 5. The First Officer moved the lever up to the next notch – Flap 15. The limit speeds on the airspeed tape did not do what the captain expected, and with full thrust the airspeed was increasing faster than it normally does. Worried that he was going to bust the flap speeds, he looked over at the EICAS to see if there was a flap fault of some sort.

- Thirty-two seconds later First Officer repeatedly calls **Pull Up.**

- Thirty-three seconds later at about 1300 RA, the V/S is -8536fpm and the pitch attitude is 17.74° Nose-Down.

- Thirty-nine seconds later, pulling 2.66G, they turn the corner into climb at 748 RA

Thirty-two seconds. Doesn't sound like much, right?

Captain?

Yeah. But hand-flying in IMC, thirty-two seconds is forever.

For sure. And they're **way** out of equilibrium.

TOGA thrust. And he's worried about busting flap speeds. Just like Fly Dubai.

Yes. Here's the data, and the timeline I made:

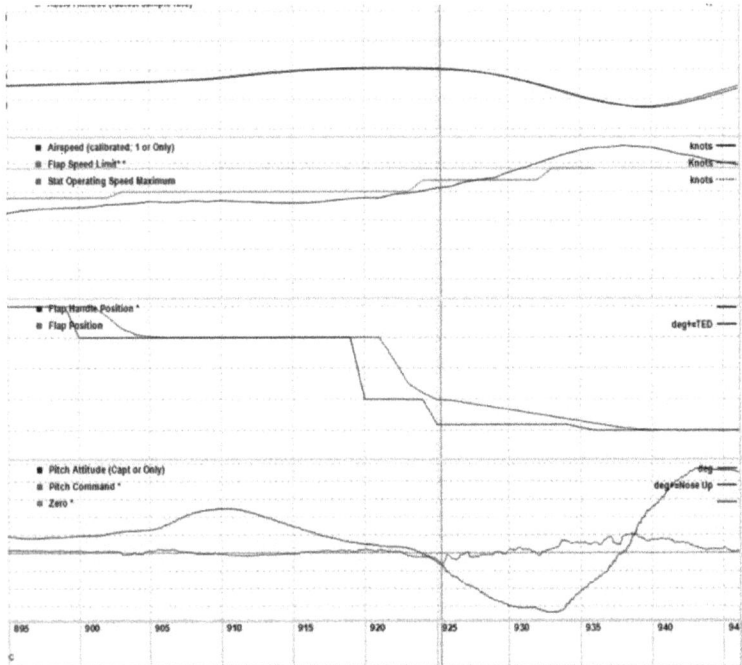

Time	Sec	RA	V/S	Flap Sel	Flap Pos	Pitch Att	A/S
14:49:33		Takeoff			20		
14:50:18	901			15		+5	175
14:50:38	921	144		5	15	2.37	
14:50:40	923			1	5		
14:50:43	926	2082	-1648			-2.9	200
14:50:48	931	1745			Pull Up		
14:50:50	933			0			
14:50:50	933	Mo-ment of Recog-nition	-8536	*see below			
14:50:51	934	1386					275
14:50:57	940	748		2.66G	0		

*14:50:50   933   **Moment of Recognition**

- First Officer senses cloud breakout (OGG METAR: BKN009 OVC020)

- First Officer sees pitch angle is "8° to 10° nose down"

- First Officer repeatedly calls **Pull Up**

- Captain pulls, pitch attitude starts to move nose-up

(This timeline is derived from the Narrative description of flight data that follows the strip chart in the United Airlines email, and from the Captain and the First Officer's statements.)

Nice. And *Moment of Recognition* to *save* is six seconds. Not much margin there . . .

I can tell from the rhythm of her words. She is going somewhere.

Chris, back there somewhere you said *start with the incontro-vertible*. Is it time to – ahh – go further? On our own?

Yes. But we don't have to. I didn't even see this at first, when I was digging around for the timeline. Shows how focus isn't everything, especially when you don't notice other stuff that could be more import-ant. This is at the end of the First Officer's statement. It's still his voice, but he is going into the *why*.

> **Flight Crew Debrief Narrative:** Once we got around the weather and up to cruise, we debriefed the departure and event. The Captain said he never announced Flaps 15, but asked for Flaps 5 twice, indicating a miscommunication on our flap retraction. The Captain said he was focused on the flap setting and was looking at our EICAS waiting for a flap malfunction to appear and was unaware of our pitch attitude until I queried him. The Captain said he did pitch forward, but didn't think he pitched forward enough to cause such a dramatic pitch change and concluded we must have hit windshear or a downdraft. Neither of us heard or witnessed the Predictive or Reactive windshear warnings but we did hear the GPWS cautions and warnings. Neither of us witnessed airspeed trend or VSI indications of a windshear event.

Wow. So he **was** looking at the EICAS for thirty-two seconds.

Looks like it.

We are both re-reading the *Debrief Narrative*. It is unequivocal. The Captain *"was unaware of our pitch attitude until I queried him."*

It's not just curiosity, she says. It's fear.

Of the ASRS.

Sure. Just like Fly Dubai. Hoping that the flap speed bust will go away, even though you know it won't.

And as a crew – they still have a miscommunication that is unresolved.

We read it again. How they explain the pitch attitude. The captain concludes it must have been windshear or a downdraft, but neither of them *"heard Predictive or Reactive windshear warnings"*.

Chris, let's go back to the data. How the hell do they get so far nose down? There's a little nose down nudge at second 923, and at 925 it's up to about 2.5 nose down . . .

But the pitch-down starts much earlier, at 910. It just gets faster at 925.

Wait – yes – at 926 the V/S is already -1648 fpm. And the attitude is 2.9 nose down. Nose down!

Yup.

Oh oh.

Yeah.

You think he had his thumb on the trim?

Yeah.

She is puzzling through how the A320 would react with its C* and autotrim.

Chris, the Triple Seven has C*U, right?

Uh huh.

So if he *did* have his thumb on the trim, all he is doing is changing U_{ERR}? Not moving the stab?

Yes. That's right.

So to move the stab he'd have to use those alternate trim handles on the pedestal?

Yes.

Unlikely.

Yes. I can feel her going way back. To braided steel cables.

I've got it, she says. There are no braided steel cables. That captain's control column trace is not elevator movement.

No. And we don't have that data, and never will.

Whoa. So let me run through this . . . his trims a bit nose-down. Or more than a bit. We **know** U_{ERR} changes. C*U is going to fly the airplane to a lower AoA, a higher speed. Like a C-172 if you take your hands off and trim nose-down. It'll pitch down.

Yes. But without the data we don't know exactly how C*U does that. Probably elevator first and stab later.

I agree. But we'll never know – well, unless someone does it or simulates it or goes to Boeing and persuades them to . . .

Yeah.

Oh, I know. That's never gonna happen. OK. But the airplane is *acting* like it is out of trim. Like it's being flown with trim.

That's what I think. But as we said, we'd have to have elevator position and stab position and U_{ERR}, if that is even recorded.

And it's a suck-in. He's looking at the EICAS. Not the attitude. With TOGA thrust he's accelerating like a rocket. The Somatogravic Illusion. Somewhere in that worried brain of his he "knows" he's pitching up, because that's what he feels. But it's only half-conscious because he's already busted flap speeds. So he thumbs the trim.

She stops. It is the boiling in her chest. She is fighting back bad words. She wants to be done with this mess.

So – did you see that article in *The New Yorker*? she asks.

You read *The New Yorker*?

Sometimes. My Significant Other pointed it out.

What's it about?

ChatGPT.

Yeah! I read it yesterday. It has been hanging about my ears ever since. What's the title again?

A Coder Considers the Waning Days if the Craft.

Right. Right. So . . .

Well it's been hanging around my head, too. That illustration – a sunset as backdrop for:

\</end>

– that gets me where I live.

You mean *the end of things.*

Yah.

I have been neglecting my espresso, my second cup of the day. It has gone cold.

Sure, I say. The end of things. That's what we've been talking about. But there's more. I have been trying to figure it out.

ChatGPT.

Yeah. I just dismissed it outright. But for my son – the one who's the prof – it's real. The kids are using it to write assignments. He has to deal with that.

And the result is highfalutin' garbage.

Yes. Mostly. And a friend of my lawyer son has written a program to detect the traces of ChatGPT. The friend is also a prof. He wants to just flunk his students.

But that gets a little sticky.

Yes. I pause to take a sip of my room-temperature espresso.

So we dismissed it outright, she says.

We did. But I found myself following the author through his *changing of mind*. His learning.

The author's friend got a subscription to GPT-4. Twenty bucks a month.

Yeah. and the friend started using it to write **code**. That was my *aha!* moment.

Maybe it's good at writing code.

Yeah.

She is turning a corner. Thinking.

What about us? she says. Can they put **us** into the database? Will they?

I shrug. It all seems a bit much.

And what are they going to put in? she goes on.

I nod.

Stick and Rudder? Handling the Big Jets? Hey, this book for that matter.

Yeah. I doubt it.

I think we've still got the Andy Grove problem. The chain of experience. Is it even possible to put experience in a database like that?

I don't know.

Well I'm dubious. They'll put in all those so-called facts that live on in those exams we have to take. Time has moved on and maybe those facts have, too. Like Fly Dubai. It's like if when I was still my old engineering self I designed both doppler radar and the *Warning – Windshear Ahead* stuff. Before I became a pilot.

Hah! I like it!

Before I could see the difference between a normal cold front and a dry microburst. Before **you** told me about *Ground Speed Mini*. Before **you** got me reading about EAL 304. When it was the *Civil Aeronautics Board*. Before NTSB.

I lean back in my oak armchair, basking in her rant.

Back before I was born, when accident reports might contain actual *experience*, like explanations from test pilots who actually knew their shit. Before accident reports were sanitized, redacted, and emasculated by comments. Before . . .

I feel relaxed, content. Peaceful, even.

. . . before – I mean even if ChatGPT swallows NTSB whole, does that deliver our collective aviation experience?

All good rants end in absolution. The ranter is released from her existential angst, at least for a while.

No. It wouldn't deliver our collective aviation experience. It would only be sanitized stuff since 2007.

I have blurted it out. Just because it came into my head. I already regret it. I feel her angst returning like a rising gorge.

I'm sorry, I say. I loved your rant. It's just that I remembered a story my friend Mark told me.

ChatGPT?

No, NTSB.

Oh, OK. And something happened in 2007?

Yeah. Or thereabouts. Mark and a few people he knew became aware that the new young NTSB crew were looking at throwing away all the old paper stuff. Cartons of it. Truckloads.

Throwing away? Erasing the record, effectively?

Yeah. So they went to bat for history. They persuaded Embry-Riddle Aeronautical University to take the paper.

Did they save it? Digitize it?

Yes, thank goodness. And I checked. It's in their Hunt Library. Accessible online at *guides.erau.edu*.

Could you find Eastern 304?

Yes, one page. *Full narrative not available.* So either my bad, or it's not all digitized.

But we have the facsimile, right? The typewritten pages?

Yes.

But if ChatGPT swallowed **them**, would it understand them?

I don't know.

She is quiet for a while. The rant energy must be receding again. Or maybe just a feeling of *WTF are you going to do?*

Chris, you know OpenAI?

That the company that made ChatGPT?

Right. They're not *open* anymore. Big Tech moved in. New Board of Directors. Including Silicon Valley insiders and a very well-known guy known for *applying free-market theory where it doesn't fit the circumstances.*

ClosedAI. Now open only to the very few.

Yeah. Screw them.

•

I have been looking for a way to summarize what we have learned together through *Einsteinian thought experiments* and *Socratic dialogue.* I could list all the *Pilot Commandments* and proverbs, and elaborate on all the dos and don'ts of our trade, but that's not the right way to go.

Something Captain said in her last rant has stayed with me. She posited her former engineering self as having invented the "doppler radar and the *Warning – Windshear Ahead* stuff". Now that she is a pilot she can appreciate the difference between a normal cold front and a dry microburst. What has changed?

As an engineer her job was to build a system. As a pilot she has become part of a system.

And, as we have seen, art imitates life. Uncle Eric's pioneering Inertial Navigation System used technologies and parts available at the time – weights, springs, potentiometers, gyros, and vacuum tubes. The equivalent today uses captive ruby lasers to measure rotational acceleration. The spinning gyros can be dispensed with. This new "strapdown" system does more than navigate. It is also an AHRS – an *Attitude and Heading Reference System.* And that six-accelerometer system (three linear and three rotational) almost (see Glossary) mirrors what we pilot creatures have in each middle ear. The good news is that it allows us to be bipeds and to steady our perception. The bad news is:

a) There is a threshold below which we do not feel rotational acceleration, and

b) We can sense the direction of local G, leaving us

susceptible to the *Somatogravic Illusion.*

The bottom line is that becoming part of a system is a non-trivial task.

The engineer designing a control system must incorporate *feedback*:

> *I have moved this control surface. What happened?*

Now that the pilot is part of the system, she too must use feedback loops if she is going to be a good pilot. She must *fly the airplane, and not let it fly her.* In fact, there is a series of feedback loops – something like this:

> *FPV <—> Attitude <—> Control Movement*

The pilot has to *imagine* the Flight Path Vector (unless she has *taken the bird* in an aircraft so equipped). She also has to *imagine* what she wants the airplane to do. If the actual FPV diverges from her plan, she has to *fly by the numbers*, using Attitude and Power (remember P + P = PP?) to fly the FPV to the tune of her plan.

So she moves controls. Gently, watching attitude. That is the first feedback loop. Then she waits, to see if this new attitude (and possibly new power) is achieving the change to the FPV that she wanted. That is the second loop. She waits again. For equilibrium. Then she trims.

She is a good pilot. A closed-loop pilot. She moves – almost unconsciously – back and forth along the chain of feedback loops:

> *FPV <—> Attitude <—> Control Movement*

She is an integral part of the aircraft.

Notice also what she does **not** do. She does not fly by feel. (A more specific definition of *fly by feel* is *let the airplane fly you.*) Nor does she fly by trim. She is very aware of the airplane being out of equilibrium (accelerating in some way) and waits for equilibrium before trimming.

What she does is not trivial. It is not learned overnight. She can get instruction to help her pass tests, but that is not the same as learning. If she is lucky she will have mentors who help her to learn – who will lead her to a deeper understanding of her trade. With that understanding comes confidence.

But that's not the full story. Just as Flight Control Computers monitor themselves, so must the pilot, because *she is an integral part of the aircraft systems.*

In the trade we speak of *situational awareness* and *pilot judgement.* But these qualities are just a part of the miracle of human perception. What we speak of as *reality* is something we construct in our heads using perception and memory and . . . and other things we are barely beginning to understand. If we are a two-pilot crew, my reality is quite similar to yours. But the two realities are not identical. If we are a good crew we try to merge our realities and act on the result, like two Flight Control Computers comparing their outputs.

Well, not exactly. What the pilot has to do is more analogous to a single Flight Control Computer on the A320. As we have seen, each FCC has two channels – one runs on an Intel CPU and the other on a Motorola CPU. Each channel has its own software, right down to assembly language. If one channel diverges from the other, the FCC declares itself invalid.

Now comes the hard part. The human pilot must know how to *declare **herself** invalid.*

Whoa! you say. She is flying an airplane. She can't just quit flying the airplane!

You are right, of course, and this is where it gets sticky. If she is part of a two-pilot crew, she can say *You Have Control.* If she is solo, she can engage the autopilot. But sometimes that doesn't work, either. We saw that with the PC-12 out of Reno, where the autopilot disengages in heavy turbulence *by design.*

She is in serious overload and she has spatial disorientation. No backup crew member. No autopilot. As we have seen, her only way out at this point is to fly attitude. Which instrument? *Primary Flight Display* or *Standby Horizon*? That's her *Command Decision.* And she flies **attitude** to the best of her ability. Straight and Level. She breathes. Slow and deep. Until, hopefully, her perceptual horizons broaden and she can do more than fly straight and level. Maybe reverse course.

If that has happened to you, you know what I'm talking about. If it hasn't yet, you may not believe it. You may not be **able** to declare yourself invalid.

> *It can't happen to me. What that accident pilot did? Pilot Error. It couldn't happen to me.*

Pilot confidence is essential, but its definition does not include *it can't happen to me.* Humility will save your life.

•

Learning, not knowledge, is the engine of intelligence.

Or does it mean, as it seems to me, that we must accept the idea that reality is only interaction?

One of my 14-year-old grandsons is, among other things, a coder. He has used the pay version of ChatGPT – subscription GPT-4 – to write code. His opinion is a qualified *meh.*

His father led me to another New Yorker article, about the *Godfather of AI*, Geoffrey Hinton. He was a generation before today's AI developers. His career was the study of *neural networks*. When he retired he bought an island in Georgian Bay and now lives there in the more clement seasons. He is the source of that first quote: *Learning, not knowledge, is the engine of intelligence.*

My friend since kindergarten – who showed me his derivation of *e* and who reads Richard Feynman slowly, like me – is now reading Carlo Rovelli, as I am. Like Feynman Rovelli is a mathematician and physicist, but a generation later. Feynman worked on – or even invented – Quantum Electrodynamics. A generation later, that mathematics may not be well understood, but it is central to much of what we take for granted, starting with transistors. But, says Rovelli, these equations remain mysterious, *for they do not describe what happens to a physical system, but only how a physical system affects another physical system. What does this mean?*

Rovelli's answer is the second quote above. But he immediately points out that that is **his** answer. It may not be right. Or it may be incomplete. There is always doubt. There is always room for more learning.

Or does it mean, as it seems to me, that we must accept the idea that reality is only interaction?

Certainly learning is interaction. Like love, it takes two. And that brings us to another phenomenon predicted by the mathematics of quantum mechanics, the one that Einstein called *spooky action at a distance*: **entanglement**. The idea is that if two particles interact somewhere in time and space, they are forever connected. Perhaps *you* and *I* are like that. Communicating between generations. Re-linking the chain of experience.

•

A memory: I was teaching ground school in an IFR course. I asked the class to imagine a concept – *safe airspace*. We would start with the obvious – minimum safe altitudes in all their VFR and IFR guises, and move on progressively – first to tricks for reducing the load on the poor pilot's brain, and then to images which are more metaphorical but can be a help in assessing risk.

While we are hand-flying an airplane – especially in IMC – we are not too good at arithmetic. So we simplify. Perhaps you plan a descent by using ETAs instead of distances. And you imagine your *safe airspace* shrinking as you burn fuel. And I realize only today what led me to the idea of shrinking airspace as a metaphor for shrinking options – the fatal accident at Heber City, Utah.

On January 2, 2006, a Beech Debonair (straight-tail Bonanza) left Billings, Montana for a VFR flight to Spanish Fork, Utah. The first hour or so was uneventful as the non-instrument-rated pilot followed highways to stay over lower elevation areas in this mountainous terrain. Then the weather started to deteriorate. He descended to stay under the lowering ceilings and followed the I-80 South-Southwest, probably joining it somewhere near Fort Bridger. Flight Following warned him of snow beginning along his route, and he said, *I'll just pick my way along here.* He probably knew the roads well, because he turned left 90° at the intersection with the I-40 to follow it SSE toward Park City. At this point his altitude was less than 300 AGL and the visibility was two miles or less in snow. Perhaps he didn't remember the terrain all that well, because he tried a U-Turn to the right, rather than to the left over the Jordanville Reservoir. To the west, where he turned, the ground rises steeply to a peak at 9363 MSL.

In those years I was still skiing and snowboarding with family. I remember driving back to California from Park City along those highways in bad weather. I guess the image stayed with me. A pilot staying stubbornly with the original intent, flying down a shrinking cone until even the U-Turn option vanished. At that point the only option that remained was to land straight ahead on the I-40 and hope for the best. And hope that he didn't kill anybody on the ground.

•

I might as well tell you about the flight. The flight of my dreams.

It was typical of my recent flying. In my attempt to stay current I file Instrument Flight Rules and fly a round trip to a small airport forty minutes away. That is just enough time to climb to my Bonanza's most efficient altitudes (8000 and 9000 feet) and stay for long enough to use *lean find* on the EDM 830 engine monitor, switch fuel tanks, enter the instrument approach in the Garmin GTN 650 GPS, and practice holding altitude and using track steering. A complete flight profile, doing it – as much as is possible in a changing world – *the same way every time.* Perhaps I record some of each leg on my iPad in ForeFlight for my self-debriefing the next day.

Because there is always something. But this time I make the same mistake on both flights: I forget to set climb power.

The IO-470N engine in the Bonanza is limited to 2625 RPM for takeoff. The prop governor is set to keep that RPM with the throttle and prop controls both full forward. My procedure is to wind the prop back to 2500 RPM after passing the IFR *400 Above Ground Level* mark where you can turn on course. It is a busy time. The gear has just been retracted and the pilot is still thinking *engine failure drill*: attitude down immediately from 10° to – perhaps not the minus 5° you would need with the gear down – but at least to 0° or maybe minus 2°. By 2000 feet that pressure has eased and you have turned on course, and there is time to call Terminal Control and get the IFR clearance. By 3000 feet that is usually done and I am continuing climb to my cleared altitude. That's when my scan picked up the RPM. Two flights in a row. Both flights that day.

It's not that I have ruined the new engine. I haven't. It's not even that big a deal, technically. But it's not procedure. Procedure is to leave full throttle until *Top of Descent*, going oversquare on Manifold Pressure during the initial climb. On that day's flights, by the time I set 2500 RPM at 3000 feet, the full throttle Manifold Pressure is down to 25 inches, so MP and RPM are pretty much square.

A term – RPM – had dropped from my close-in situational awareness space. Like the two small onions. No biggie, perhaps – but a sign. Because the next day's review revealed something more serious.

It's usually only after a night's sleep that a *post mortem* can reveal stress level and let you evaluate how close you came to overload.

It began with the clearance.

On the way back I always file via *ABCDE*, an intersection close to my home airport. The reason is the nearby *Glider Area*, which is quite large and goes up to 7000 feet. My intersection keeps me clear of that area. My re-clearance (on initial contact) was direct *XXXXX* (a 45° left turn) then direct destination. No sweat, I thought, this has happened before. This terminal area, almost adjoining my home terminal area, has climbs and descents going on, so I am a nuisance until I get to 9000 feet. They'll give me direct *ABCDE* when I level off.

But when I did get to cruise, I forgot, and so did the controller. I forgot because I was near saturation. It's not that it was unexpected Instrument Meteorological Conditions – it was more than that. It was like the JFK Jr. situation – at night over Long Island Sound. What he could see looked like the inside of a black sphere covered with a million points of light. There was no way he could distinguish between stars and lights on the ground. There was no way to resolve a horizon. No wonder he got disoriented.

Although you can see something in conditions like this, looking outside is no help at all. Looking out is a dangerous distraction.

Back to today. Smoke from forest fires had concentrated at higher altitudes. Below 5000 feet there had been good Visual Meteorological Conditions. And 8000 feet on this morning's outbound flight had been good, too. But here at 9000 feet there is no horizon. I can see the ground if I look straight down, but that is no help at all in flying the airplane.

So I'm working. Cruise Check. Lean Find. Switch tanks. Don't take your eyes off attitude for more than two seconds, or you'll find yourself in a 20° bank. The Bonanza is like that. A fighter plane in roll. I remember now how – when I was really current and proficient, flying across the continent for the nth time – I would keep her balanced with aileron trim. On those two or three-hour flights it was part of fuel management. Right tank when the analog clock was pointing right, left tank from :30 to on the hour. Aileron trim frequently adjusted. But I didn't think of it until it was almost time to descend. And here I was, almost at *XXXXX*. My clearance direct destination (a 45° right turn) put me right over the Restricted Area. I requested descent. Terminal switched me to Center. Center acknowledged me, and cleared me to 7000 feet. A minute later he came back with *This route really messes with your descent. Contact Terminal 124.65.*

Now I am over higher ground north of my destination. The smoke is still thick. I am in IMC. Or, as I might put it, IMC with visual distractions. The NEXRAD radar on my iPad shows showers between me and my home airport. But Terminal Control – that voice I know well from my airline days – has it all under control. He vectors me 30° left. Oh, good, I think, he is going to get that Restricted Area out from under me and descend me.

He does. As I clear the Restricted Area he gives me progressively lower altitudes and turns to the right until I can go direct destination.

My dream is about this descent with smoke and rain showers. Except in the dream the descent is a physical object, somehow. It is only in that slow emerging into wakefulness after the third night that I definitely connect this object with the descent. It is because of the pleasure I feel. This is something I love to do.

For the last few days one of our teenage grandsons has been visiting. In the dream I am his age, probably because I have been basking in the wondrous reality of the young. I am also basking in the pleasure of this descent object. I feel that it is right to love it, to want to be with it, to want to be there. Like a beer or two after a flight, I think.

But you can't drink and drive. It is my father speaking to me. Lecturing. Explaining. Being practical. I should leave this object alone. Let it go.

Then I realize it is not my father, now long departed. It is I. Me, this old grandfather.

Then I am a teenager again, thanking the old man. You're right, I say. I agree with you.

Then I wake up on the third morning. I know exactly where I am in my own story. I am descending through five thousand feet in smooth air at 180 knots, going through the carwash of a rain shower, direct destination. The NEXRAD shows the feathery edge of the shower has drifted south almost to the airport. The controller lets me down to 2800 feet. *Let me know when you can cancel,* he says.

A couple of minutes later I have the airport in sight. I cancel. The controller tells me there is one aircraft in the circuit. I am in position for the preferred circuit entry: overhead from the inactive side, halfway down the runway. I descend to circuit altitude and slow down to gear and flap speed. I announce myself. I see the traffic – turning base leg, a Cessna 150 I think. I activate the visual approach in the Garmin GTN650. That way I'll have a glideslope as a crosscheck. Abeam the threshold on the downwind leg I extend the gear and do the *Before Landing Check*. I extend flaps to 10° and pull the Manifold Pressure back to 15 inches – the target for descent and approach. The C-150 passes abeam on final. I wait a minute or so and start a turn to base leg, announcing it. I turn final and announce that. I Select Flap Full and pre-trim to about 12° UP. That way I'll be in trim at the flare. Glide-slope good. C-150 has touched down. Looks like he'll make the Delta taxiway. Good. One more gear check at 400 feet. Green and nosewheel tape. Announce short final. C-150 has turned around. Did he miss the Delta? G-ABC going in the Echo, she says, and does so, clearing the runway. I am at the flare. I continue, making sure I don't miss the Delta. I am a bit rattled. As I clear in the Delta, I key the mike and say, *Aircraft in the Echo, thank you.*

Five minutes later, as I bring out the tug to put the airplane in the hangar, a light rain begins. I get a bit damp putting her away.

•

Chris? Are you there?

Yeah. Still here. For the moment, anyway.

I am relieved to hear her voice, feel her presence.

How've you been? I ask.

Huh. I've been having dreams too. For days.

Like a series?

Yeah. Like you. Only I'm on a roller coaster. Know how they climb slowly, then over the top they're free, accelerating so you're almost zero G?

Sure.

I like it, you know. I feel that I'm at the top of my game. That's a good feeling.

Of course. And you are.

And I'm not scared. I'm a pilot, right? This is fun. In a moment I'll be going real fast and start a pullup. Maybe a couple of G's worth. Whee!

Yeah. Sounds good!

But it isn't. Suddenly I am conscious of the longer term. This is a ride. It's going to be over. Not now, maybe. But someday.

It washes over me. What she is feeling. Has felt, maybe, over several nights. It goes from zest to disaster. The bottom drops out.

Just the other day – after my dream series, during hers – there was a light aircraft crash. The pilot was doing circuits, maybe touch and goes. To keep in practice. Maybe there was a tailwind on base, and he overshot the centreline. Maybe he added some rudder to tighten the turn. Then some top aileron so as not to over-bank. Then as the nose dropped he pulled. Classic spin entry. At the break, the nose drops as he rolls inverted. In the few hundred feet left, the rotating aircraft falls almost straight down. The pilot follows the heavy engine through the hangar roof. Making the hole in the roof uses just enough energy so the wings don't follow. Somehow there is no fire. The pilot survives.

I saw that too. Are we still dreaming?

Maybe. It has that dream-like non sequitur.

Huh. The non-sequitur that actually has a sequence. Just not a logical one,

Yeah. What do you think it is?

That it's not the end. Looks like it's gonna be the end, but it isn't. Life goes on.

We keep silence. I have never met her, but we are companionable in peace. Our thoughts are not that far afield from each other.

Chris, I hope you don't mind . . .

Not at all. Go ahead.

When you were getting a bit damp. Putting the Bonanza in the hangar.

OK.

What were you feeling? Right then?

Abashed. Embarrassed. Like a naughty puppy. I should have gone around. It was too close.

And then you had your dream sequence. A three-night debriefing. Maybe you are no longer a naughty puppy.

No.

See, I've been worrying about you. Well, about me, too, obviously. But you – your flight and your reactions – have been gnawing away at me. That's why I had my own dream sequence.

I don't need to say anything. She is thinking it through. The whole day's flying as I described it. And my dreams.

Chris, if I'm getting too . . .

No, not at all. Tell me what you think.

Well, you were not at crisis overload, but you were close.

Definitely.

So maybe you actually did the right thing.

I did?

Yeah. If you're falling, you're going to grab a branch. Hang on to something that's solid, right here and now.

She has taken me back to the moment of the flare. I touch down early, eager to get the weight on the wheels. Not rough, but not pretty, either. I briefly skid a wheel in my eagerness. There will be no trouble making the Delta. Ahead of me, she has cleared in the Echo. I feel rattled. I pull off into the Delta and key the mic. It is my branch. The Delta, not the mic.

Yeah. See, we pilots are pretty good at risk management.

Uh huh. It's what we do.

And we're fast. We decide in a fraction of a second.

Again, I am re-living it. That other option – the long tunnel ahead which is go-around. Eyes out front as I smoothly bring in full power. Strong push with the left arm until I can get that trim from 12° nose-up to about 3°. Strong push with right leg to keep the ball centred against the strong leftward pull of the prop disc at high power and high Angle of Attack. Hoping I don't get a cramp in the leg. Or the arm. Gear. Flaps. Radio. Take a few deep breaths on downwind and do the whole thing again. And don't forget anything.

My point. Risk management. You grabbed the branch. Took the bird in the hand.

Doing a go-around in my state was the riskier option.

Yes.

I realise that I have already come to the same conclusion. But I may have been distracted by the consequences: if the go-around was too risky, maybe I shouldn't be in that position. Again.

•

For the whole book, the entirety of our time together, we have been discussing aircraft accidents and learning. And the difference between learning and training. And my own decisions during my long career.

You sound a bit . . .

Captain?

Yes. You sound a bit sad.

We wait. We are used to it, she and I. Wait for what, I don't know. Perhaps for time to move, and with its magic render the sad, the bad, or the irreconcilable . . .

. . . acceptable, she says aloud.

Yes.

We wait. It is the communion before acceptance. We are in no hurry. I find myself relaxing in my old oak armchair, gazing out the window at wondrous and beautiful Nature as she endures a Montreal winter.

Chris, you're saying goodbye, aren't you?

Uh. Yes. I suppose I am.

We wait. We each have our own imperfect compassion for the sins if the world.

I hope you don't mind my tears.

Emotion washes over me. I welcome it and go with it, like body-surfing a breaking wave.

No, I say. Me, too. They're good for an old man's tear ducts. Healthy. Sometimes I feel that it's cry or die.

I find myself trying to get a picture – not so much of her as her situation. Is she sitting at the kitchen table, like me? Is she looking out the window? If so, maybe she sees the bare branches of hibernating trees, like I do. She's in the same city, after all. Is she real?

Chris, ever wondered why learning has to be so painful?

A gentle breeze comes up, stirring the cedar limbs. A late, lost leaf flutters down from somewhere, crossing my field of vision. I will not fly again. I wish the leaf a safe landing.

§

Epilogue

A Dearth of Skills Here

Learning is still the key. It has to continue. Knowledge has to be passed on. Sadly, there is not enough of that going on in our trade today.

There is plenty of regulation. There is plenty of training. Far too much, some airline executives would say.

23 MAR 2024	SWA 147	KLGA	B737
11 APR 2024	SWA 2786	PHLI (Lihue, Kauai)	MAX-8
19 JUN 2024	SWA 4069	KOKC	B737-800

This trifecta of incidents says otherwise. All of them were, like Waterloo, a damn close thing.

This book has looked carefully into many accidents and some incidents with the hope that we can learn from them. In Chapter Nine I wrote "I could list all the *Pilot Commandments* and proverbs, and elaborate on all the dos and don'ts of our trade, but that's not the right way to go." I still believe that. But this trifecta of incidents, all at the same airline, and each one illustrating the lack of a different essential pilot skill, demands to be considered as a whole:

- SWA 147 came very close to hitting the control tower in LaGuardia in bad weather

- SWA 2786 came very close to hitting the ocean south of Lihue during a missed approach

- SWA 4069 came very close to hitting the town of Yukon northwest of Oklahoma City during a night visual approach to Runway 13 at KOKC in CAVOK conditions

All this happened within a three-month period this Spring

(2024).

Why?

Let's start with clues:

The approach in use at LaGuardia that day was the ILS to runway 04. Here is the notes section for that approach:

NEW YORK, NEW YORK — AL-289 (FAA) — 241

LOC/DME I-LGA 110.5 Chan 42	APP CRS 044°	Rwy Idg 7001 TDZE 21 Apt Elev 21	ILS or LOC RWY LAGUARDIA (LG.

RNP APCH - GPS.

▼ Rwy 4 helicopter visibility reduction below RVR 5000 NA. Inop table does not apply to
△ S-ILS 4 all Cats, S-LOC 4 Cats A and B and WARIN fix minimums Cats A and B.
For inop ALS increase S-ILS 4 all Cats visibility to RVR 4500. Going below glidepath
may not provide obstacle clearance inside DA. Crossing Rwy threshold below charted
TCH may not provide required visual area obstacle clearance. DME from LGA VOR/DME.
Autopilot couple approach NA. Circling NA northwest of Rwy 4 and southwest of Rwy 13.
* RVR 2400 authorized with use of FD or HUD to DA.

MALSR
(A)s

MISSED APPROACH:
Climb to 2000 on LGA
VOR/DME R-043 to
GREKO INT/LGA 5.7
DME and hold, contin
climb-in-hold to 2000.

D-ATIS ARR 125.95 D-ATIS DEP 127.05	NEW YORK APP CON 120.8 263.0	LAGUARDIA TOWER 118.7 263.0	GND CON 121.7 263.0	CLNC DEL 135.2	CPDLC

Notice the fine print. Second-to-last line in the largest box: **Autopilot couple approach NA.** (Flying the approach on autopilot is *Not Authorized.*)

That's for the first incident, the one at LaGuardia in bad weather.

The clue for the second incident, the one at Lihue, is simply the fact that it happened during a missed approach. Remember SkyLink, Fly Dubai, and Atlas Air? Remember United Airlines 1722 at Maui? The latter was not on a missed approach, but **was** doing a full-power takeoff. That also is a clue.

The clue for the third incident, the one at Oklahoma City, is here:

Runway edge lights: medium intensity
RUNWAY 13
Latitude: 35-24.276483N
Longitude: 097-36.954543W
Elevation: 1278.7 ft.
Traffic pattern: right
Runway heading: 131 magnetic, 135 true
Declared distances: TORA:7800 TODA:7800 ASDA:7800 LDA:7800
Markings: nonprecision, in good condition
Visual slope indicator: 4-light PAPI on left (3.00 degrees glide path)
Runway end identifier lights: yes
Touchdown point: yes, no lights

It is perhaps not a direct clue, but it is evidence. The runway SW 4069 intended to land on, Runway 13, had a Visual slope indicator: a 4-light PAPI. Was it not turned on? Did the pilots not ask for it? Or did they only notice the PAPI once all four lights were red?

●

I was an early fan of Southwest Airlines. At the time I was working on the logistical problem of assigning aircraft and crews to flights. I thought: *Genius business plan. One aircraft type. Any crew can operate all aircraft!*

I was also a Boeing fan. I had flown the B-727 and was now a First Officer on the B-767. During an eastbound transcontinental flight we had an engine slowly spool down and overtemp at FL410, so we had to shut it down. The captain – great guy, may he rest in peace – let me continue as PF. So I did a real single-engine landing in Winnipeg. Not only was it fun – the captain taught me by example. He delegated where possible so he could maintain an overview of the entire operation.

Now forty years have somehow slipped by. Some good ideas have aged gracefully. The B-767 copied many good system designs from the DC-9, also a twin. The B-767 was a good airplane. So was the next Boeing clean-sheet design, the B-777, which went into service ten years after my single-engine landing in Winnipeg.

Then things began to come unglued. The B-777 was Boeing's last good airplane design. Or at least the last aircraft launch without loads of problems.

Meanwhile, Boeing and Southwest Airlines had unwittingly become each other's nemeses.

●

In ancient times the gods walked among us. They were not perfect. They bickered with each other as we do. They mingled with us, sometimes to the point of progeny. They played with us, often tipping the scales of our life decisions for their amusement. As if we were the cast of a TV series and they could make writer and director decisions on the fly.

As intimated above, some people were *godlike*. Achilles – and many others – were godlike because they were of mixed blood. Achilles' mother was the sea-nymph Thetis. Because she was a god, she knew her son's fate. That was her tragedy.

You didn't have to be a god to experience that kind of tragedy as a parent. Daedalus was a master craftsman. When he and his son Icarus were imprisoned, Daedalus collected feathers and beeswax. He made wings for them so they could fly away. In his pre-flight briefing, Daedalus was careful to point out that if they flew too low, near the sea, the feathers could get wet and drag them down. If they flew too near the sun, the beeswax could melt.

Icarus immediately loved flying. The experience was so wonderful he forgot that their mission was to escape. The higher he got the more wonderful flying was. Until the wax melted. Then he fell into the sea, leaving only a scattering of feathers. His father was left with that ultimate tragedy: the death of a child.

Narcissus, everyone agreed, was beautiful. But he turned away all suitors. The gods, sensing *hubris* – the sin of overweening pride – caused him to fall in love with his own image in a pond. So passionate was he that he beat his chest purple with frustration at being unable to join the object of his love, and finally died by the pond.

Hubris, defined as *arrogance before the gods*, was countered by *Nemesis*, the goddess of retribution. The process was always in the form *Hubris => Nemesis*. The hubris was brought on by the hero becoming too conscious of his gods-given gifts and thinking those gifts were his property. So the gods brought things into balance with the gift of *nemesis*: always tragic and always related to the gifts of which the perpetrator was so proud.

●

From a pilot's point of view, LaGuardia is one of the most challenging airports in the system. It has two intersecting 7000-foot runways. Two of the runway thresholds are on piers that jut into the East River. From the threshold of Runway 31 you can see the waves of Flushing Bay lapping the rock fill. The threshold of Runway 04 is almost a part of the Grand Central Parkway.

LaGuardia is the opposite of the normal, large acreage airport. Buildings – terminal, control tower, hangars – are very close to the runways. Aircraft speed is very evident. It is like driving at freeway speeds on a downtown street. Once, years ago, after a perfectly normal 130- knot touchdown on Runway 04, an irate passenger waited for us to emerge from the jetway. He yelled at me. I was irresponsible, flying **way** too fast.

The weather awaiting the crew of Southwest 147 on that day in March 2024 was bad in several respects. The visibility was about one mile, variable above and below minimums for the approach. There was a ragged ceiling of about 600 feet. The wind was north at 16 knots. At 40° left of the runway, the wind components were a headwind of 12 knots and a left crosswind of 10 knots.

There was more. A pilot on approach, if he glanced at the top left of his NAV display, might have noticed that his groundspeed (GS) was 10 knots or so greater than his True Air Speed (TAS). There was *windshear*, defined as a change of wind speed and/or direction with altitude. Here, at 2000 feet on approach, he has a tailwind. With the higher groundspeed, he needs a greater rate of descent to stay on the glideslope. So he is using less power than he would when winds are calm. But now things are going to change quite rapidly. At the shear, where the wind changes, there will be a few sharp bumps and the GS will slow by 20 knots. Given the momentum of the airplane, that slowing will take time, but the immediate effect is the indicated airspeed jumps up 20 knots and the aircraft sinks below the glideslope. Pilots call this situation *increasing headwind shear*. What's needed is an immediate increase in thrust, but this is counter-intuitive if you're looking only at the airspeed. There is more. He will drift to the right, because the heading he had been holding is no longer tracking the runway centreline.

No surprise, then, that there were many missed approaches that day. Sometimes flights did go-arounds before reaching minimums.

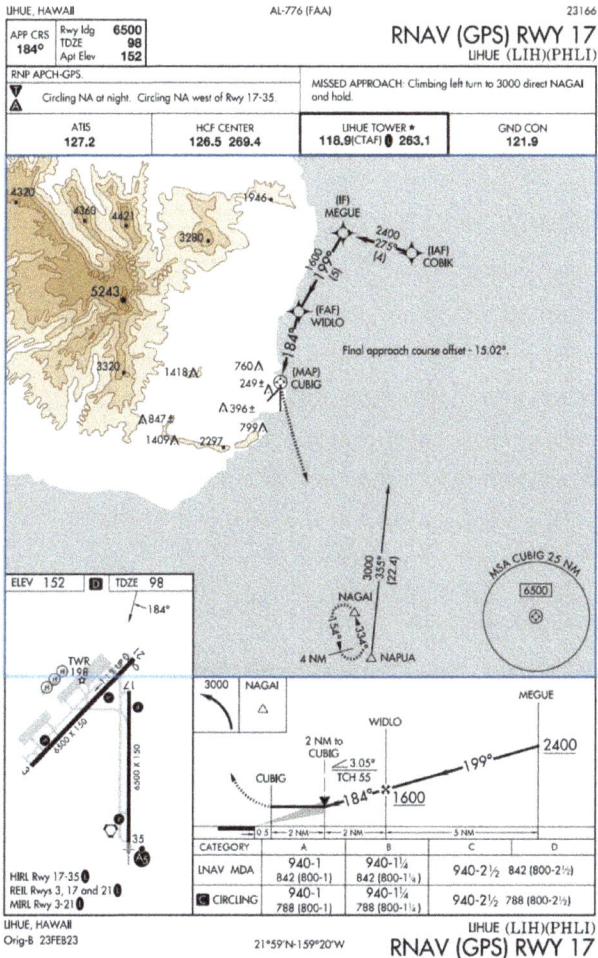

Southwest 2786 was a flight from Honolulu to Lihue, Kauai. At Lihue the visibility was 2½ miles in fog. The wind was 120 at 13 knots. There is high terrain to the west, and a ridge to the south of the airport. Southwest 2786 was flying the RNAV (GPS) RWY 17 approach. The wind components for landing on Runway 17 were an 8-knot headwind and a 10-knot left crosswind. The First Officer was flying.

I am including an image of the Approach Plate for this approach because it clearly shows the terrain of this volcanic island. The approach also (and for that reason) has an offsets on the two final legs. The note (although not in bold typeface on the approach plate) says:

Final approach offset – 15.02°

It is instructive to put ourselves in the pilot's position and imagine what he sees as he nears the minimum altitude two miles from the runway threshold. He doesn't *break out*, because there is no ceiling. There is obscuration and fog. He could see the ocean if he looked straight down. Of course he is looking ahead, looking for a runway. But because of the offset he will have to turn his head 15° left to see the landing runway. And the first runway he will see (if he sees anything) is Runway 21, angling off to his right by 15°.

It is not airline practice to fly visual approaches at night without some sort of glideslope. There are just too many illusions that can lead you astray. Most of the time (as was the case with the runway SW 4069 intended to land on, Runway 13 at Oklahoma City) there is a PAPI (*Precision Approach Path Indicator*). Or there is an IFR approach with a glideslope. If there are parallel runways, the pilot **must** fly the IFR approach to avoid lining up with the wrong runway. Or with a taxiway, as in the very near miss event of Air Canada Flight 759 at San Francisco on July 7, 2017.

If there are none of these aids, it is incumbent on the pilots to calculate a rough glideslope using the one-in-three rule: to maintain a 3° glideslope, be at 1000 feet above ground three miles from the runway.

One of the many illusions awaiting the pilot flying at night is called the "Black Hole". In the classic case the airport itself is the black hole and there are brighter lights beyond, like the lights of a city. To evaluate what the pilots of SW4069 saw, you would have to fly the approach on a clear night in an airplane or a simulator. There are lights underneath them – the lights of the town of Yukon – and there are lights to their left. Ahead, the airport is dark, but beyond it are the lights of South Oklahoma City.

Looking at the RNAV (GPS) RWY 13 approach overlaid on a VFR chart, you can see that the Intermediate Fix (IF) WABUT is over the town of Yukon. This is the position where SW4089 reached its minimum altitude of around 500 AGL. WABUT is 8.7 miles from the runway threshold. Using the one-in-three rule – or the approach plate – a 3° glideslope would require 4000 MSL at WABUT, or 2804 AGL. They were about 2300 feet too low.

•

The Southwest business plan worked. The airline was profitable for 47 consecutive fiscal years, from 1973 to 2019. Southwest also has an impressive safety record. Not one passenger has died in a Southwest aircraft accident. The airline carefully cultivates its image as "fun" and "playful".

Herb Kelleher was the man with the vision. He went his own way, eschewing Robert Crandall's hub and spoke for a point-to-point system. He sought productivity from airplanes and flight crew, mainly by reducing airport turnaround times using various free-seating methods instead of assigned seats.

The company began as an intra-Texas airline, avoiding regulation so it could set prices to undercut competitors. Lawsuits brought by other airlines failed to stop Southwest. The low-price, low-cost strategy caught on, and the young company flourished. When deregulation came along in 1978, the only effect on Southwest was to bless this strategy and free the airline to expand into neighboring states. It did so with alacrity, and grew to become effectively the largest USA domestic airline, by virtue of carrying the largest number of domestic passengers. It also boasted the world's largest fleet of B737 aircraft. Passengers loved the image of the feisty little airline that does better at just about everything and costs less to boot. Big and small at once. Everything to everyone. What could possibly go wrong?

There were signs. In the 1990's Southwest successfully lobbied against high speed rail in Texas. There were accidents. People died. Innocent people on the ground, or passengers who were not declared dead until after arrival at the gate. Nevertheless the carefully cultivated image of the fun, feisty little airline with the perfect safety record persists, even to this day. What could possibly go wrong?

Success. Power. The passage of time.

Herb Kelleher was president and CEO until 2001. By that time Southwest had the world's largest fleet of B737s. Only B737s. The B737 was a generation old. Southwest's business model *required that the fleet be only B737s.* Meanwhile newer airplanes and engines were more fuel-efficient than the older B737 and Southwest's business model required that the fleet be only B737s *so the pilots and flight attendants would not have to train on a newer type.* Boeing was made very aware of this requirement. We want the fuel efficiency, but the new, efficient airplane *must be a B737.* And to meet Southwest's no-training requirement, the new airplane *must be certified on the original 1967 Type Certificate.* A cascade of non-negotiable requirements from Boeing's largest B737 customer. What could possibly go wrong?

In or around June 2011, Boeing decided they would not design a *clean sheet airplane.* Instead their solution would be a new version of the B737 called the B737 MAX. This was partly in response to the Airbus A320 neo, which used the new LEAP engine. Boeing, too, would hang LEAP engines on their old (in Boeing's case *very old*) airframe.

In the execution of this plan, Boeing made a very dangerous and very stupid mistake. Five years after the first crashes, the mistake is still there, covered with layers of band aids.

●

20 July 2024

The good news (if you can call it that) is that the Southwest flight that experienced *dutch roll* back in May had been damaged by a storm while on the ground in New Orleans. So most likely the incident was not related to the troubled history of the B737 rudder hydraulic unit. But there was substantial damage to the rudder, begging the question *Why was this damage not caught on a walkaround check?*

The bad news is there has been another low flying incident where the aircraft got very low on approach and was warned by ATC after their radar gave an alert. Very similar to SWA 4089 in KOKC, but lower. In this one, last Sunday (July 14, 2024) SWA 425 got down to 275 feet above Tampa Bay just inside ZEXYY, the FAF for the KTPA RNAV RWY 10 approach. That point is 4.8 nm from the threshold of runway 10. It is right over the Campbell Causeway.

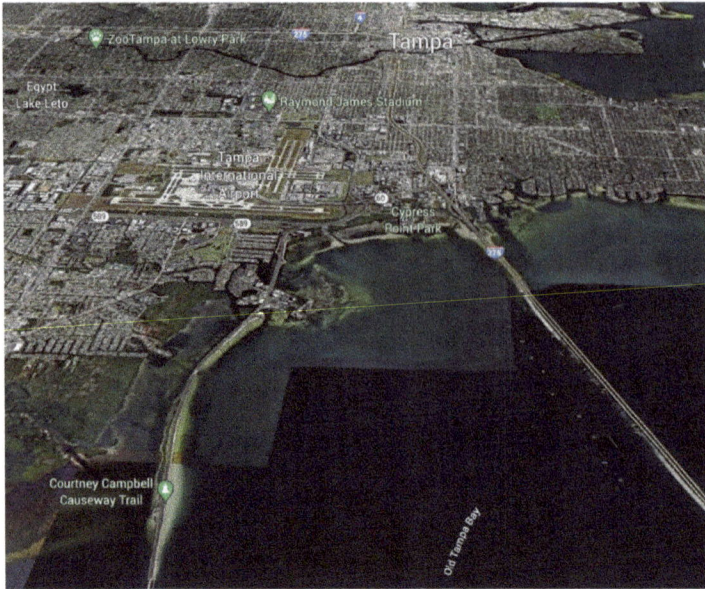

When are pilots likely to be overconfident? It has been a subject for opinion and discussion, but the truth is it can happen to anyone, at any level of experience. That has been one of the themes of this book.

Some time back I wrote a note to myself: *We are never in the clear. It is a fight to the last flight.*

Now I am on the other side of my last command decision. I have taken in my shingle. Sold my airplane. Let my licences and ratings expire. I will no longer live in that world I have known and loved for almost sixty years.

The memories are still there, of course. That is a feature of old age. Today I remembered what a senior captain on the DC-8 said to me in 1979 about flying a descent and approach in bad weather. I still think of him as *Bird of Prey*. He said:

> *When the weather's bad, get down early. Don't fuck around.*

The way I see it now, 45 years later, Bird's definition of bad weather includes a lot more than just low ceilings and visibilities:

- It's midnight and you're tired.

- Have you flown this approach before in good weather?

- How well do you know this pilot you're flying with?

The list of threats goes on. So what did Bird really mean?

Don't hot dog. Get down early and slow down early. Give yourself time to breathe and accomplish one thing at a time in good order. And:

DON'T FLY A VISUAL APPROACH!

It might be worthwhile to listen to the ATC tapes for SWA 4089 at KOKC and SWA 245 at KTPA. Not the tower tapes, but the previous frequency, where they asked for and received an approach clearance, because we are almost certain they were both flying visual approaches. Was that their clearance? Or had they cancelled IFR?

In both cases the tower got a low-altitude alert from their radar system. At Tampa the controller said: *SWA 245, low altitude alert, check your altitude. Tampa altimeter 30.14.* Then, almost a minute later, a hint: *SWA 245, you plan to go around?*

SWA 245 was almost certainly lining up with the Campbell Causeway. Runway 10 was almost certainly obscured by rain showers. Their altitude was certainly as low or lower than the minimum for the RNAV approach. And they're flying a visual?

SWA 4089 was also flying a visual. The crew were tired. It was midnight. Were they also lining up with something that wasn't the runway? Like old Highway 4 out of Yukon? That would explain why they didn't see the PAPI lights. And why they got so low.

●

The McDumbass virus first infected Douglas. The effects were plainly written in the history of a twin-aisle, widebody trimotor. A generation later, the government – perhaps unwittingly – forced the same McDumbass virus onto Boing. The proud series – from the seven-oh to the seven-seven – was at an end.

Where did the McDumbass virus come from?

Adam Smith proposed, described, or perhaps idealized, a system that now has been with us for centuries, long enough for corruption to creep in and multiply in a process similar to myiasis, where maggots feast on living flesh.

Adam Smith spoke of the *invisible hand* of the market, which would balance transactions to the benefit of all participants. But this *invisibility* could also be used to cover corruption. Corrupt actors could put their finger on the scale and say, *"It's just the market"*.

The genus of these market disruptors is not some invisible force. It is humanity. In 1887 Lord Acton wrote, in a letter to his bishop:

> *Power tends to corrupt and absolute power corrupts absolutely.*

Power, in other words, is addictive to human beings. And power and wealth are facets of the same thing. A lot of power, or a lot of money, is never quite enough.

Conman Ican was an early corrupt, adept at what later came to be called the *leveraged buyout*. At one point he owned an international airline. When he was done, the airline was an empty shell, an exoskeleton whose innards had been eaten. But the idea caught on: *the purpose of business is not business, but shareholder(s) profit*. Soon the Famous

Business School was teaching this dogma, and up-and-comers lined up to get their MBAs so they could go out and re-invent the whole gamut of corruption, finding ways to extract wealth from healthy companies.

But how could someone steal wealth from other shareholders in a company? Aren't the shares equal in their trading value?

Well, not anymore. Preferred shares. Non-voting shares. But the real breakthrough was bankruptcy. Spin off divisions and value. Re-organize. Then, when the balance sheet has been shaved of assets, declare bankruptcy. Bingo! The shares are now worthless and no longer a liability.

The techniques have gone through many iterations, and the practitioners are now known as *Vulture Capitalists*. Though the techniques vary, the result is always the same: a healthy company, formed to make something or do something, is slowly stripped of assets, whose value is pocketed by the VC. Then the empty shell is abandoned. But there is collateral damage: the knowledge, skill, and experience that was needed to make something or do something is gone.

Boing is such an empty shell. The progress has been steady since the infection with the McDumbass virus; the waypoints and markers along that road being the peregrinations of the corporate headquarters. First to the Midwest, as *we're only in this for the money* took hold. Then to the shores of the Potomac, as *our real business is lobbying* took over from just making money. The factory floor is now a continent away and institutional memory there has been leached out as engineers leave or retire. It is an empty shell.

•

Boypilot was not a test pilot. Boypilot was not an engineer. But Boy-pilot was an important link with the regulator who was going to allow the airplane to fly. Boypilot was also a drinker, which is not surprising given the position in which he found himself.

The airplane was certified by the regulator, and cleared to fly with the stupid mistake on board. Moreover, because of Boypilot's ministrations, there was no simulator training required on the new variant, and there was no mention, anywhere, that the stupid mistake was on board. The customer pilots who flew the airplane had been duped. Boypilot left Boing to go fly for one of its airline customers.

Then there were two crashes. Three hundred-forty six people died. Since the crashes did not happen in North America, much was made of the fact that the pilots were – well, not American. But the fact that the American regulators did not have primary access to the recorders and their data also meant that those data became and remained available. So we know exactly what happened. The stupid mistake acted, in each case running the horizontal stabilizer to full nose-down. For many, many reasons well-known in the history of aviation, this condition is not recoverable from low altitude, no matter what was said about *pilot error*.

The airplane was grounded world-wide for twenty-two months. There was finally a *fix*, and the airplane flew again. But the *fix* was a fix. Regulators felt duped, because they had been. Each weighed in with complicated conditions. In the end, though, the stupid mistake was still there. Except now it had a diaper and a pacifier.

Unsurprisingly, regulators were pissed off. They had been well and truly had, and they knew it. First they went after Boypilot, charging him with four counts of wire fraud. Despite the evidence, he was acquitted, amid accusations of *scapegoating*.

So the United States of America, by and through the Department of Justice, Criminal Division, Fraud Section, took their evidence to the Empty Shell, which hereby submits and enters into this plea agreement . . .

The very dangerous and very stupid mistake is still there. The spin has evolved through *pilot error*, the *fix*, and *scapegoating*, and finally to a de facto admission of guilt. But only of fraud. There is no mention of the stupid mistake.

It's not over yet. The Empty Shell also has problems with its obligations in Project Artemis, the effort to again put men on the moon. The government agency which achieved that in the late 1960's has bet everything on the Empty Shell.

You mean NASA.

What?

I'm so glad you gave us the links!

I am startled. I have been thinking about NASA's future, because NASA/Boeing has just successfully landed an empty Starliner in New Mexico.

Um, links?

Yeah. I read that part you edited out. I wanted more. You put the links in the glossary. Thank you!

Captain?

Yeah.

I am struck dumb. There is an awkward pause.

I exist, you know.

Yes . . . of course . . . I . . .

Just because we said goodbye, and I cried . . .

Yes. It was hard . . .

. . . and you doubted. Even though you cried, too. You asked yourself, *is she real?*

I don't know what to say. My own sense of loss washes over me. For my vocation, my trade. For my airplane, now sold. For Captain. For my belief in her, maybe not lost. In any faith, there is doubt . . .

Exactly. So can we get on with it, for fuck's sake?

I laugh. It's like the old days.

I'll take that as a yes. So . . . first I read your factual account, now deleted. It ends in mid-thought. So I went to the plea agreement. It wasn't hard to find, but thanks for the link. I read all of Attachment A-2, the *Statement of Facts*.

Yes. It's all there. Or most of it.

Huh. There's more. A lot more. It's in the UK 737 post. Thanks for that link. I never would have found it.

I found it because . . . I got curious about the fix. How it got flying again after twenty-two months. I think . . . well, until then I really didn't want to know . . .

Yeah, I can see why you deleted that version and didn't research the fix. You didn't want to know. You probably **still** don't want to know.

I feel a swirling sensation. She has got me in the gut. Nailed it.

OK, she continues. For example. In the so-called *fix*. Now we use two AoA vanes. Duh. But there's all this stuff!

Stuff?

Yeah. In the so-called *fix*. *Split Vane Monitor. Mid Value Select*. And there will be a hypothetical *Future 3rd Synthetic AoA Source*, whatever that means.

Uh huh. Don't hold your breath.

Yeah – and take Sully and the Canada Geese. *Both* engines spool down. In seconds. What's to say a large flock of small birds doesn't take out *both* AoA vanes? And if they do, *both* vanes will send max *AoA* signals. We know that from Ethiopian 302.

Right.

So *Split Vane Monitor. Mid Value Select. Cross FCC Monitor*. All useless.

Yes.

You don't want to know. *The diaper and the pacifier.*

I sigh.

No – I liked that! The shit's still there, but he's not crying. And by the way, I'm sure you'll agree those FCCs are not Flight Control Computers.

Well, they can call them that. But I'm pretty sure they're not C*U.

She laughs. We are peaceful together, like before. It is lovely.

Sooo . . . Chris . . . LaGuardia . . .

I sigh. Yeah.

Any idea *why* ILS 04 can't be flown on autopilot?

Well, apparently, the signal is a bit wavy. Not sure if it's localizer or glideslope or both. Maybe a consequence of so many structures close to the antennas. Not to mention vehicles zipping by under the approach lights on Grand Central Parkway. So – flown by hand, the human pilot wouldn't struggle to follow each little wave. In theory. Provided the frequency of the wave was such that the pilot's perception could be aware it was a wave.

Whew!

I wait. She is thinking about the weather. And the shear.

OK, Chris. You set it up well. The shear, and the consequences. Everybody was having a hard time. There were lots of go-arounds.

Yes. It was a challenge. In many respects.

Yeah. At the shear, if you don't get the power up right away, you're gonna scare the crap out of yourself.

Yup.

And if you're just watching airspeed, you're *not* going to push the power up.

No.

She's thinking again. Second approach. Airplane gets *way* low. Below minimums. And *way* off to the right. The localizer deviation is off-scale.Chris, they were exactly where they would be if the Pilot Flying did exactly nothing.

I react, but non-verbally. Maybe a snort. She sighs.

Maybe the guy just can't hand-fly an ILS?

Yes. Sure looks like it. But we don't know everything. Were they using the autopilot? If so, was it coupled to the ILS? What were they saying to each other during those two approaches?

But we know a bit more about number two incident, don't we? Lihue, Kauai?

We do. But it's by chance. A leaked internal memo at Southwest. That's how we know the First Officer was flying, and that he did the go-around and got distracted setting the power. Didn't want to overboost.

So we're pretty sure it was another Somatogravic Illusion. Where attitude awareness is lost because of worry about something much less consequential. Flap overspeed. Engine overboost.

Yup. Well put. There have been too many of those.

An unintended consequence of the airline's parameter exceedance monitoring.

Absolutely.

Huh. And numbers three and five. How do you explain those? Hot boy-pilot thinks it's cool to hot-dog? Do the world's quickest approach? Get this sucker on the ground *now* and make for a fast turnaround?

For a moment I struggle with how to apply her analysis to number five in Tampa.

Uh, yeah. I can see getting sucked in by what you see, or think you see, in Okie City. With Tampa you're probably in a rain shower and you're flying level along the causeway at minimums or lower. You haven't landed on it, though. Maybe you have some doubt. But you fly like that for fifty seconds – fifty seconds! – and even then it's ATC who says *you planning to go around*? Like it's '*just a suggestion . . .*'

Boy-pilot is not really open to changing his mind.

True enough. Almost a minute of causeway cruising.

Chris, we've talked about this. About making that split-second decision. When threats appear. When suddenly all is not what it seemed to be. It's a pilot thing.

A pilot thing notably lacking in both these cases. ATC has to get in there and save them from themselves.

She sighs. She's moving on.

Number four. Portland. I'd give them a let on not being aware that the runway was NOTAMed closed.

 Oh, me too. For years I have been ignoring the FAA and Nav Canada, where you have to pick out the needle in the haystack. I have been using ForeFlight, where NOTAMs are presented in some order of relevance . . .

Maybe they were distracted by being able to talk to Boston Center on the ground in Portland. It's always a plus to discover those airports . . .

Sure. But you said distracted. Is that really an excuse? I mean, just because the tower is closed – I think they knew that much – doesn't mean it's not a Mandatory Frequency. I mean, there were other aircraft movements on the ground. They obviously hadn't heard anything on the MF.

I can feel her chest tightening. I think of a legendary DC-8 captain, now departed, who was of Basque origin. *I can't help it*, he would say. *Some things just make my blood boil*. This Captain, in the here and now, is working up to a rant.

And the one you haven't given a number to. The *Dutch Roll* in cruise.

OK . . .

So a tornado rolls through New Orleans overnight. The airplane is parked at the gate. In the morning, it is still parked at the gate. Anyone do a walkaround? Anyone think that might be important because there could well have been 100 mph gusts?

I don't know what to say. I also hate to interrupt a good rant.

And sure, you're not going to see the damage to the backup rudder servo mechanism. But the rudder skin is wrinkled, right? A flight control surface with wrinkles. What the fuck?

I take a breath. I think she does, too. There is something liberating about that peaceful moment after a rant. That breath of air. We've seen what we're going to see. We're still here.

She takes another long breath.

Chris, you know what just came to me?

Uh . . .

It's a thought. Tell me what you think.

OK . . .

Maybe we're not going to learn any more. About any of these.

Yeah . . .

No DFDR, no CVR, and especially no parameter exceedances.

Yes . . .

Because as you say in the glossary, these latter are the property of the airline, and can be made to go away.

There. She said it. Our work is done, at least for now. I find myself in that curious state which occasionally visits me in my old age: peace with doubt mixed in. Will I even still be around when *what we think we know* goes through yet another upheaval?

Chris?

Sorry. I'm here.

And?

I have nothing to add. I believe you're right. There won't be any final reports. But tell me about you. You still on the Bus?

I'm on course.

Oh, neat! Tell! You still gonna do line indoc? Do you know?

Yeah. They asked me to go on the MAX. More money.

And?

I respectfully declined.

Oh, OK . . .

So they asked me if I'd do line indoc on the A220. Same money. I said sure.

Wow! Good for you!

So I guess I'm going to see if I like C*U.

You're gonna love it. It's a good airplane. I'm jealous. I can't wait to hear what you think.

Hah! You will. Count on it.

I look out the window. It has been warm for September. Beautiful days like we used to have in Summer. Except the horse chestnut leaves are turning brown as the trees shut down photosynthesis for the year. The world of green is mostly still here, but it is not a June green or even an August green.

OK, I get it. You're done. Fair enough. But don't say goodbye.

You're not gone yet, and *what we think we know*, as you like to say, is still a moving target. All this shit is still worth thinking about. I'm still thinking about it and I know you are too.

Yeah. I sigh.

Our understanding is still in flux. For example, Colgan. With those six-bladed props in fine pitch, they were decelerating like crazy. Somatogravic, but the reverse: it would feel like the nose was dropping. Another reason he wanted to pull.

Yes!

And AF447 was ballistic. Zero G. It would feel like the bottom was dropping out, because it was.

You're right. At least while they're still ballistic. Before they get to terminal velocity.

Huh. Terminal!

'Fraid so.

And no stall warning?

No. They got it briefly again when the left-seat pilot took control and used nose-down sidestick to get the AoA briefly to less than 47°.

That scared them. And 47° is the cutoff.

Yes. From somewhere around 15° to 47° is the stall warning range.

'Cause the AoA could never possibly be more than that.

Right.

And there are no AoA indicators.

No. As you know. Not direct indicators, anyway.

The quiet is better than *the German* saying STALL STALL STALL.

They didn't try another recovery.

Shit, Chris. There they are in their closed Einsteinian box. At one G. Everything feels normal. Or almost. But I said quiet . . . I bet it sounded different. Unusual. Like something you never heard before.

Yeah. The airflow is vertical, not longitudinal. Different white noise.

So how much time did they have left?

Oh, I'd have to check. Maybe two minutes.

Maybe enough time. Maybe. So – what's the recovery?

Get the FD's off.

So you can clearly see attitude.

Yes. Then power to idle.

Helps get the nose down . . .

Yes. Then call up the Flight Controls page on ECAM.

So you can see the position of the stabilizer. Or – excuse me – *le plan horizontal.*

Oui. Exactement. Then use the big wheels. Roll them forward until the stab is in the green band.

Wait for a decent airspeed and pull out.

We are quiet for a minute, thinking about those pilots – and those passengers – in their elevator with the cables cut.

But they don't pull out. Didn't they call for the captain to came back to the flight deck?

Yes. But by the time he got there they were falling through 10,000 feet.

Shit. Too late.

Yes. And if you look at the CVR transcript, I think you'd say that at that point the captain knew.

I feel like we're looking each other in the eye. Maybe we are, in some way. I know we are in the same space. On that flight deck, with those three pilots. In those last seconds before we hit the water.

Captain. I won't doubt her again.

§

Glossary

ACARS   Aircraft Communications Addressing and Reporting System. (CH. 9 p.230)

ADF   Automatic Direction Finder.   LF (Low Frequency) avionics system with both rod and loop antennas. The cockpit indicator points at the station. Superimposed on a slaved compass, it gives a bearing to the station. That setup is called an RMI – Radio Magnetic Indicator. You can also use the ADF to listen to AM radio.

ADIRU   Air Data Inertial Reference Unit.   These are IRS units that also contain an AHRS unit. In the initial A320 installation the IRS position was updated by DME/DME, or VOR/DME. As VORs and TACANs were retired, inertial update was handed over to GPS. See **AHRS**.

ADS-B   *Automatic Dependent Surveillance – Broadcast* is the latest version of what began in World War II as *IFF – Identification – Friend or Foe*. IFF was the first *transponder*, a piece of avionics which adds function to *primary radar*. The latter bounces a signal off the airframe and reads the energy that bounces back, and with a rotating antenna positions the target in both *azimuth* (direction) and distance. IFF was the first so- called *secondary radar*. It listens for queries from the ground and transmits replies, which can contain the coded identity of the aircraft. Later (1960's) the reply contained a 4-digit octal code, which could be set by the pilot at a controller's request. In the 1970's the aircraft's altitude was added to the reply, greatly facilitating the work of both controller and pilot. With the arrival of *inertial navigation* and *GPS*, the aircraft knows more about itself than the controller does: viz. position, altitude, and the *Flight Path Vector*. This begs the question: *why not just ask the aircraft for that information?* In a word, it has the potential to render primary radar obsolete.

AERODYNAMIC CEILING   Like *Service Ceiling, Aerodynamic Ceiling* (AKA **Coffin Corner**) is determined by *Density Altitude*. But the limitation is not necessarily available thrust. Rather, it is an aerodynamic limitation of the wing. As altitude increases, the *Stall* Speed in Indicated (*Calibrated, to be precise) Airspeed* stays the same but the speed of sound decreases. Meanwhile the limiting *Mach Numbers* for the airplane remain the same. If you are climbing and watching the numbers on the airspeed tape on the *Primary Flight Display*, you will see M_{MO} (*Mach Max Operating*) sliding down toward V_S (*Stall Speed*) until they become the same. (By the way, this is not recommended. See AF447. The airplane is outside its *Flight Envelope*. It is no longer flying. That's why it's known as **Coffin Corner**.)

AGL   Above Ground Level

A/H   Artificial Horizon.   This is the instrument that makes instrument flying possible. At its heart us a gyro with a vertical axis. Change in pitch or roll is resisted by the gyro, so as the airplane banks or pitches the gyro's axis stays vertical. Gyros *precess* for many reasons (see **Precession**), the simplest being friction in the gyro's bearings. We'll look at the vacuum-driven A/H that was ubiquitous in the era before glass and MEMs. (see **Glass** and **MEMs**). Precession is corrected by an ingenious set of vanes which produce jets of air which nudge the gyro's axis. The direction of the jets is 90° (in the direction of spin) before the direction of the desired nudge. Over time, the gyro will erect to the G Vector. (see **G Vector**). How *completely nuts* is it to put your faith in such an instrument? If you fly in circles long enough, it will show that you're straight and level! So it is a matter of faith. Believe in the instrument, because there will be times when there is nothing else. At those moments it is *believe or die*. Did I mention that instrument flying is exciting? See also **Malcolm Horizon.**

AHRS   Attitude and Heading Reference System. (p.51) This term came into use with IRS systems. With IRS the aircraft's attitude and inertial parameters are known. By adding the traditional pitot/static parameters, Angle of Attack, and heading, a complete set of flight parameters is made available. See **ADIRU.**

ALT* (ALT STAR) Airbus altitude capture mode. (See discussions Ch. 6 p. 166-169, 173, Ch. 7 p. 194-200)

ALTERNATE LAW   Fly-by-Wire system operating law reverted to after some sensor failure(s). No Flight Envelope Protection.

ALTIMETER SETTING   The value of Mean Sea Level Pressure can be set in the small window of a barometric altimeter. The units are millibars or inches of mercury. This in known as **QNH**. (See **Q Codes**)

ATIS   Automatic Terminal Information Service. Broadcast as a tape loop on a dedicated frequency, ATIS is a verbal reading of the latest weather and airport conditions. In the present day ATIS usually also available via ACARS.

AUTOPILOT   **1. Gyros**   The autopilot was invented in 1914 by Lawrence Burst Sperry, using gyro instruments. His father, Elmer Ambrose Sperry, had invented the true-north-seeking gyro compass in time for use on navy ships in World War One. As we saw talking about Richard Feynman, gyros are a perplexing phenomenon. In 1910 Elmer Ambrose was truly ahead of is time. His gyro compass used the rotation of the earth to align to True North, just as a strap-down ruby laser IRS (1982) does today during its alignment phase. Gyros don't like having their spin axis change. They resist. And if forced, they react in a very non-intuitive way. Piece of cake, mathematically, at least according to Richard Feynman. You merely assume *Preservation of Angular Momentum* and do the math. If that is not an option for you, imagine that the force changing the spin axis is applied to a certain point on the rim of the spinning gyro disc. The gyro axis will change alignment, *but as if the force were applied 90° or pi/2 radians later in the rotation.* Of course this too is imaginary, because the force is not applied to a point on the disc. The disc is spinning at high speed. Instead the force is applied to the gimbal in which the gyro spins. How does this happen? What would apply such a force? Well, the student in my ground school course would twist the bicycle wheel and feel the squirrely response. And there is also a change in the orientation of the axis – called *precession* – caused by the drag in the bearings supporting the spinning gyro. Again a piece of cake for Feynman – he does the math. But what else could cause precession, seemingly out of the blue? It was the genius of the senior Sperry – Elmer Ambrose – to see that this is *frame of reference* problem. The gyro is of the Earth – somewhere on the surface, in the case of a ship. But Earth is also spinning. And depending on the gyro's orientation relative to Earth's spin axis, there is a component of this precession-causing force which is dependent on *latitude*. I know. Whew! Sometimes a *reductio ad absurdum* can help. Imagine a gyro with a vertical spin axis at the True North or True South Pole. At Earth's spin axis, in other words.

They have the same spin axis, so there will be no precession.

All *Frame of Reference* problems can be truly perplexing, as we saw (starting on p. 20) with the *Coriolis Effect*. And that is why Einstein employed the *thought experiment* technique.

AUTOPILOT   2. First Autopilot   But back to Lawrence Burst Sperry and his autopilot. He used a vertical-axis gyro to sense attitude – the *Artificial Horizon* – and a horizontal-axis gyro to sense change of direction – *Turn and Slip*, or *Needle and Ball*. Lawrence is credited with the invention of the *Artificial Horizon*, and his father the *Turn and Slip*. But father already had many inventions to his credit, including a gyro stabilization system for ships (1911) and a much smaller and lighter system for aircraft (1913) which was the basis for his son's autopilot (1914). So in reality they were a team, son building on father's achievements and implementing them in aviation. By the 1960's most autopilots used a single gyro where the gimbal axis was about 30° from horizontal, so it sensed change of direction but also reacted to movement in roll. This was the *Turn Co-ordinator*. Its information could drive a *Wing Leveller*. With the wings level, the airplane will hold a *heading*. To that you can add a *Turn Knob* to command turns. And if you have a *heading bug* on your directional gyro, it can be used to command turns to a heading. A simple vertical system can be made with just a small pressure-sensing bellows which commands small pitch changes to hold altitude. From that you can build a vertical speed command – see the Sperry SP-50 on the DC-9 (p. 105). Yes – still called Sperry, although Lawrence Burst tragically died on December 13, 1923 in a crash into the English Channel on a foggy day. He was not quite thirty years old.

AUTOPILOT   3. Auto – *Pilot?*   Do autopilots know how to fly? No. They do not. They are ingenious tools which can be used to reduce a pilot's workload. But their successful use depends on two conditions, both of which involve the human pilot:

1)   She must know how to fly.
2)   She must understand how her autopilot works. In great detail.

A recent accident is a case in point. What? Another accident? *In the Glossary?* Yes. A young woman gets her Private Pilot Licence in a Cherokee. Then she buys a high-performance single. It is a Debonair – the straight-tail version of the Bonanza. It is from the early 1960's, like my Bonanza. Like mine, it has an Aspen PFD. But unlike mine, it has an autopilot. She becomes focussed on learning how to use the autopilot. She documents her progress with 3-camera videos which she posts on YouTube. We can be grateful to her for that because she has left a trail for us to follow – like DFDR and CVR and ADS-B-Out, but better. We see an instructor who is not helping her. He spends his time punching autopilot buttons for her and looking at his phone. He does not see that she does not understand basics like pitch and power.

P+P=PP *(first seen on p.62)*

She changes instructors. The new guy tries to return to basics, but she has become obsessed with trying to learn how the autopilot works. It is the wrong approach. She has no chance of understanding her autopilot if she does not know how to fly. She does not understand P+P=PP, and that is very evident in the videos. But she has her Private Pilot Licence! Doesn't that mean she knows how to fly? Well, obviously not. We have the data. It is unfortunate, but true. She does not know how to fly. In the tragic final flight – documented by ADS-B-Out – she kills herself and her non-pilot father in (most likely) an out-of-trim dive into the ground at 213 knots – well above V_{NE}. The real tragedy? She has not understood that her job as a licensed pilot is survival, and that no autopilot is ever going to do that for her.

ASRS Aviation Safety Reporting System. This is ostensibly an anonymous, voluntary reporting system for flight crew and others to use to share data on threat events, AKA close calls. However, airlines can intercept data bound for the DFDR and transmit that data in real time – via Satellite ACARS, Inmarsat, or Iridium, via another shared link such as those used for inflight entertainment or electronic flight bag for the pilots – or can access the data on the ground via a Quick Access Recorder. In all cases the data can be processed within 24 hours and searched for parameter exceedances as part of the airline's Flight Operational Quality Assurance program. United Airlines **did** share the data flagged on UAL 1722 at Maui when so requested by the NTSB. They **did** redact the pilots' identities. Note, however, that a) the pilots' identities are known to the airline and b) the data itself is controlled by the airline and can be made to disappear.

A/T   AutoThrust.   This is the part of automated flight which handles the throttles or thrust levers. It is also the least understood. Pilots are especially vulnerable to misunderstanding when they change types from Boeing to Airbus or vice-versa, because there is no commonality of design or even lexicon between manufacturers. There have been many accidents and incidents where ignorance of autothrust status is a factor, even though that status is displayed on the FMA.

BIRD   The "**Bird**" is the symbol on a *Primary Flight Display* or a *Heads-Up Display* depicting the *Flight Path Vector*. The latter is *where the airplane is going relative to the surface of the earth*. It is a stylised aircraft as seen from behind – a circle with stubby wings and a vertical tail.

Black Hole   One of many **Visual Illusions** likely in night flying causing the pilot to think he is too high. Captain "Ike" Jones taught me about that (and many other things) in my first year on the line in the DC-9. Bless him. May he rest in peace. This particular illusion (you think you're high) happens when there is a 'black hole', an area without lights, with perhaps city lights beyond. An airport at night, with its subdued lighting, is a classic black hole. The bottom line, as Ike said, is "look here b'y – at night, if there's no glideslope, make yer own. Always. Use 1000 AGL is 3 miles".

Braided Steel Cables   There is some poetic licence here. This is my name for the steel control cables ubiquitous in aircraft before fly-by-wire became the norm. They are all compound cables, composed of wires making up strands which are wound in a helix about a central strand. For example, the 7 by 19 cable consists of six strands of metal wire laid around a center strand in a clockwise direction. The wires composing the seven individual strands are laid around a center wire in two layers. The center core strand consists of a layer of six wires laid around the central wire in a clockwise direction and a layer of 12 wires laid around this in a clockwise direction. Did you really want to know all that?

C*   Control Law for *Fly by Wire* aircraft. (ref: *A New Lon-*

gitudinal Handling Qualities Criterion, presented at the May, 1966 Aerospace Electronics Conference in Dayton, Ohio.)

C*U   Control Law for *Fly by Wire* aircraft. A recent article on both **C*** and **C*U** can be found at *https://www.engineeringpilot. com/post/2018/10/15/c-an-unknown-star*.

CAVOK   Ceiling And Visibility **OK**.   Informal term for *no low cloud and no reduced visibility*. Close synonym for **VMC**. Also **CAVU** for Ceiling And Visibility Unlimited; and **FABO** in Quebec for **Fait Beau**.

CEILING   The highest *Density Altitude* an airplane can (safely) reach.

C of G   Center of **G**ravity (also **C/G**). The picture I like best is a large man and a small woman sitting on a seesaw. The heavy man is sitting closer to the pivot point than the lighter woman, so the seesaw remains balanced. As a wit in one of my classes observed, they are "sharing a moment". The *moment* – the torque around the pivot point – is expressed as weight times length of moment arm. The units are inch/pounds or metre/kilograms. Most aircraft achieve stability in pitch by placing the Center of Gravity just forward of the Center of Lift. This creates a nose-down moment about the lateral axis of the aircraft (think of that as a line from wingtip to wingtip). That moment is counteracted by the horizontal tail surfaces, which produce a downforce. They *fly upside down*, so to speak.

C of G RANGE   Center of Gravity **Range**. (also **C/G Range**).

C of L   Center of Lift. (also **C/L**)

Coffin Corner   See **AERODYNAMIC CEILING**

CVR   Cockpit Voice Recorder.

DENSITY ALTITUDE   *Density Altitude* is *Pressure Altitude* corrected for temperature. The (slightly simplified) equation for air density is:

$$Density = Pressure/Temperature$$

In turn, the definition of *density* is:

$$Density = Mass/Volume$$

But Earth's atmosphere is a mix of gases held to the planet by gravity. There is no fixed volume. So what we learned in high school about Boyle's Law and Charles' Law does not exactly apply (p. 37). The bottom line is both equations are true, but wing and engine performance depend on how close together the gas molecules are at a given point in the atmosphere. So *Density Altitude* is used in many performance calculations. See also **WAT**.

DIRECT LAW   Fly-by-Wire system direct operating law. No Flight Envelope Protection. Control surface movement corresponds directly to sidestick deflection. This is the most degraded mode. The airplane handles, according to some, like a wet fish.

DME   Distance Measuring Equipment. (p. 34) This is an avionics unit which measures the distance to a ground station with a query/response on **UHF**. It is called a **Slant Range**, because directly over the ground station it will read altitude (**AGL**) in **Nautical Miles**.

DUTCH ROLL   All swept-wing aircraft are subject to Dutch Roll, which is an instability where yaw and roll are linked. This is known as *oscillatory instability*. As altitude increases, Dutch Roll becomes more likely. Jet transports have full-time yaw dampers to counter this instability.

EYEBALL BOUNCE   It has been pointed out to me that the analogy between the rotational accelerometers in our middle ear and the ring laser gyros on IRS systems is not an exact one. Unlike the rotational accelerometers in IRS systems, the semicircular canals are **very heavily damped** by both the viscous liquid therein and the very tiny diameter of the canals. In fact, their purpose may be quite different from that of the rotational accelerometers in IRS systems. Research has shown that the canals have a linear output between 0.1 and 5 hertz, and that most likely our perception uses this information to stabilize the image on our retina.

ENVELOPE PROTECTION   See **FLIGHT ENVELOPE PROTECTION**

Equilibrium   In unaccelerated flight. The aircraft is not turning, and Lift = Aircraft Weight and Thrust = Drag.

FAF   Final Approach Fix. (p. 14)

FCU   Flight Control Unit. (p. 20)

FD   Flight Director.   Indication on the Primary Flight Display which shows what the autopilot is commanding (or would command if engaged).

FLIGHT ENVELOPE   The range of airspeeds and G loadings where the airplane is within its design limits and the wing is not stalled. In other words, it is still flying.

FLIGHT ENVELOPE PROTECTION   The basic strategy for staying within the Flight Envelope is having a pilot. Having, by design, positive aerodynamic static and dynamic stability in all axes makes the pilot's job easier. Fly-by-wire aircraft have the option of ignoring aerodynamic stability and achieving an acceptable controllability through software. Some early fighter planes took this route. C* airplanes (Airbus) do not have aerodynamic speed (AoA) stability and so require Flight Envelope Protection. C*U airplanes (B777 and A220) have AoA stability through software but still have Flight Envelope Protection for other reasons. None of this – as we have seen – is an absolute guarantee of safety.

FLIGHT LEVELS   FL350=**Flight Level Three-Fife-Zero**. For takeoff and landing, the barometric altimeter is set to the *altimeter setting* for the airport. This is so the altimeter will read the *field elevation* above *Mean Sea Level* when the airplane is on the ground. The code for this is **QNH**. At higher altitude and at jet speeds it would be impractical to change the altimeter setting every fifteen minutes, so instead we set the altimeter to 29.92 inches, or 1013.2 millibars, which is the pressure at *Mean Sea Level* in a *Standard Atmosphere*. This is called **QNE**. We are following a pressure gradient as we fly across the country, and because we all use the same reference pressure we maintain vertical separation from each other. Simple, huh?

FMA	Flight Mode Annunciator.	The information is presented in a strip across the top of the Primary Flight Display.

FPM	Feet per Minute, usually in reference to Vertical Speed.

FPV	Flight Path Vector. (pp. 21,22). The term itself is redundant, but what it describes is so important that it doesn't matter. The FPV is the airplane's velocity *in reference to Earth*. It where and how fast the airplane is going in 3-D (the flight path). The FPV is important because is the pilot's job to visualize that invisible arrow. Not a simple task.

G Vector	The direction (and strength) of local gravity. Sitting in your kitchen chair, or in a parked airplane or a flying airplane that is in equilibrium, you experience one G and its direction is vertical. Other times in an airplane, local G can be more or less than one and may ***not be vertical with respect to either Earth or the airplane***. Hard to understand? You bet.

Gates, Dominic	Aviation reporter for the Seattle Times. He has been exemplary in his accurate and detailed coverage.

Glass	Refers to cockpit displays that use an electronic screen to display aircraft parameters.

GPS	Global Positioning System. (p. 22)

GPS Accuracy Prediction   A GPS avionics unit calculates its spherical error with each position, about once per second. Using the number and geometry of the satellites it is using, it also predicts what the accuracy ***will be*** for the next 90 seconds. This is to establish a very high confidence that the accuracy will remain within spec for the approach, from the FAF to Minimums. See **GPS Lockout**.

GPS Lockout	If the **GPS Accuracy Prediction** is not within the specification for the approach in use, that approach will be *locked out*. The approach will disappear from the **PFD** and be replaced by an error message.

Horizon   Plane tangent to the surface of the Earth.

HUD   A Heads-Up Display (p. 14) is a *Primary Flight Display* projected onto the windshield and focussed on infinity. The pilot can look out the windshield and see the flight parameters and symbols (including "**the Bird**") superimposed on the real world outside. This is particularly useful during an instrument approach, where the pilot can fly the bird onto the runway symbol. As visual ground contact is made, the pilot does not have to *look up*, because he is already doing so. He will see the real runway emerging under its symbol.

ICAO   International Civil Aviation Organization.

ILS   Instrument Landing System.

IMC   Instrument Meteorological Conditions (p.30). See also   **VMC**

INS   Inertial Navigation System. (p. 23)

IRS   Inertial Reference System. (p. 23)

ISA   International Standard Atmosphere. At Mean Sea Level in a standard atmosphere, the pressure is 29.92 inches of mercury, or 1013.2 millibars . The temperature is 15° Celsius.

The "**Leans**"   Pilot disorientation caused by the middle ear accelerometers. (The vestibular system). .

LF   Low Frequency.

LOC   Localizer.

Local G   What the pilot (or passenger) feels. In an aircraft in **equilibrium** (no acceleration) This is one G oriented vertically relative to the horizon. See **G Vector**.

MAC   Mean Aerodynamic Chord.   Basically draw a line from the leading edge of the wing to the trailing edge. Or more precisely, the distance between leading and trailing edges in the direction of the airflow. The location of the Center of Gravity and the Center of Lift are often given in **%MAC**, or distance from leading edge divided by chord length.

Mach Number   Mankind has always been interested in the speed of sound. My own interest was kindled at the lake cottage my grandfather built. You could look across the bay and clearly see someone with an axe or a hammer, and hear it land only after an obvious delay. In Ancient Greece some opinion held that higher-pitched sound travelled faster. The Seventeenth Century brought several scientific experiments, and in the Eighteenth, the Italian doctor Bianconi showed that sound traveled faster in warmer air—probably the first time the speed of sound was linked to air temperature. In the *Principia* (1687) Isaac Newton computed a speed of 978 feet/sec, or 580 knots. This is about 15% too low. Lagrange and Euler both tried and failed to explain the discrepancy between this calculation and the experimental values. Sound waves in air are a compression and rarefaction which produce local temperature changes—heating on compression and cooling on rarefaction—which remain local and do not transfer to the surrounding air. This is known as an *Adiabatic* process. An example from weather science is the lifting (by wind over hills, for example) of a parcel of warm, moist air. Rising, it expands and cools. When the temperature drops to the dew point, the water vapour condenses, releasing the Latent Heat. In other words, the change of state from vapour to liquid releases energy, which heats the parcel further and makes the system unstable, increasing the vertical velocity. Carried into the Stratosphere, the expanding and cooling can trigger a second change of state—to ice crystals—adding still more energy. Eventually the system runs out of juice, and converts all that energy to work, as a tremendous downdraft falls to the ground and spreads out in what is called a microburst. The first to understand that the air temperature fluctuations in a sound wave are adiabatic—that is, they do not transfer to the surrounding air—was Pierre-Simon Laplace. The limit of this non-transfer is now known as Laplace's Coefficient. Laplace's insight brought Newton's calculation into agreement with experiments. Ernst Mach (1838-1916) was a polymath who among many other things worked on sound effects observed during the supersonic motion of a projectile. The ratio of the speed of the projectile (or aircraft) to the local speed of sound is named for him: the *Mach Number*.

Malcolm Horizon   Invented by Dr. Richard Malcolm in the 1970's, it is also known as PVHD, or Peripheral Vision Horizon Display. Quoting from the Wikipedia article: The development of the PVHD was driven by a high incidence of military aircraft accidents due to "attitude awareness issues." Does that ring a bell? Malcolm's solution was genius: mimic the subliminal awareness of horizon the pilot experiences in CAVOK conditions. The pilot doesn't think about the horizon or even look at it, but he using it nonetheless. Nor, sometimes, is he aware when that horizon gradually – or suddenly! – becomes unresolvable. Malcolm's invention steps in to provide that subliminal horizon artificially by projecting a laser beam across the whole instrument panel. It has a little tick mark in the middle to show which way is up. Setting it up, the pilot turns down the intensity so the tick mark just disappears in his foveal vision. But that faint line – aligned with the real horizon – is still there in his peripheral vision, where perception is sensitive to movement. Just as with a clear day, the pilot doesn't have to look at something. But he is aware – or his perception is aware – of movement in pitch or roll. PVHD was used extensively in the military. One application was in the SR-71, where it was used during aerial refuelling where the pilot's concentration is on the probe. What a pity this wonderful invention is unknown in the airline world to this day!

MCAS   Maneuvering Characteristics Augmentation System. This is the infamous piece of software that caused the MAX crashes in 2018-19. Because of the new larger engines hung further forward on the wing there is a negative stick force per G at high AoA. A pilot would have to push the yoke forward to avoid going to an even higher AoA. Left to its own devices, the aircraft would continue into aerodynamic stall. Of course this is a no-no for certification. (Necessary background here is to consider that the MAX is certified on the original type certificate granted in 1967 for a 100-passenger aircraft with JT8D engines producing 12,250 to 17,400 pounds of thrust. The MAX 9 of today is a 300-passenger aircraft and uses LEAP-1B engines producing 23,000 to 29,000 pounds of thrust. Three times the passengers and twice the thrust. Same aircraft regarding certification?) In 2018 the original MCAS was a single point of failure system, meaning that failure of any component meant failure of the system. The necessary sensor, unsurprisingly, is an AoA vane. In both crashes the AoA sensor sent an erroneous high AoA signal, causing the MCAS to run the stabilizer to full nose-down. For many reasons discussed elsewhere in this book, this situation is unrecoverable from low altitude. During the 20-month grounding of the aircraft, a parallel system was added using the other AoA vane. You would think this makes it safer, and indeed it does, at least statistically. But Captain Sullenberger's airplane encountered a flock of geese, taking out both engines. There is a real chance that a MAX could fly through a flock of much smaller birds, which could disable both AoA vanes. The final point – and one essential to remember – is that the B737 is a 1960's airplane, however many modern bells and whistles have been patched on. And the essence of the essential is this:

> MCAS is not Flight Control Software because <u>it has no feedback</u>

> MCAS does not provide Envelope Protection (to put it mildly)

(See Chapter Seven for discussions of what Flight Control Software really is.)

As long as MCAS senses that the AoA is too large, it will continue to move the stabilizer to *full nose-down*. MCAS does not know how to fly. All it knows is how to move the most powerful aerodynamic control into the suicide position. And MCAS is there to allow certification?

Melvill Jones, Geoffrey   (see Ch. 6, p.154)

MEMs   Micro Electro-Mechanical devices.

METAR   (p. 33) The **MET** is for **Met**eorological. The **A** is for either **A**erodrome or **A**viation. The **R** is for **R**eport or **R**outine – take your pick. It is produced once per hour in a format that is common world-wide. Example:

METAR CYHZ 290200Z 35019G27KT ¼ SM R14
2600FT/N +SN VV002 M06/M06 A2962 RMK SN8

CYHZ: ICAO Code for Halifax, N.S.

290200Z: 29th of the month, time 0200 Zulu
(co-ordinated universal time)

35019G27KT   wind from 350° Magnetic at 19 gusting to 27 knots

¼ SM   Visibility one-quarter Statute Mile

R14 2600FT/N +SN   Runway Visual Range 2600
feet (steady) in heavy snow

VV002   Vertical Visibility two hundred feet
(see **Obscuration**)

M06/M06   Temperature minus six Celsius, Dew
Point minus six Celsius

A2962   Altimeter Setting 29.62 inches of
mercury

RMK SN8   Remark: Snow obscuration 8 octas,
or the whole sky

MSL   Above **Mean Sea Level**. See also **AGL**. MSL altimeter setting is **QNH**.

NM (nm)   Nautical Mile. One minute of Latitude, or 6000
feet.

NORMAL LAW   Fly-by-Wire system normal operating
law. Flight Envelope Protection is active.

NOTAM   Notice To AirMen. Promulgated by
the FAA in the USA and NavCanada in Canada, these notices are
more useful as butt-covering for non-pilots than they are as aids to
pilots. In any day there are a zillion of them. Only a handful are relevant to today's flight. Nevertheless, pilots really want to know that
their planned landing runway is closed. ForeFlight to the rescue!

OBSCURATION Back in the day there was a code for *sky obscured*. For example, **W0X0F** meant *indefinite ceiling zero obscured and visibility zero in fog*. An airport with this condition was technically known as *flat on its ass*. With today's **METAR**, the clue is **VV**, or Vertical Visibility. Awareness of this condition (essentially obscuration going right to ground level with fog or heavy snow) is extremely important because, although a pilot may see lights on the ground, she has *no vertical guidance whatsoever*.

OTOLITH The linear accelerometer(s) in our middle ear.

PAPI Precision Approach Path Indicator. Four sets of lights, usually on the left side of the runway near the touchdown point. Essentially four VASIS (see **VASIS**) set at slightly different angles. On the glideslope the pilot sees two white over two red. Three red and you're a bit low. Four red and you're very low. Et cetera. The are much easier to fly accurately than VASIS, and have now largely replaced the latter.

PF Pilot Flying.

PFD Primary Flight Display.

PM Pilot Monitoring.

PNF Pilot **N**ot **F**lying. (Term no longer in use. Now known as Pilot Monitoring.)

Q Codes:

QNE Altimeter is set to standard sea level pressure

QNF Altimeter is set to indicate zero when the air craft is on the ground.

QNH Altimeter is set so that when the aircraft is on the ground, it indicates Airport Elevation.

Precession A comparatively slow gyration of the rotational axis of a spinning body about another line intersecting it so as to describe a cone.

RMI   Radio Magnetic Indicator.   (see also **ADF**)

SEMI-CIRCULAR CANALS   The rotational accelerometers in our middle ear. It has been pointed out to me that the analogy with the ring laser gyros on IRS systems is not an exact one. Unlike the rotational accelerometers in IRS systems, the semicircular canals are very heavily damped by both the viscous liquid therein and the very tiny diameter of the canals. In fact, their purpose may be quite different from that of the rotational accelerometers in IRS systems. Research has shown that the canals have a linear output between 0.1 and 5 hertz, and that most likely our perception uses this information to stabilize the image on our retina, just as the camera software in your mobile phone does today, or like the Steadicam systems did in the movie industry. (Steadicam was invented by Garrett Brown in 1975.) So what pilots call eyeball bounce is more likely caused by G forces outside the linear output frequency range of the canals rather than physical distortion of the eyeball itself. See also **EYEBALL BOUNCE.**

SERVICE CEILING   The *Service Ceiling* is the *Density Altitude* where the *Rate of Climb* drops below a certain minimum – usually 100 feet per minute or 50 feet per minute. It is determined by available thrust.

Somatogravic Illusion   First described (although not by this name) in the seminal article in *Aerospace Medicine* in August, 1965. Geoffrey Melvill Jones and co-author J. F. Martin describe the mechanism through which changes to the Local G Vector can produce the dangerous illusion that the airplane is rearing up like the Ferrari horse. (A pre-requisite for the illusion is lack of attitude awareness. See also **Malcolm Horizon**). The article was in response to the two DC-8 crashes, months apart, in 1963-64. The article was pooh-poohed in airline circles at the time. Sadly, airlines have experienced about one loss of life accident per year (where the *Somatogravic Illusion* is almost certainly a factor) since the article was published, and that pace continues to the present day. See also **EYEBALL BOUNCE, SEMI-CIRCULAR CANALS.**

Speedbrake   Jet aircraft are slippery. They really don't want to slow down or go down. Or stay down once on the ground. The solution is panels on the wing just ahead of the flaps and/or ailerons. They are hinged at their forward ends. They can be lifted (usually hydraulically) to reduce lift and add drag. In the air they generally can extend to about 35° and are called **speedbrakes**. On the ground after landing they extend to about 60°, so with flaps extended you can see right through the wing. This kills lift and puts all the aircraft's weight on the wheels so brakes can have the maximum effect. In this *after landing* situation the panels are called **spoilers**.

Spherical Error   Accuracy of a position in three dimensions. Analogous to triangulation in two dimensions. Often displayed along with a GPS position. See also **GPS Lockout** and **GPS Accuracy Prediction**.

Slant Range   Distance from an aircraft in flight to a point on the ground.

Spoiler   see **Speedbrake**.

Spread   Temperature/Dew Point spread. If the two are equal water vapour is condensing

Strapdown   An IRS system is *strapdown* because the accelerometers are not on a gyro-stabilized platform, as in INS, but in a fixed attitude compared with the aircraft's axes. To make this work, in addition to the linear accelerometers, there must also be a rotational accelerometer for each axis. The benefit is that the IRS also knows *attitude*.

TLA   Three-Letter Acronym. As you can see, there a zillion of them in aviation. There are also large groups of them such as **V speeds**, **Airspeeds**, **Minimums**, and **Q Codes**. And also, of course, airport identifiers. ICAO identifiers are four letters, but are often known by three: KSFO becomes SFO. Not exactly a TLA, but there you go.

TOGA   Takeoff and **Go-Around** Thrust

TRK/FPA   Track/Flight Path Angle. Airbus FCU mode. The autopilot will *inertially* navigate a ground track and a vertical track of the selected number of degrees to the horizontal . Usually used in descents and approaches. See Chapter 6.

Troposphere   The lowest layer of the atmosphere, where temperature decreases with altitude. Its upper limit is called the **tropopause**. Above that is the **stratosphere**, where the temperature is either steady or gets warmer with altitude. Through my career I have been aware that the pollution that my airplane produces while in the stratosphere will remain there.

UHF   Ultra **H**igh **F**requency.   300 Mhz to 1 Ghz. Used for aviation, cell phones, GPS, bluetooth, and satellite phones, etc.

VASIS   Visual Approach Slope Indicator(**s**)   A white light inside a box. The glass front facing the approach is divided: clear on top and red on the bottom. The vertical position of the light in the box determines the glide slope. Flying it, you want to see white with the occasional hint of pink. Now largely replaced by the more accurate PAPI. (See **PAPI**.)

VECTOR   A moving object has both speed and direction – a velocity. That object also experiences acceleration. These qualities could be described by scalar values like Miles per Hour and Northeast, but that gets complicated when direction is not on a surface, but in a space, in three dimensions. In aviation, then, vectors are the simpler way to describe velocity and acceleration. A vector is an arrow. The scalar quantity is the arrow's length.

VISUAL ILLUSIONS   There are many of these. **Black Hole**. **Whiteout**. Obscuration causing 'duck under'. Any many more, some waiting to be discovered by the unwary. The bottom line is: *fly instruments, especially at night*. Today your GPS can give you a distance to the runway, so there is no excuse for getting too low. The latest GPS software even has visual approaches which give you a LOC and at 3 miles out, a 3° Glideslope. (Not to be used as an Instrument Approach, but could save your butt on a dark night or landing into a setting sun.)

VHF   Very High Frequency.   108.0 Mhz to 135.975 Mhz for aircraft use. Defined as 30- 300 Mhz for all uses.

VMC   Visual Meteorological Conditions.   Visibility sufficient to allow the pilot to define a horizon by looking outside.

VNAV   Vertical **Nav**igation.   FMGC mode that enables programming a descent profile.

VOR   Very High Frequency Omnidirectional Radio Range

VORTAC   VOR with **TACAN**, a UHF system used by the military.

WAAS GPS   **W**ide **A**rea **A**ugmentation **S**ystem. Various propagation errors are corrected by a ground station at a fixed and surveyed position. The ground station generates and continuously transmits an *Error Vector*, allowing an aircraft receiver to achieve an accuracy of about *one meter spherical error*.

WAT   Weight Altitude Temperature.   *WAT Charts* are used in calculating takeoff and landing performance. *Pressure Altitude* and *Temperature* determine *Density Altitude*. So if current aircraft weight, altitude and temperature are known, various takeoff and landing numbers can be calculated – e.g. runway distance required, V Speeds, and Rate of Climb.

Accidents and Incidents

Date	Flt	Location	Type	Ch/ Page
29 Nov 1963	TCA 831	Ste-Thérèse	DC-8	6/154
25 Feb 1964	EAL 304	Lake Pontchartrain	DC-8	6/154
01 OCt 1966	West Coast Air	Near KPDX	DC-9-14	4/107
12Apr 1977	DAL 1080	KLAX	L1011	8/220
26 JUN 1978	AC 189	CYYZ	DC-9	4/104
26 Jun 1988	Air France	Mulhouse/ Habsheim	A320	7/200
19 Jul 1989	UAL 232	Sioux City	DC-10	3/84
26 Sep 1989	Skylink 070	CYXT	Metro III	2/40
14 Feb 1990	Indian Airlines	Bangalore, India	A320	7/196
30 Jun 1994	Airbus Test	Toulouse ALT*	A330	6/161
16 JUL 1999	JFK Jr.	Long Island Sound	PA-32	6/138
31 JAN 2000	Alaska 261	Ocean near KLAX	MD82	8/220
12 Nov 2001	AA587	KJFK	A300-600	6/174
06 JUL 2008	USA Jet 199	Saltillo, MEX	DC-9-15	4/108
12 Feb 2009	Colgan	KBUF	DHC-8-Q400	2/60
01 Jun 2009	AF 447	ITCZ	A330	1/05, 2/48

06 Jul 2013	Asiana 214	KSFO	B777	1/15
08 MAR 2014	MH 370	Southern Ocean	B777	9/231
31 Oct 2014	SS2	KMHV	Space-ship	5/115
29Mar2015	AC 624	CYHZ	A320	1/25, 6/130
19Mar2016	Fly Dubai 981	Rostov-on-Don	B737-8	1/5, 3/85
03Aug2016	UAE 521	Dubai	B777	7/187
29 oct 2018	Lion Air 610	Jakarta, Indonesia	MAX-8	N/A
23 Feb 2019	Atlas Air 3591	KHOU	B767	2/36, 3/76
10Mar2019	EA 302	Addis Ababa	MAX-8	3/83, 3/86
18 DEC 2022	UAL 1214	PHOG	B777	5/112, 5/113
22 Feb 2023	Executive Acft	KLIT	King Air 200	5/123
30Nov2023	Private Aircraft	KGAI	Mooney	2/70
15 Jan 2023	Yeti Airlines	Pokhara, Nepal	ATR-72	5/119
26 JAN 2023	Alaska Airlines (2 aircraft)	KSEA	B737-900, MAX-9	5/129
24 Feb 2023	Executive Acft	KRNO	Pilatus PC-12	5/126
07 DEC 2023	N5891J	Near Pukaski, TN	Beech Debon-air	Glossary Autopilot
	SW 147	KLGA	B737-800	Epilogue
11APR 2024	SW 2786	PHLI	MAX-8	Epilogue

19 JUN 2024	SW 4069	KOKC	B737-800	Epilogue
25 JUN 2024	SW 4805	KPWM	B737-700	Epilogue
14July2024	SW 425	KTPA	MAX 8	Epilogue

Accidents and Incidents Reference

Final Reports Links

		Location		Reference (final Report)
29 Nov 1963	TCA 831	Ste-Thérèse	DC-8	Report of Commission of Inquiry https://reports.aviation-safety.net/1963/19631129-0%20CF-TJN.pdf
25 Feb 1964	EAL 304	Lake Pontchartrain	DC-8	https://en.wikisource.org/wiki/Aviation_Accident_Report:_Eastern_Air_Lines_Flight_304
01 OCt 1966	West Coast Air	Near KPDX	DC-9-14	https://asn.flightsafety.org/wikibase/332291
12 Apr 1977	DAL 1080	KLAX	L1011	https://www.tristar500.net/library/flight1080.pdf
26 JUN 1978	AC 189	CYYZ	DC-9	https://asn.flightsafety.org/asndb/328840

26 Jun 1988	AF	Mul-house-Habsheim	A320	https://asn.flightsafety.org/reports/1988/19880626_A320_F-GFKC.pdf
19 JUL 1989	UAL 232	Sioux City	DC-10	https://libraryonline.erau.edu/online-full-text/ntsb/aircraft-accident-reports/AAR90-06.pdf
26 Sep 1989	Skylink 070	CYXT	Metro III	https://asn.flightsafety.org/asndb/326203 Youtube Videos: https://www.youtube.com/watch?v=nSm-x5gaFVE, and https://www.youtube.com/watch?v=bEyOXur-3zLQ
14 Feb 1990		Banga-loreIndia	A320	https://www.dgca.gov.in/digigov-portal/Upload?flag=iframeAttachView&atta-chId=dz01VHjtbmk-Wa9TGKn5TSg%3D%3D
30 Jun 1994	Airbus Test	Toulouse ALT*	A330	https://asn.flightsafety.org/asndb/324952
31 JAN 2000	Alaska 261	Ocean near KLAX	MD82	https://asn.flightsafety.org/reports/2000/20000131_MD83_N963AS.pdf
12 NOV 2001	AA587	KJFK	A300-600	https://asn.flightsafety.org/reports/2001/20011112_A306_N14053.pdf
06 JUL 2008	USA Jet 199	Saltillo, MEX	DC-9-15	https://asn.flightsafety.org/wikibase/321684

Date	Flight	Location	Aircraft	Report
12 Feb 2009	Colgan	KBUF	DHC-8-Q400	https://asn.flightsafety.org/reports/2009/20090212_DH8D_N200WQ.pdf
01 Jun 2009	AF 447	ITCZ	A330	https://asn.flightsafety.org/reports/2009/20090601_A332_F-GZCP.pdf
06 Jul 2013	Asiana 214	KSFO	B777	https://www.ntsb.gov/investigations/AccidentReports/Reports/AAR1401.pdf
08 MAR 2014	MH 370	Southern Ocean	B777	https://asn.flightsafety.org/reports/2014/20140308_B772_9M-MRO.pdf
31 Oct 2014	SS2	KMHV	Space Ship	https://www.ntsb.gov/investigations/AccidentReports/Reports/AAR1502.pdf
29 Mar 2015	AC 624	CYHZ	A320	https://www.tsb.gc.ca/eng/rapports-reports/aviation/2015/a15h0002/a15h0002.html
19 Mar 2016	Fly Dubai 981	Rostov-on Don	B737-8	https://mak-iac.org/upload/iblock/1e8/report_a6-fdn_eng.pdf
29 Oct 2018	Lion Air 610	Java Sea near Jakarta, Indonesia	MAX 8	https://asn.flightsafety.org/asndb/319547
23 Feb 2019	Atlas Air 3591	KHOU	B767	NTSB/AAR-20-02

10 Mar 2019	EA 302	Addis Ababa	MAX 8	https://asn.flightsafety.org/reports/2019/20190310_B38M_ET-AVJ.pdf
JAN 2021	The FIX	Return to Service	B737 MAX	http://www.b737.org.uk/mcas.htm#fix
18 DEC 2022	UAL 1214	PHOG	B777	https://data.ntsb.gov/Docket?ProjectID=106734
15 Jan 2023	Yeti Airlines	Pokhara, Nepal	ATR-72	https://www.tourism.gov.np/files/1/9N-ANC%20FINAL%20Report.pdf
26 JAN 2023	Alaska Air (2 aircraft)	KSEA	B737-900, MAX-9	https://www.seattletimes.com/business/boeing-aerospace/after-alaska-airlines-planes-bump-runway-a-scramble-to-pull-the-plug/
22 Feb 2023	Exec Acft	KLIT	King Air 200	https://asn.flightsafety.org/asndb/318692
24 Feb 2023	Exec Acft	KRNO	Pilatus PC-12	https://asn.flightsafety.org/wikibase/308758
30 Nov 2023	Pvt Acft	KGAI	Mooney	https://www.avweb.com/aviation-news/no-injuries-after-mooney-tangles-with-powerlines/
07 DEC 2023	N5891J	Near Pukaski, TN	Debonair	https://www.youtube.com/watch?v=66z-726rQNxc
July 2024	Boeing Plea Agreement	Fort Worth, TX	B737 MAX	https://www.justice.gov/criminal/media/1361546/dl?inline

Acknowledgements

You know who you are. Some of you have already departed, but you are still in my heart. You were kind to me when I was a green first officer on the DC-9. And when I was a slightly different shade of green on the DC-8, B-727, L1011, or B-767.

You taught me and mentored me. I remain profoundly grateful. Ours was an apprenticeship trade. For that, too, I am profoundly grateful.

This book is my attempt to pass on some of the enormous gift you gave me.

§

I have known this man since kindergarten. That is now seventy-five years and counting. This photo[1] is from 1983, when he was one of the First Canadian Astronaut Finalists. He got a degree in Physiology before deciding he wanted to work directly with people. He went back to school and studied medicine. He got his M.D. and practiced Emergency Medicine for thirty-some years.

Now in retirement he studies Mathematics and Physics. He also studies the lives of the extraordinary men and women who have built those disciplines — some acknowledged, some not. He has a special feeling for the humanity of genius.

It is only through Allan that I know of Dr. Geoffrey Melvill Jones. They met at McGill when Allan was studying physiology, and remained friends. They are both pilots and even flew together out of the old Edmonton Municipal Airport. Melvill Jones' 1963 paper is the origin of what came to be called the *Somatogravic Illusion*, the still-not-widely-known cause of many accidents and incidents. As far as I know, he is

1   Credit NRC Digital Repository

still with us. He turned 102 in January.

Allan and I both turned 80 last year. Over the last two years he has spent an enormous amount of time reading this book and writing a page by page (and sometimes word by word) set of notes of commentary, suggestions, and questions. We have had hours of discussion both on the phone and in person. This book would not be what it is without Allan's detailed and probing critique. Or without his generous encouragement.

§

Last — but far from least — is Captain. Yes, I needed her for dialogue. Yes, I imagined her. But as our friendship deepened, I began to long for her company. She gave me courage in those moments when I felt I couldn't address another human tragedy alone.

When I decided to stop flying and sell the airplane, she was holding my hand.

I still look up at a blue sky with low cumulous clouds and want to be up there among them. But thanks to her cheerful and sometimes badass presence over these last years, I feel the joy of that sky and not the emptiness where my trade for nearly six decades used to live.

My life is not empty. I have family, friends, music, and writing. And I also have a growing certainty: Captain is real. Our paths may have crossed, or nearly so, at the same airline. If we didn't share the exact co-ordinates in spacetime, it was pretty close, and I am grateful.

§

www.ingramcontent.com/pod-product-compliance
Lightning Source LLC
Chambersburg PA
CBHW041820090426
42811CB00009B/1045